teach yourself...

UNIX

Includes Languages and Power Tools

RUTH ASHLEY
JUDI N. FERNANDEZ

ADVANCED COMPUTER BOOKS

MANAGEMENT INFORMATION SOURCE, INC.

COPYRIGHT

P.O. Box 5277
Portland, Oregon 97208-5277
(503) 282-5215

First Printing

ISBN 1-55828-017-0

Library of Congress Catalog Card Number: 89-31749

TABLE OF CONTENTS

INTRODUCTION

So you are ready to teach yourself Unix. You've made a good start by opening this book. It is structured so that you can practice using Unix as you learn it. By the time you complete this book, you'll be able to use Unix to create files, run programs, manipulate files and directories, and communicate with other Unix users.

Unix is an operating system that helps you communicate with a computer. There are several different operating systems based on Unix; one of the most popular is Xenix. In this book, we cover basic Unix; what you learn here will work on virtually any Unix-derived operating system. Many variants, such as Xenix, include additional commands, enhancements, and features, but the basic Unix commands work just fine. Later on you'll be able to check the documentation for your system and build on what you learn from this book.

This book assumes you are new to Unix, but not to computers. You might be a programmer who has used another operating system, for example. Or you may be experienced in PC DOS and regularly use a word processor and spreadsheet. In either case, you have enough background to benefit from using this book.

You'll encounter hands-on exercises several times in each chapter. If you are reading while sitting at a terminal, feel free to try out commands as you go along. When you come to an exercise, make a point of working through it. If you don't have continual access to Unix, go back and work through the exercises when you can.

Chapters 1-4 give a good basis for using Unix; you'll be able to function fairly well at a Unix terminal by the time you have completed these chapters. Chapter 1 starts right out with using Unix. You'll learn to log in and use the shell to execute basic commands that handle files and make Unix work for you. Chapter 2 introduces you to the Unix directory system. You'll learn to create files and directories, then manipulate them as needed. You'll learn to access files in any directory using the commands covered in Chapter 1.

Chapter 3 deals with Unix security measures. You'll learn to change your password, provide or change access to your files, and create links among files to which you have access. Chapter 4 covers Unix communications. You'll learn to use the built-in electronic mail system as well as to send messages to other users who are online at the same time you are.

Chapters 5 and 6 cover somewhat more advanced techniques and commands that make you more efficient during your Unix sessions. Chapter 5 shows more ways you can manipulate files and data using techniques to get input from a nondefault location or send output where you want it. You'll learn to sort data and perform several different operations that compare files or count or classify file elements. Chapter 6 covers the use of patterns or strings in Unix. You'll learn to locate lines containing specific characters, and to specify processing based on whether or not a pattern is located in a line.

Chapters 7 through 9 cover the use of the visual editor provided with Unix. If you will be creating and printing files under Unix, these chapters will be very useful to you. Chapter 7 introduces you to the editor and shows the basic commands you need. Chapter 8 continues with additional commands for editing files. Chapter 9 deals with the text formatter you'll need to get anything other than default printing from your edited files.

Chapters 10 through 13 are concerned with programming and system administration. If you are a programmer or if you just want more control over how you interact with Unix, these chapters will be very useful. Chapter 10 covers command file programming using the Bourne shell, while Chapter 11 covers command file programming using the C shell. Chapter 12 is for programmers; you'll learn to use the C programming tools provided at most Unix installations, such as the compiler and the makefile utility. Chapter 13 covers the very basics of Unix system administration so that you have some idea what goes on behind the scenes.

Before you can start using Unix, you'll need a user ID and possibly a password. You'll also have to learn how to get a terminal connected to Unix. This may be as simple as turning one on. It may require you to dial in from a remote site. Contact the person in charge of your Unix installation to get the information you need.

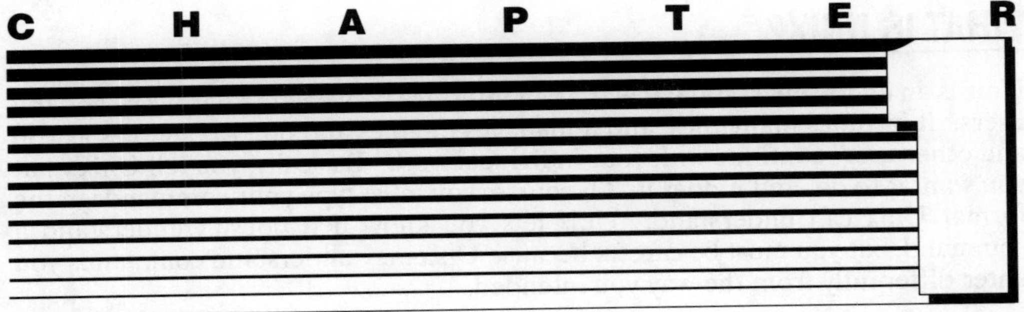

GETTING STARTED WITH UNIX

In this chapter, you will learn to use the most commonly needed Unix commands in their basic forms. While most commands have more options, the stripped-down versions introduced in this chapter will meet your immediate needs. By the time you finish this chapter, you will be able to log on and log off Unix. You'll also be able to perform basic file management operations, including such tasks as creating a file, displaying file contents, copying a file, renaming a file, and listing the files in a directory.

WHAT IS UNIX?

Unix is an **operating system**; it acts as an interface between the hardware and the users. It includes many files, and it manages the files and other resources as you and other users continue with your individual work. Basically, you tell Unix what you want it to do, and it does it. Of course, you must type your commands in the format Unix can understand. Unix lets you know if it doesn't understand a command, but you must be careful because Unix may understand commands you enter differently from the way you intended.

Unix is not unfriendly, but it is very terse; it uses as few messages to you as possible. While this is a bit disconcerting at first, it saves a great deal of time in the long run.

In this book, the assumption is that you can get to the **login prompt**; that is, your terminal is ready for you or you know how to get it that way. Most likely, anyone in the computer room can give you a hint here, but the procedure varies from one Unix installation to another. Once you reach the login prompt, most Unix commands work the same way, whether the Unix operating system is installed on a microcomputer, a minicomputer, or a mainframe.

THE LOGIN PROCESS

Before you can use Unix, you must have a **user ID** and a **password**. If you don't have these, see your system administrator. The administrator will tell Unix to expect you and set up certain parameters so that you can use the system. Once you have these values, you are ready to get started using Unix.

When you see the login prompt on your terminal, you are ready to start logging in (the terms "log in" and "log on" are used interchangeably in this book). Here is what you might see:

```
unixtype!login: _
```

You type your user ID and press **Return**. The system is case sensitive, so use uppercase and lowercase letters exactly as the value was given to you. Unix sends another message, just below the login prompt:

```
Password: _
```

Now you type your password. This is a bit more difficult than typing your user ID because, for security reasons, the characters don't appear on the screen as you type. You can change your password later; you'll see how in the Chapter 2. If either the user ID or the password is incorrect, you'll get the *Login incorrect:* message and see the login prompt again. You must then enter both user ID and password over again. If you can't get past the login process, see your system administrator; you probably have the wrong user ID or password.

Once you enter the correct user ID and password, you'll see the **shell prompt** and be ready to start using Unix proper.

UNIX SHELLS

Unix has several shells that can be used; the ones available to you depend on your particular Unix version. The shell is the interface between you and the Unix system. It provides the prompt when you can enter a command. The two most common shells are the **Bourne shell** (part of standard Unix) and the **C shell** (originally developed for the Berkeley Unix system). When the system administrator sets up a startup file for you, a specific shell was specified; you can ask for that shell to be changed if you want.

Each shell displays a different prompt to indicate that Unix is ready for another command. The Bourne shell uses the dollar sign ($) as a prompt while the C shell uses a percent (%) sign with a counter that keeps track of how many commands have been executed, so you see 1% right after you log in, 2% after your next command, and so forth. At the basic level, the two shells work about the same. More sophisticated features may be different between the shells. In this book, you will be informed if a command has different effects in the different shells as that command is discussed.

Some installations have more complex shells. Some even provide menus from which you can choose commands and options; however, specialized shells are beyond the scope of this book.

Figure 1.1 (see following page) shows how the login procedure looks with two different Unix systems and two different shells. Both shells are supported by most Unix systems, however. You'll see the Bourne shell prompt ($) most of the time in this book.

Whenever you see your shell prompt, Unix is waiting for input from you. You can type a command to Unix whenever you see this prompt.

```
xenix386!login: ashley
Password:

                    Welcome to SCO XENIX System !

                                 from

                    The Santa Cruz Operation, Inc.

Terminal type is ansi
$ _
```

```
login: carson
Password:
        Welcome to UCXX Unix.
1% _
```

Figure 1.1 Login displays

LOGGING OFF

When you finish with a Unix session, you must log off. This frees up the terminal for someone else to use. If you don't log off, someone can use the terminal and have immediate access to all your files. For security reasons, you'll want to be sure to log off before leaving the terminal unattended. When you have logged off correctly, the login prompt appears on the screen ready for the next user.

The logging off process varies a bit among shells. The Bourne shell ($ prompt) uses the **exit** command while the C shell (% prompt) uses the **logout** command. In some installations, either command works. For example, if you have the % prompt and type **exit**, Unix may respond with the **logout** command for you. But if you have the $ prompt and type **logout**, you'll see the message *logout: not found*, indicating that logout is not a valid command. When you have entered a valid logoff command, you will see the standard login prompt on the screen.

Most Unix versions recognize the **Ctrl-D** command at the prompt as a logoff request as well. If you hold down the Ctrl ("Control") key, which may be labeled "Cntl," and simultaneously press the D key (uppercase or lowercase will work), Unix logs you off immediately. Because the **Ctrl-D** key combination terminates several other Unix processes as well, some large Unix installations have disabled it for the logout process.

COMMAND-LINE ENTRY

When you type at the shell prompt, you are entering characters into an area of memory called the **command-line buffer**. When you press **Return** at the end of the command line, Unix accepts the contents of the buffer as the command line and processes it. (Your keyboard's equivalent to the Return key may be labeled "Enter," "RET," or "NEWLINE" or may have an arrow pointing down and to the left.) If Unix can't tell what you want, you'll see a brief error message, such as *command: not found*. When that happens, just examine your command; you will usually be able to tell what you did wrong at a glance. For example, if you are in the C shell and you type **logoff** as a command, you'll see a message and can figure out that you typed **logoff** instead of **logout**.

You can make corrections in the command line at any time before you press **Return** because the characters are still in the input buffer. Use your keyboard's **Backspace** or **Delete** key to erase characters. If your keyboard has a **DeleteLine**, or "line kill" key, that key removes the entire command, and you can start over. If not, you can often get the same effect by pressing the **Ctrl-U** key combination (hold down the Control key and simultaneously press the U key). In either case, you won't get another prompt, but the cursor moves down to the next line.

Unix System Exercise 1.1

Purpose: Log on to Unix and log off.

1. Get the login prompt.
2. Type your user ID.
3. When you see the password prompt, type your password.
4. Notice the resulting prompt; do you use the Bourne or C shell?
5. Type your user ID as a command on the command line, and then press **Return**. Read the error message and the shell prompt.
6. Now log off to restore the login prompt.

continued on following page. . .

Exercise 1.1 continued. . .

If it doesn't work:

A. If you see the *Login incorrect* message, enter your user ID and password again. If it still doesn't work, see your system administrator to verify the values.

B. If your prompt isn't $ (Bourne) and doesn't end in % (C), check with your system administrator so you know which of the two standard shells yours is similar to.

C. If you have trouble logging off, try **exit** if you see the $ prompt or **logout** if you see the % prompt. If you don't see either prompt, try **Ctrl-D** .

STANDARD INPUT AND OUTPUT

Unix uses the keyboard and the terminal screen for its standard input and output devices. It always expects input from the keyboard and sends output to the terminal unless you tell it differently. Much of the time, you'll be happy with these standard devices. But sometimes you might want to save your output to a file instead of just show it on screen. Or you might want to use the output from one command as the input to another command. There are various ways to handle these functions. Later in this chapter, you will examine **redirection**, which lets you send screen output directly to a file on disk. But, for now, just remember that if the command you enter doesn't specify otherwise, input comes from the keyboard and output appears on the screen.

BASIC FILE MANIPULATION

Like all operating systems, Unix stores data and programs in **files**. In Chapter 2, you will see how the files are named and stored and how file directories are structured. In this chapter, you will work with the directory you are placed in automatically whenever you log in—the **home** directory. While working in the home directory, you will need to display file contents and copy, move, rename, delete, and print files. You'll also need to be able to display a list of all your files. In this section, you'll learn commands to do all these things.

Entering Unix Commands

When you want to enter a command line, just type it at the keyboard. Unix is case sensitive, so if the command is **cp**, you can't type **CP** and expect it to work. Once you have typed the command, press the key that ends a line; on many keyboards it's the **Return** key, others may label it "Enter," "RET," or "NEWLINE" or use an arrow pointing down and to the left. This key will be called **Return** in this book, but press the equivalent key on your keyboard.

Checking the Date and Time

One of the simplest commands in all Unix systems lets you check the current date and time. Just type **date** at the shell prompt and press **Return**. The bottom of the screen will look something like this:

```
$ date
Thu Jun 1  12:54:42  PDT  1989
$ _
```

The shell prompt returns and Unix waits for your next command. The **date** command requires no additional information from you to do its work.

Listing Files in a Directory

When you are in Unix, some directory is always the **current** directory, and until you change it, the current directory is your home directory. You can enter the **ls** command at the shell prompt from your keyboard to **l**i**s**t the directory contents on the screen. If you are a new user, you won't have any files in your home directory yet, so when you type **ls** and press the **Return** key, you'll just see the prompt again. If your directory contains some files, you'll see a listing such as the following:

```
$ ls
addresses
paint.memo
save_them
$ _
```

The files are listed alphabetically by file name. You can specify various options to produce a listing with different contents or in a different format. Figure 1.2 shows some of the options you can use in the **ls** command. These options are common to virtually all Unix versions and installations. Your version may have additional options or shortcuts you can use to modify the sequence or otherwise affect the format. In the next chapter, you'll learn to specify certain files or directories when you use the **ls** command.

Command: **ls**

Purpose: List files in directory.

Format: **ls** [*options*] [*file-list*]

Options:

-a	List all files, including hidden ones.
-d	List directory names only, not ordinary files.
-g	Show group information with listing.
-l	Show long listing with extended information.
-r	List in reverse order.
-s	List in order of increasing size.
-t	List in order of time, most recent first.

Examples:

1. `ls`
2. `ls -l`
3. `ls -ra`
4. `ls -ls`

Result: Files that make up a directory are listed on screen, with options applied.

Figure 1.2 The **ls** *(list directory) command*

Many Unix commands accept or require options or arguments. *Options*, as you can see in Figure 1.2, are generally single-character entries that specify a variation in the basic command. While a hyphen must precede the first option, you can combine the options in any sequence. The most used option is **-l**, which produces a long listing such as the following:

```
$ ls -l
-rwxr-xr-x   1  ashley       14334    May 19    14:58  addresses
-rwxrw-r-x   1  ashley        1298    May 22    09:32  paint.memo
-rw-rw-rw    1  ashley        8900    May 22    09:56  save_them
```

Figure 1.3 shows the details of the extended output format listing. You'll learn to interpret various parts of the extended directory listing as you continue in this book. For now, just note that the actual file names are on the rightmost end of the line and that the date and time the file was last changed appear just to the left of that.

access permission	links	user	size	date last modified	time last modified	file name
`-rw-rw-r--`	1	ashley	8900	May 22	09:56	save_them

Figure 1.3 Long directory listing format

Some versions of Unix may display a slightly different format from the one in Figure 1.3. For example, you may get the group name in addition to the user name on the line.

The other options shown in Figure 1.2 limit or expand the number files that are listed. Each directory contains hidden files in addition to the names you see displayed. If you specify **-a** in the command, you'll see the hidden file names as well as the standard ones; **hidden** file names always begin with a period. You can combine options to specify **-la** to get extended information about all the files. The **-g** option causes the group name rather than the user name to appear in the listing. You will learn the effects of the **-d** option in Chapter 2.

Displaying a Calendar

Unix lets you display a calendar of one or more months by typing the appropriate **cal** command; some versions of Unix treat this command a bit differently, but you will still be able to display something on screen and use it to create some files to practice with. When you type **cal**, some Unix systems show you the calendar for the current month and one month before and after it. Other systems don't recognize **cal** without any arguments. Figure 1.4 (see following page) shows the standard format of the **cal** command. Most Unix commands have much the same format; they invoke a Unix utility program and supply various arguments and/or options to it.

Command: **cal**

Purpose: Display a calendar.

Format: **cal** [*month*] *year*

Examples:

1. `cal 1990`
2. `cal 3 1989`

Result of example 2:

```
          Mar
 S  M Tu  W Th  F  S
          1  2  3  4
 5  6  7  8  9 10 11
12 13 14 15 16 17 18
19 20 21 22 23 24 25
26 27 28 29 30 31
```

Figure 1.4 The **cal** *(display calendar) command*

In the format of the command, you'll see a value in square brackets; square brackets indicate an optional part of the command and should not actually be typed. In this case, you can include a month value (from 1 to 12) before the year to limit the calendar to a single month of the specified year. For the year, use all four digits; **cal 90** is not the same as **cal 1990**. If you use a month value such as 6 without a year, some systems give you the calendar for that month in the current year; others might give you the calendar for 1906 or 2006.

Redirection

You can send any screen output, such as the calendar listing, to a file in your directory by using **redirection** in the command line to redirect the output from the terminal screen to a file. The redirection symbol is a greater-than sign (>). If you type **cal 1990 > year1990**, the calendar for the year is not sent to the screen; instead it is sent to a file named **year1990** in your directory. If you type **date > save.date**, the information normally displayed on screen is sent to a file named **save.date** instead. You won't see any confirmation on the screen if the redirection works correctly, but the file will appear when you list the directory. If Unix can't interpret your command, you'll see a brief error message.

In the same way, you can create a file containing a directory listing. The command **ls > myfiles** creates a file named **myfiles** in your directory and stores the file listing produced by the **ls** command in the file **myfiles**.

When you redirect output to a file, if you name a file that doesn't exist yet, Unix creates that file and stores the screen output in it. You must be careful with redirection, however; if you name a file that already exists to hold the redirected output, Unix quietly destroys the contents of the existing file by replacing it with the command output. You won't get an error message because Unix expects you to know what you are doing. For example, if you already have a file named **myfiles** and then use the command **cal > myfiles**, whatever was in **myfiles** is overwritten by the calendar output. You can avoid this problem by first checking to see if the name you are going to use is in the directory listing.

Another redirection option lets you specify that the new file contents should be added to the end (appended) of an existing file. You do this by doubling the greater-than sign (> >) used for redirection. The command **cal 1992 > > months** generates a calendar for 1992 and places it at the end of the file **months**. The command **date > > months** then adds the date line to the end of the same file. If the named file doesn't already exist, Unix simply creates a file with that name and stores the command output in it.

Unix System Exercise 1.2

Purpose: Display information and create a few files.

1. Log on to Unix.
2. Display the current date, then the current year's calendar on the screen. Notice that the year's calendar may scroll off the screen before you can read it.
3. Display the current month's calendar on the screen. You may need to specify the year as well.
4. Try typing **cal** and pressing **Return**. If you get a display, your Unix version has some extensions.
5. Use redirection to create a file named **year.file** in your directory; put any year's calendar in it.
6. Use the **ls** command to check your directory to see the files listed. Try it again to see any hidden files. Try a long listing to see the date and time you created the files. The total shown includes the hidden files as well. Don't worry about the information in these listings; just note the file names.
7. Use redirection to make a file called **this.month**, containing only the current month's calendar. Then use the **date** command to append the current date to the end of the same file.
8. List the directory again. Notice that the files are in alphabetical order.
9. Use redirection to store the long current directory listing in a file named **new_directory**.
10. Practice more with the **date**, **cal**, and **ls** commands if you want; then log off.

If it doesn't work:

A. If your system doesn't generate onscreen calendars, make sure you used **cal 1990** and **cal 1 1991** as the formats.

B. For the redirection, use a format such **cal 1990 > year.file** in item 5, **cal 4 1990 > > this.month** in item 7, and **ls > new_directory** in item 9.

MANIPULATING FILES

At this point, your directory should include at least three files: **this.month**, **new_directory**, and **year.file**. In this section, you'll learn to display the contents of a file on screen, copy files, move or rename files, delete files, and print them.

When you enter commands, Unix normally does what you request and returns the prompt for the next command. You'll see a brief error message if Unix can't interpret the command, but you won't see any confirmation if the task is completed as requested.

Copying and Renaming Files

You can copy a file and give the copy a new name, resulting in two identical files. The **cp** command lets you **copy** files. When you enter the **cp** command, the original file (i.e., the one you want to copy) is called the **source** file. The copy is called the **target** file. The command **cp oldfile newfile** makes a copy of the file named *oldfile* and stores it in the same directory under the name *newfile*. The original file is unchanged. Figure 1.5 shows the format of the command.

Command:	**cp**
Purpose:	Copy a file.
Format:	**cp** *source-file target-file*
Example:	`cp accounts89 accounts.arc`
Result:	There are now two identical files with different names.

Figure 1.5 The **cp** *(copy file) command*

If you name a source-file that doesn't exist, such as **yeers**, you'll see a brief error message, such as *cp: cannot access yeers*. If you name a target-file that does exist, you won't see an error message. Unix assumes you know what you are doing and overwrites the existing file with the contents of the source-file. Be sure you provide a unique file name for the target-file if you don't want to destroy any existing files. Check the directory listing as often as necessary to be sure you don't overwrite important files.

You can rename a file with a similar command, as shown in Figure 1.6. The **mv** command **moves** the contents of the source file to a target file with a new name and then erases the original file. This has the effect of renaming the original (source) file, resulting in a single file under the target name. This command can also be used to move a file into a different directory.

Command:	**mv**
Purpose:	Move or rename a file.
Format:	**mv** *source-file target-file*
Example:	`mv accounts89 accounts.arc`
Result:	One file with the target name exists.

Figure 1.6 The **mv** *(move or rename file) command*

As with the **cp** command, you'll get an error message if you name a source file that doesn't exist, and you can destroy an existing file (intentionally or unintentionally) if you name a target file that is already present.

If you use the basic form of the **mv** and **cp** commands, as shown in Figures 1.5 and 1.6, the target file remains in the same directory. In Chapter 2, you'll see how to copy and move files into other directories.

Deleting Files

You can use the **rm** command to **rem**ove or delete a file from a directory; the format is shown in Figure 1.7. You can name several files in this command; they will all be removed. As with other commands, you'll see an error message if you name a file that doesn't exist. If you name a file that is present in your directory, you won't get any confirmation, but Unix removes it immediately. Be sure you really want to delete a file before you use the **rm** command, because you can't easily retrieve it once it is gone.

Command: **rm**

Purpose: Remove a file.

Format: **rm** [*option*] *file(s)*

Option:

-i Ask before deleting.

Example: `rm accounts89`

Result: The file is no longer listed or available.

Figure 1.7 The **rm** *(remove file) command*

Note that the **rm** command allows an option. When you specify **-i**, Unix asks for confirmation before deleting each file. This allows an extra measure of security.

Using the cat Command

You will often want to see what is in a file before you delete it or otherwise process it. You can display the contents of any text file on your terminal screen by using the **cat** command as shown in Figure 1.8 (see following page). This command has many different uses and effects; one use is con**cat**enation (combining files)—hence the command name.

If you specify **cat** without any arguments, it uses the standard input and output devices. You type a line at the keyboard and press **Return**, and then the line you typed is repeated on the screen. If you use redirection and name a new file, you can create a file directly from keyboard entries. If you name a file in the command, it is used as the input file and listed as output to the screen. You can also use **cat** to combine or concatenate files with redirection (>) and append (>>) symbols.

Command: **cat**

Purpose: Display or create files.

Format: **cat** [*source-file*] [*symbol*] [*target-file*]

Examples:

1. `cat this.month`
2. `cat`
3. `cat > new.file`
4. `cat oldfile1 oldfile2 >> new.file`

Result: File displayed on screen, lines echoed on screen, or lines sent to redirected file.

Figure 1.8. The **cat** *command*

Displaying File Contents with the cat Command

When you enter **cat this.month** at the keyboard, the file is displayed on the screen until the end of the file is reached; the early part of the file may scroll out of view if the file contains more than one screenful of information. When you use this command to display a file, you usually just want to verify the file's general contents. (Soon you will learn to use the **more** command, which is more useful if you really want to read everything in the file.)

If the file you name doesn't exist, you'll see an error message; Unix may report that the file can't be opened or that you don't have access. In any case, the message means the file is not available to you at the location you indicate.

If the file you name contains more than one screenful of information, you may want to cause the display to stop before it reaches the end of the file. Just press **Ctrl-S** (hold down the Ctrl key and simultaneously press the S key) and the display pauses; press **Ctrl-Q** to start it up again. In many systems, pressing any key restarts the display following **Ctrl-S**.

Copying and Combining Files with the cat Command

You can use **cat** to copy a file or combine files if you use redirection. For example, **cat this.year > one.year** has exactly the same effect as **cp this.year one.year**; it copies one file into another without changing the original file. You can combine files as well, with commands such as **cat this.year next.year > two.years**. In this case, the two files (**this.year** and **next.year**) are sent to the redirected file (two years) in sequence. A command such as **cat another.year > > two.years** adds the contents of still another file to the end of **two.years**. Note that the redirection (>) or append (> >) symbol precedes the target file, which is always the last file in the list. All source files named before the symbol are sent to the target file in sequence.

Creating a File from the Terminal with the cat Command

You can also use the **cat** command to create a new file directly from the terminal. As previously mentioned, if you use **cat** with no arguments, it simply repeats what you type to the screen. In the following example, you type the first of each repeated line. Unix sends the second line to the standard output device, and the screen will look like this (bold type represents characters typed by the user):

```
$ cat
This is a sample
This is a sample
of what happens when
of what happens when
you use cat without any arguments.
you use cat without any arguments.

_
```

Unix continues to give you a cursor at a new line for entering text and then sends whatever you enter back to the screen. You can terminate this effect of **cat** by pressing **Ctrl-D**.

If you use redirection, you can use **cat** to send the lines you enter to a file instead of to the screen and thus create a new file. For example, if you enter the sequence of lines that follow, Unix creates a new file named **my.address** in your directory (or replaces it if a file named **my.address** is already present). As usual, you can use **> >** to append the lines to an already existing file.

```
$ cat > my.address
Ruth Ashley
Apartment 777
777 Old Barkla Way
San Diego, CA  92000
$ _
```

Only the lines you type appear on the screen. The cursor appears at the left of the blank line. When you press **Ctrl-D**, the **cat** command is terminated, and the newly created file is closed. If you then use the command **cat my.address**, exactly what you entered on the screen is displayed as the file contents. You can make corrections to lines in a file as you type them just as you can on the command line; however, once you press **Return**, you can't change the line. You'll want to use the editor instead of **cat** to create files of any length or complexity.

Using the more Command

The **more** command is available in most installations; it has a single purpose and requires you to name a file. It displays the first screenful of the file you name and then pauses with a message such as *--More--* and a percentage value that indicates how much of the file has been displayed. When you press **Spacebar**, you'll see the next screenful and a new percentage value. The output also lets you see the next line by pressing **Return**. If you type **more addresses**, for example, the first part of the **addresses** file is displayed.

Printing Files

You can print files in several different ways. The easiest way to print a file is to send the file to your installation's standard line printer. The location of the line printer depends to a great extent on what your system administrator has decided. Unix has an internal spooler that manages the separate print requests of different users. When you request a printout, the request is sent to the print queue, where it waits its turn. You may find that printing is quicker at certain times of the day or week at your installation. Eventually, you'll get a feel for how long you have to wait. If you happen to have a printer dedicated to your terminal, you won't have to wait at all.

The **lpr** command requests a printout of a text file's contents from the **l**ine **pr**inter. You cannot print out executable programs or binary files, but if you can display the contents of a file at your terminal, you can print it. Figure 1.9 shows the format of the **lpr** command. The **-m** option asks that you be notified when the printout is ready; you'll see a message on screen alerting you to go pick up your output. The other options affect the disposition of the file being printed. If you specify **-c**, Unix makes a copy of the file before it is printed, which ensures that the file is printed in its current form. If you don't include **-c** and then make changes to the file before it is actually printed, the changes will appear in the printed output. If you specify **-r**, the file is deleted automatically after being printed; you would do this if it is a one-shot file or if you have a separate version of the file specifically for printing.

Command: **lpr**

Purpose: Print file on local printer.

Format: **lpr** [*options*] [*files*]

Options:

-c	Copy file first.
-m	Use mail to report when printing is finished.
-r	Remove file after printing.

Examples:

1. `lpr my.address`
2. `lpr -c save_it`
3. `lpr -r new.file this.year`

Result: File is sent to printer queue and eventually printed; if specified, file is copied before printing or removed afterwards.

Figure 1.9 The **lpr** *(print file) command*

You can name one or more files in the **lpr** command; the named files are printed in sequence when the printer is free. Suppose you use the command **lpr my.address**. You'll see a message on screen that indicates that the file is sent to the print queue. The screen might resemble the following:

```
$ lpr my.address
request id is prop-9 (1 file)
$ _
```

The **print ID** (**prop-9** in the example) can be useful later if you want to remove the print request from the queue. In the above example, the command **cancel prop-9** removes the job from the print queue. If the job has already started, the printout will be stopped in the middle.

The print output may be preceded or followed by a banner page, which specifies the user and the print ID of the file; the contents and even the presence of the banner page is determined by your system administrator. If you order several files printed in one command, only one banner will appear. The printout produced by **lpr** is not formatted; the text is printed continuously, even over the perforations on continuous-form paper. If you want to control the format of the output, you must use the **vi** editor or a text formatting program; these topics are covered later in this book.

Unix System Exercise 1.3

Purpose: Use file management commands.

1. Log on to Unix if necessary.
2. Display your directory, and then make a copy of **new_directory** called **direct.two** and a copy of **year.file** called **this.year**.
3. Change the name of **year.file** to **what.year**. Check your directory listing again.
4. Add the calendar of 1999 to the **this.year** file.
5. Try to delete a file named **next.year** (if you already have a file named **next.year**, use a name that isn't on your directory). Delete file **direct.two**; use the **-i** option so Unix will ask you to confirm it after the command is issued.
6. At this point your directory contains these files: **new_directory**, **direct.two**, **this.month**, **this.year**, and **what.year**. Use the **cat** command to create one called **my.address** that contains your address in at least three lines.

continued on following page. . .

Exercise 1.3 continued...

7. Display the contents of a few of your files on the screen.
8. Create a new file named **many.years** that holds the contents of **this.year** and **what.year**. Then in a separate command, add the file **my.address** to the end of it and display the result.
9. Display the contents of **many.years**; try to pause the display with **Ctrl-S**. Then try displaying it with **more**. When you're finished, delete this file.
10. Request a printout of one or two files, then log off.

If it doesn't work:

A. Practice a bit more and re-read appropriate sections in this chapter if you have trouble. Basic file maintenance operations are crucial to maintaining the files in your directory.

B. Item 8 can be solved with **cat this.year what.year > many.years**, followed by **cat my.address > > many.years**.

C. Check with your system administrator if you don't know the location of your line printer.

SUMMARY

In this chapter you've learned to do the following:

- Log on and log off at your terminal.
- Enter commands at your shell prompt.
- Check the system date and time with **date**.
- List directory contents with **ls**.
- Display a calendar with **cal**.
- Redirect and append output to a file with > and > >.
- Copy files with **cp**.

- Rename files with **mv**.
- Delete files with **rm**.
- Create, combine, and display files with **cat**.
- Display screen output one screenful at a time with **more**.
- Print files with **lpr**.

Many of these commands are covered in more detail in later chapters.

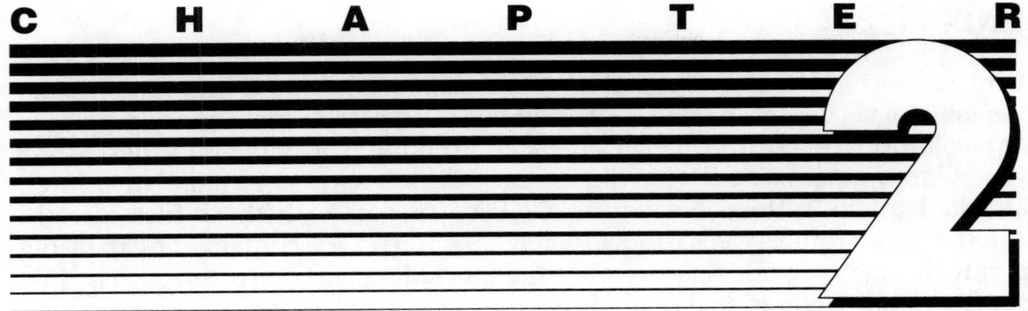

UNIX DIRECTORIES AND FILES

The Unix operating system is based on files, which are stored in directories. When you log in to Unix, you are automatically placed in your home directory; in Chapter 1, you learned to use several commands to manipulate files in that directory. In this chapter, you will learn how the Unix directories are structured and how to create, manipulate, and name directories.

You will also learn to apply your directory knowledge to the basic commands you already know how to use. In the process, you'll learn many more ways to use the basic file handling commands during a Unix session.

UNIX FILES

Unix supports several types of files. You became acquainted with the ordinary file in the last chapter; **ordinary files** contain such data as text, binary programs, or any information stored in eight-bit bytes. Another type of file is the **device file**; your Unix system has a device file for each device, such as terminal or printer, attached to the system, but you won't have to deal with these files directly. Another major file type is the **directory**. A directory contains not data but **pointers**, which provide links to other files, including other directories. The first section of this chapter deals with directories in a Unix system.

UNIX DIRECTORY STRUCTURE

The Unix operating system uses a treelike, or hierarchical, structure of directories for storing files. The primary directory, called the root directory, is at the top. Each directory can contain other directories as well as files. Figure 2.1 shows a diagram of a simplified Unix system. The **root** directory is at the top. Within it are various subdirectories that Unix needs to function. For example, the **bin** directory contains utility program files, the **dev** directory includes files that describe various devices that Unix can use, including terminals and printers. The **usr** directory contains a directory for each user ID recognized by the system. Any given Unix system will have many more directories than are shown in the figure, but you won't have to deal with most of them.

Each box in Figure 2.1 represents a directory, and each box contains that directory name. The root directory is always named /, as shown in the figure; note that it is a *forward* slash character. The names outside of boxes represent some of the files in each directory. Note that a directory can contain other directories as well as files. Each directory (except for the root directory) has one parent. A **parent** directory is the one directly above another directory. A directory may have several directories directly below it; these are **child** directories. The term **subdirectory** is often used to refer to a child directory, but it is also correct to just call them all directories.

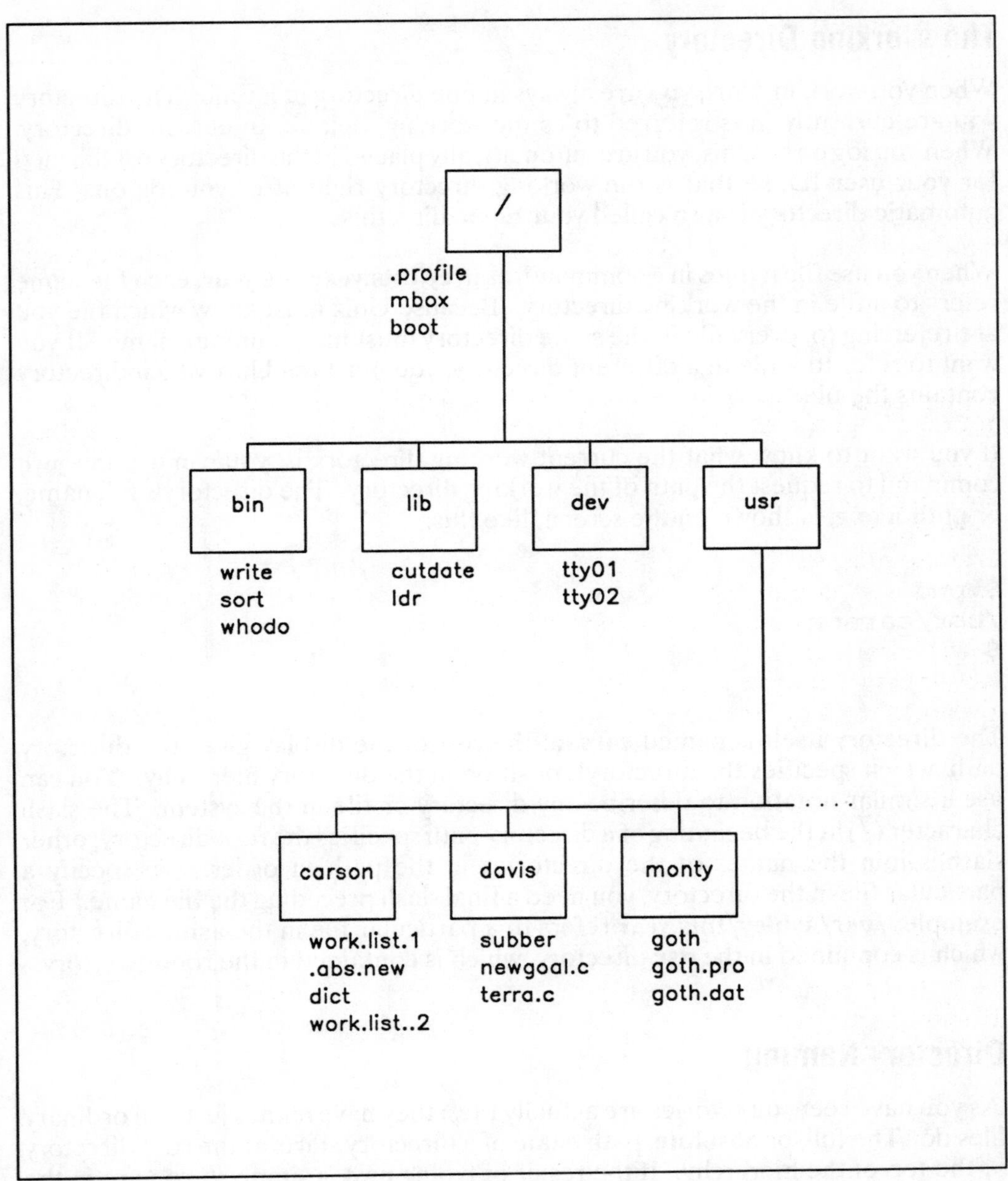

Figure 2.1 Unix directory structure

The Working Directory

When you work in Unix, you are always in one directory at a time. The directory you are currently in is referred to as the working, default, or current directory. When you log on to Unix, you are automatically placed in the directory established for your user ID, so that is the working directory right after you log on. This automatic directory is also called your **home** directory.

When you use file names in a command, as in **cp this.year one.year**, each file name refers to a file in the working directory. Because Unix must know which file you are referring to, every file in the same directory must have a unique name. If you want to refer to a file in a different directory, you must tell Unix which directory contains the file.

If you want to know what the current working directory is, you can use the **pwd** command to request the **p**ath of the **w**orking **d**irectory. The directory's full name, or **path name,** is shown on the screen, like this:

```
$ pwd
/usr/carson
$ _
```

The directory itself is named **carson**; the rest of the display gives the directory path, which specifies the directory's position in the directory hierarchy. You can use a similar notation to describe any directory or file in the system. The slash character (/) at the beginning of a directory path specifies the root directory; other slashes join the names of the directories in the path in order. To specify a particular file in the directory, you need a final slash preceding the file name. For example, **/usr/ashley/this.year** refers to a particular file in the **ashley** directory, which is contained in the **usr** directory, which is contained in the root directory.

Directory Naming

As you have seen, directories are actually files; they have names just like ordinary files do. The full, or **absolute**, path name of a directory starts at the root directory or the top of the hierarchy. If the result of typing **pwd** is simply **/**, you are in the root directory. This character always appears at the beginning of an absolute path.

The / character also joins directories in any path. For example, the path **/usr/carson** says to start at the root, go to directory **usr**, and then go to directory **carson**. If this directory contains another directory named **schedules**, the path would be **/usr/carson/schedules**.

A relative path begins at the working directory, without the / character. For example, if the working directory is **usr**, you could use **carson/schedules** to refer to **/usr/carson/schedules**.

Your automatic working directory is often called the home directory; this is the one you are placed in automatically when you log on to Unix. Your login ID value is your home directory's file name. In the Bourne shell, you can always refer to your home directory by the name of **$HOME** as well. If your login name is **monty**, you can use the name **$HOME** instead of **/usr/monty**. Typing **$HOME/schedules** is the same as typing **/usr/monty/schedules**. A directory path that begins with **$HOME** is an absolute path because **$HOME** is equivalent to beginning with the root directory and progressing to the current user's home directory. In the C shell, **%HOME** has the same effect.

Listing a Non-Working Directory

As you know, you can use the **ls** command to list the files in your working directory. You can also use it to list files in other directories. For example, you can use **ls /usr** to list the contents of the **/usr** directory. **ls /** lists the contents of the root directory. **ls /usr/monty** lists the files in the home directory of the user with login name of **monty**. Because directory names look just like ordinary file names, you can't tell from a simple listing which entries are directories. And just as ordinary file names must be unique within a directory, so must directory names also be unique. The subdirectories and ordinary files contained within a single directory must all have unique names.

To see which files are directories, use the **-l** option. The very first character in each file name line shows a **d** if the file is a directory and a hyphen (-) if it is another type of file. Following is an example:

```
$ ls -l
-rwxr-xr-x   1  ashley    14334   May 19   14:58  addresses
drwxr-xr-x   2  ashley     1298   May 22   09:32  projects
-rw-rw-rw-   1  ashley     8900   May 22   09:56  save_them
$ _
```

The second file listed represents a directory named **projects**, as shown by the first character in the line. The **-d** option of the **ls** command is also useful in identifying directories because it limits the display to directories only. In this example, only the directory files are listed:

```
$ ls -d
projects
$ _
```

You can also use the **-d** option in combination with others:

```
$ ls -ld
drwxr-xr-x   2  ashley     1298   May 22   09:32  projects
$ _
```

The result is an expanded listing of just the directory files in the current working directory.

Files in Directories

When you refer to a file in the working directory, you can just use its file name, as you did in Chapter 1. If you want to refer to a file in another directory, you must use the directory path as a file name prefix. Suppose your home directory is **carson** and that of a co-worker on the same project is **davis**; the absolute path names of the two directories are **/usr/carson** and **/usr/davis**. To print a file named **marchand** from your own directory, you'd use the command **lpr marchand**. To print a file of the same name from the **davis** directory, you would use **lpr /usr/davis/marchand**. You can refer to any file in any directory by prefixing it with the absolute path name. (Of course, you must be permitted access to the file; access and security will be discussed in Chapter 3.)

Any Unix command that lets you specify a file name permits a path name to be included if it is needed to identify which file you are referring to. For example, the following commands are all valid if the named files exist:

```
lpr /usr/davis/time.sheet
cat /usr/davis/michael.out
cp /usr/davis/time.sheet davis.time
cp my.time /usr/davis/ashley.time
```

```
mv my.time /usr/davis/ashley.timeout
rm /usr/davis/ashley.timeout
```

The directory names in the six previous commands qualify the file name and identify exactly which file is being referred to.

Copying and Moving Files to a Different Directory

The **cp** and **mv** commands allow you to specify a directory or ordinary file as the target to which you copy or move a file. Unix knows whether the target name represents a directory or an ordinary file. For example, if the system has a directory named **davis** in the **usr** directory, the command **cp marchand /usr/davis** copies the file named **marchand** from the working directory into the **davis** directory and retains the original file name, **marchand**. If the system doesn't have a directory named **davis**, the previous command creates an ordinary file named **davis** in the **usr** directory.

Similarly, you could use the command **mv marchand /usr/davis** to move a file named **marchand** from your directory into the **davis** directory. If you want to supply a new name (e.g., **marchand.over**), you can include the new name following the path name in the **cp** command and the **mv** command, as in **cp marchand /usr/davis/marchand.over** or **mv marchand /usr/davis/marchand.over**.

You can also specify more than one file at a time to be copied or moved to a target directory. But when you specify more than one file at a time, you cannot give the files new names as you copy them. When you enter the command **cp marchand.time stockwell.time mchale.time /usr/davis**, all three files are copied from the working directory to the target directory and stored under their original file names. The command **mv marchand.arc stockwell.arc mchale.arc /usr/davis** moves the source files to the target directory and assigns the original names and then removes all listed files from their original locations. If you name a target directory that doesn't exist, you'll get an error message.

As with copying and moving files within your working directory, you must be sure the target file names don't already exist in the target directory. If a file of that name exists in the target directory, it is overwritten and destroyed by the copied file. Unix doesn't notify you of this effect because it expects you to know what you are doing. When you move files, remember that the original file is deleted from its original location. And remember that if you move a file to a new directory and accidentally overwrite a file that has the same name but different contents, the target location contains only the data from the moved file; the data of the overwritten file is lost.

Special Directory Names

Unix provides special names to refer to a few directories. Just as **/** refers to the root directory, the symbol **.** as an element in a path name refers to the working or current directory. The symbol **..** as an element in a path name refers to the directory above the working directory, the parent directory. So if you want to refer to another directory on the same level and with the same parent as the current directory, you could use **..** as the beginning of the path name. For example, if you are in the **/usr/carson** directory and want to refer to the **/usr/davis** directory, you could use a reference such as **../davis** to name it. This reference is interpreted as telling Unix "start with the parent of the current directory, find the **davis** directory below the parent, and there you are." This is a **relative path**, because the **..** name is relative to the working directory; it does not start at the root directory.

By using the appropriate path name, you can display, print, and remove files from any directory, provided you have the appropriate access.

Unix System Exercise 2.1

Purpose: Become familiar with other directories.

1. Log on to Unix and display the name of the working directory.
2. Try to display listings of the **root** and **/usr** directories; if you are successful, try listings with the **-l** and **-d** options.
3. Display a listing of the **/dev** directory.
4. If you know the user ID of another person in your group, display the extended form of that person's directory (use **ls -l ../userID**).
5. Try to copy a file (not a directory) from another user's directory to your own. Name it **save**.

continued on following page. . .

Exercise 2.1 continued. . .

6. If you were successful with item 5, try to copy **this.month** from your directory to the directory of that other user; name it **from***userID*, using your own user ID.

If it doesn't work:

A. You may not have appropriate access to any other directories; if not, you can perform similar operations in Exercise 2.2 when you have created your own directory structure.

B. Don't worry about it if you can't get around in other directories; some installations require a great deal of security.

MANIPULATING DIRECTORIES

Generally, your home directory is all yours. You own all files in it and can do what you want with them. You can develop and maintain a complete hierarchy of directories below it, using **$HOME** as the first directory in the path. Unix provides commands you can use to create new directories, change the working directory, or even remove an empty directory. In this section, you will learn to create and maintain a structure of directories.

To make sure you have the correct access, use a command such as **ls -l /usr**. In the resulting listing, find the one for your user ID. It will look something like this:

```
drwxr-xr-x   2  ashley     1298   May 22   09:32  monty
```

If the line starts with **drwx**, you have all the access you need to work with this directory.

Creating a Directory (mkdir)

The **mkdir** command lets you **make** a new **dir**ectory. If you specify a relative path name (without starting with /), the new directory will be at a level below the working directory. If you specify an absolute path name, the path starts at the root directory. Suppose you are working in the **davis** directory and use the command **mkdir exercise**; Unix creates a new directory named **exercise** and places it one level below your working directory. If you then type **ls**, you will see the file name **exercise** listed with the other files. If you use **ls -l**, you'll see that **exercise** is a directory rather than an ordinary file.

The command **mkdir /usr/exercise** would create the new directory at the level below **/usr**, that is, at the same level as your home directory; you probably won't have the correct access to do this, in which case you'll see an error message. When you create directories, you will use relative paths most of the time in order to keep the new directories within your own control. You can create a complete hierarchy of your own below your home directory. For example, you could use the following series of commands:

```
$ pwd
/usr/carson
$ mkdir projects
$ mkdir research
$ mkdir projects/os_2
$ mkdir projects/dos4
$ mkdir research/troy
$ mkdir research/troy/greece
$ mkdir research/troy/britain
$ pwd
/usr/carson
$ _
```

The previous commands create a directory structure like the one shown in Figure 2.2. Notice that the top of this structure is your home directory, **carson**, rather than the root directory. The absolute path to the last directory created is **/usr/carson/research/troy/britain.** You could also specify this as **$HOME/research/troy/britain**.

After creating all the directories, you are still in the home directory, as indicated by the **pwd** command output. The two child directories (**projects** and **research**) appear as files in the home directory listing. If you get an extended directory listing, you'll notice the entries for the directories you created begin with the **d** character, indicating that they are indeed directories.

Any of the created directories can contain files. You could move or copy a file to any of the newly created directories by specifying the relative path for the target directory in a command issued from the home directory. For example, **mv athens.r research/troy/greece** moves the file named **athens.r** from your home directory to the **greece** directory.

If you specify a file or directory that already exists in the **mkdir** command, you will get a message that Unix can't make that directory. You can rename the existing file or directory or provide a new name for the one you are trying to create.

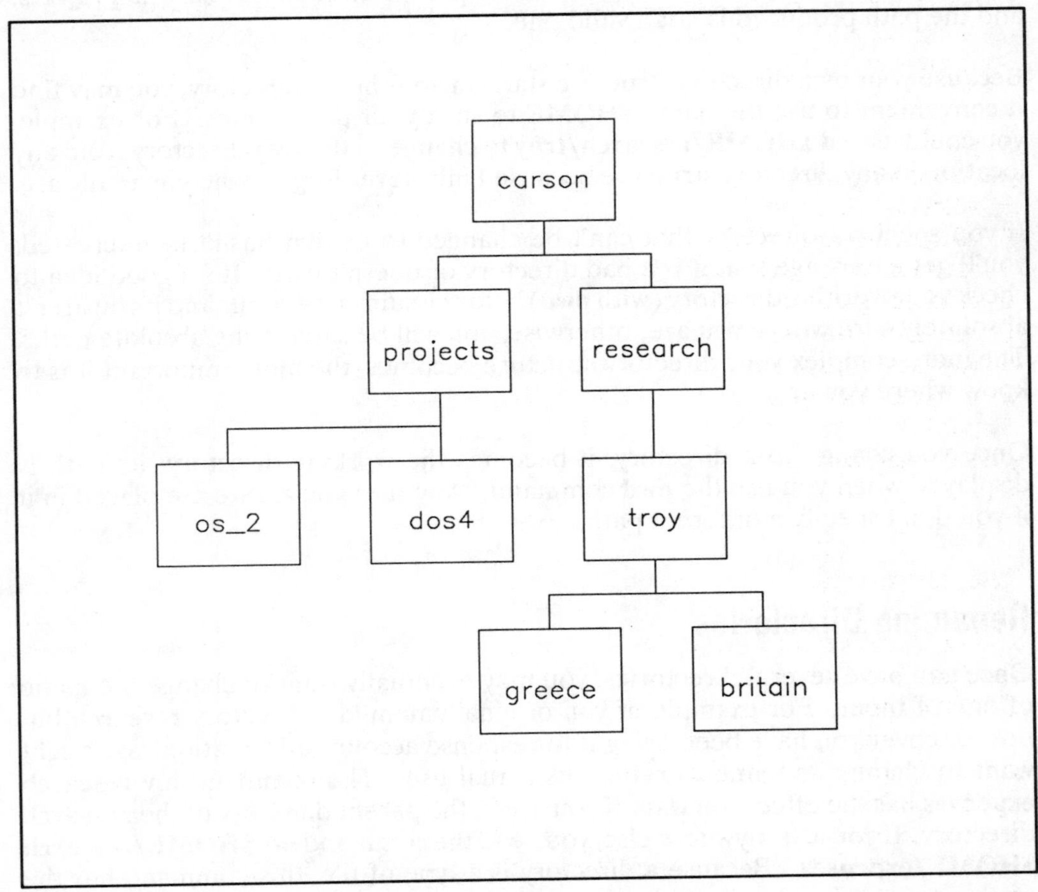

Figure 2.2 Created hierarchy

Changing Directories (chdir or cd)

You can change the working directory to any other directory to which you have access; if you have created a directory, you own it and have access to it. The **chdir** command lets you **ch**ange the working **dir**ectory to a different one that already exists; some versions of Unix require the abbreviated command **cd**. You can specify either an absolute or relative path in the command, depending on your needs. For example,entering the command **cd /usr/carson/project** has the same effect as entering **cd project** if the working directory is **/usr/carson**. The command **cd ../research/troy** could be used to change from the **project** directory to the **troy** directory. This command could not be used to change from the **os_2** directory to the **troy** directory because the parent directory of **os_2** is **projects**, and the path produced is not a valid one.

Because your own directory structure starts at your home directory, you may find it convenient to use the name **$HOME** to start your path names. For example, you could use **cd $HOME/research/troy** to change to the **troy** directory from any location in any directory structure because Unix never forgets who you really are.

If you specify a directory that can't be changed to or that hasn't been created, you'll get a message that it is a bad directory or doesn't exist. It's a good idea to check your working directory (with **pwd**) before issuing a **cd** command if you aren't absolutely sure where you are; otherwise, you will be safer using absolute paths. The more complex your directory structure becomes, the more important it is to know where you are.

Once you change to a directory, it becomes the working directory; its path is displayed when you use the **pwd** command. Any files you create are placed in it if you don't specify a different path.

Renaming Directories

Once you have several directories, you may eventually want to change the name of one of them. For example, if you originally named a directory **research** but now discover you have been using it for expense account information, you might want to change its name to reflect its actual use. The command **mv research expenses** has the effect you want if you are in the parent directory of the **research** directory. If you are anywhere else, you need the command **mv $HOME/research $HOME/expenses**. Because a directory is a type of file, this command has the effect of renaming the directory.

You can't use **mv** to physically move a directory or **cp** to copy one; only the system administrator can do that; however, you can achieve the effect of moving a directory to another location in a series of steps:

- First, make a new directory (**mkdir**) at the target location with the name you want.
- Next, move (**mv**) or copy (**cp**) all the files from the old directory to the new one.
- Finally, remove (**rmdir** or **rd**) the original directory if you don't want it in the original location.

Removing a Directory (rmdir or rd)

Once you have several directories in use, you'll need to maintain your hierarchy. Ultimately, this will involve removing directories as well as other activities. The **rmdir** command lets you **remove directories**; some versions of Unix require the form **rd** instead. Unix won't remove a directory that is the current working directory, is in the current directory's path, or that isn't empty, so you must first move or remove any files or subdirectories in the directory you want to remove. If you try to remove a directory that isn't empty, you'll see a message that it is not empty or is nonexistent. Of course, you must have the proper access to a directory before you can remove it. In general, if you created a directory, you can remove it.

The command **rmdir $HOME/projects/os_2** completely removes the **os_2** directory. If the working directory is **projects**, you could use **rd os_2** instead. You cannot remove a directory while it is the working directory. You won't have the proper access to remove your home directory.

Suppose you have a directory named **$HOME/projects/potential** containing only two files, named **ny.articles** and **archive.1900**. You want the files to be moved to a directory named **$HOME/research/newyork.** You could use the following series of commands:

```
$ pwd
/usr/carson
$ mkdir research/newyork
$ chdir projects/potential
$ cp ny.articles archive.1900 research/newyork
$ rm ny.articles archive.1900
$ chdir ..
$ pwd
/usr/carson/projects
$ rmdir potential
$ _
```

The result is that the same files are stored in a new directory with a different name and the original directory has been removed from the system. The **pwd** command was used a few times to document the current working directory.

Unix System Exercise 2.2

Purpose: Use directory management commands. *As you work through this exercise, use the* **ls** *and* **pwd** *commands whenever you need them. They help you keep track of where you are in the directory hierarchy.*

1. Log on to Unix if necessary.
2. Get a long directory listing to see your files; unless you have already experimented with the **mkdir** command, your home directory does not yet contain any other directories.
3. Create new directories named **exercise** and **text** below your home directory.
4. Change to the **exercise** directory, then create a directory named **chap2** below it.
5. Return to your home directory and list it. Then copy a file from home to the last directory you created (**$HOME/exercise/chap2**).
6. Copy two different files from your home directory to the **text** directory.

continued on following page. . .

Exercise 2.2 continued...

7. Change to the text directory and create a file named **year.1900** in it, using the calendar of the year 1900. Then copy that file to the **chap2** directory.
8. Change the name of the **text** directory to **machine**.
9. Return to your home directory. Then remove all the files in the **$HOME/exercise/chap2** directory and the directory itself.

If it doesn't work:

A. Be sure you use **mkdir**, **chdir** (or **cd**), and **rmdir** (or **rd**) as the commands to make, change, and remove directories. These commands should work. If one doesn't, try the long or short form, whichever you didn't use the first time. Remember to use paths beginning at **$HOME** (or **$home**) if you aren't in the direct path of the directory you are trying to affect.

B. Remember to use the correct path name before any file reference that is not in the current working directory.

FILE NAMES

So far, this book or your Unix system has provided the file names, but the day will come when you must create your own. In this section, you will learn to form the names; the same rules apply to ordinary file names as to directory names. You will also learn to how to get Unix to generate groups of file names so that a single file reference can apply to several files at a time.

Your Unix installation may have certain conventions you are expected to adhere to in creating names for directories and ordinary files. For example, you may be required to use certain characters at the beginning or end of names, or a particular set of characters following a period. You may be limited to a different number of characters, or to a subset of the generally allowable characters. If so, apply these guidelines when you create file names for use on your system. Consider the instructions in this book as hints to forming names, but make sure they are acceptable to your particular system.

Forming File Names

All Unix systems can handle file names of up to 14 characters; some can use names as long as 256 characters, but 14 is more standard. These characters can include the following:

- A to Z
- a to z
- 0 to 9
- _ (underscore)
- . (period)
- , (comma)

Just as Unix is case sensitive when you enter commands, it is also case sensitive with regard to file names; that is, the names **ABC**, **AbC**, and **abc** represent three different files. You can't use a space or a dash in a file name, but the underscore (_), period (.), and comma (,) are all valid. If you use a period as the first character of a file name, you create a hidden file; the file name will not appear in a normal directory listing. You can use the **-a** option of the **ls** command to show hidden files. If you use a period as the first character of a name by accident, you'll wonder where your file went. You can still refer to the file (perhaps to rename it), even if it doesn't appear in the listing.

Using the separator characters helps make the names easier for you to read; Unix can read names with or without separators. The following are all valid file names:

```
every_user
EXTRA.b
accounts.recv
Accounts.pay
Maxie.BBB
May.19.1990
abciii4tGbq900
```

The period is often used to create an extension for a file name. Many programs require or prefer a particular extension. For example, object code for the C compiler requires **.c** at the end of the file name. The C compiler generates files with extensions of **.o** and **.m** containing object code and symbolic maps. If you use any software that requires or generates particular extensions, avoid those extensions in other file names you create.

Ambiguous File Names

When referring to existing files in a Unix command, you can use special characters in the file name to refer to more than one file. For example, if you have eight files with names ending in **.c**, you might want to copy or print them all with a single command. If you have files named **chap1.unix**, **chap2.unix**, and **chap3.unix**, you might want to perform the same operation on all three. You can do this with special characters in a file name.

The character **?** represents any other character. A file specification of **chap?.unix** includes the three files mentioned in the previous paragraph, but would not include **chap12.unix** or **chap1.unixv**. The file names must match except for the characters in the position that corresponds to the position of the **?** character.

The character * represents no character or any number of characters. A file specification of **chap*.unix** represents the three files listed earlier as well as **chap14.unix**, **chap.unix**, and **chapter6.unix**. It does not include **chap1.unixv** or **CHAP1.UNIX**. A specification of * represents every file in the directory except for hidden files to prevent you from accessing these accidentally. You could use a command such as cp * **$HOME/projects/newyork** to copy all the nonhidden files in the working directory to the target directory; however, you probably wouldn't need the standard hidden files in another directory. A specification of ***.*** represents every file name that contains at least one period. You could list just the hidden files in a directory with a command such as **ls .***, which would list all files with an initial period and any other characters following that period.

Sometimes you want to match not just any character, but one of a specific set of characters. If you include such characters in square brackets, the file specification will match any one of them. For example **chap[123x].unix** will match **chap1.unix**, **chap2.unix**, **chap3.unix**, or **chapx.unix**, but no other files.

You can include as many characters as you want within the brackets; you can even specify a range with a dash. The specification **memo[a-eA-E]** matches **memoa** through **memoe** and **memoA** through **memoE**.

You can combine the various special characters to specify various combinations. Following are some examples:

***a**	All files with names ending in **a**
***[xyz]**	All files with names ending in **x**, **y**, or **z**
***.?**	All files that contain a period with exactly one character following it
??	All files with two-character names
***.obj**	All files with **.obj** as the last four characters

You can find out what files are included in an ambiguous file name with **ls** or with the **echo** command. Typing **ls** followed by the ambiguous file name produces a listing down the screen of just the file names that match the specification. To use **echo**, just type the command name followed by the ambiguous file name; the selected names are displayed across the screen. You can see more names at a time with **echo**, which is useful if you have a very full directory. The command **echo *[xyz]** lists all the file names in the current directory that end in **x**, **y**, or **z**. The command **echo /usr/a*** lists all the file names in the **/usr** directory that start with **a**.

File Names in Commands

You can use ambiguous file names in any Unix command that uses a file name. Here are some valid commands:

```
ls m*
ls -l /usr/a[acs-y]*
echo *add*
cp memo* $home/research/troy
mv Chap?.unix archive
lpr *.year
lpr chap[123456]
```

The first example lists all the file names that begin with the character **m.** The next lists all the file names in the **/usr** directory that start with **a** and have a second character **a**, **c**, or any other letters from **s** through **y**. The **echo** command lists across the screen all file names that contain the characters **add**. The **cp** command copies every file whose name begins with **memo** to the target directory; no file names are changed. The **mv** command moves all files that match the specification to the target directory. The first **lpr** command example sends all files whose names end with **.year** to the line printer, while the last **lpr** command prints files named **chap1**, **chap2**, **chap3**, **chap4**, **chap5**, and **chap6**.

When Unix sees an ambiguous file reference in a command, it generates (internally) a list of all file names in the directory that match; then it applies the command to each of them. The generated file names are processed in the order in which Unix encounters them in the directory.

COMMAND EXPANSION

The basic commands you learned in Chapter 1 can use all the features discussed in this chapter. This section provides expanded information on all those commands, with a few more examples. You'll find that you use these commands and the features covered in this chapter in virtually all your Unix sessions.

The cp Command

Figure 2.3 shows the complete format of the **cp** command. When you specify a single file to be copied to another single file, you can use any path with either the source or target file name. If you specify more than one file, either separately or with an ambiguous file name, you must specify a directory as the target without a specific file name.

Command: **cp**

Purpose: Copy a file.

Format: **cp** *source-file target-file*
cp *source-file-list target-directory*

Examples:

1. `cp accounts89 accounts.arc`
2. `cp account6 payments $home/archives`
3. `cp account* archives`

Result: Two identical files with different names or all specified files are copied to target directory.

Figure 2.3 Expanded **cp** *command*

If you specify a directory as the target, all the source files are copied to that directory and given the same file names they had originally. If you want to change the name of a file in the copy process, you must copy it individually.

The mv Command

Figure 2.4 shows the complete format of the **mv** command. When you specify a single file to be moved or renamed, you can use any path with either the source or target file name; the result is a single file at the target location with the specified name. If you specify more than one file, either separately or with an ambiguous file name, you must specify a directory as a target without a specific file name. The source files are then stored in the target directory with the same file names they had originally.

Command: **mv**

Purpose: Move or rename a file.

Format: **mv** *source-file target-file*
mv *source-file-list target-directory*

Examples:

1. `mv accounts89 accounts.arc`
2. `mv payments $home/archive/payments.89`
3. `mv account6 payments $home/archive`
4. `mv acc*.89 archives`

Result: One file with the target name or all specified files moved to the target directory.

Figure 2.4 Expanded **mv** *command*

The ls Command

You can name a specific directory in the **ls** command to get a listing of the files in that directory. The command **ls -l /usr/monty/process** results in a long listing of the **process** directory. If **process** is an ordinary file rather than a directory, you'll see only one line in the output. You can also use an ambiguous file name to see a listing of the files that match that name. For example, if you use the command **ls chap*.unix,** you'll see a listing of just the files in the working directory that match the ambiguous file name.

The cat Command

You can name many files in the **cat** command, either separately or with an ambiguous file name, and you can include a path where appropriate. The files are listed in sequence on the screen. If you use redirection, as in **cat chap?.unix > all.chaps**, all files that match the file specification are sent (in alphabetical order) to the target file to create a concatenated file containing all of them.

The rm Command

You can remove many files with a single **rm** command, either by listing them separately or by using an ambiguous file name. You can include a path in any separately listed name or preceding an ambiguous file name. Using the **-i** option so that Unix asks you to confirm it before each specific file is removed helps to ensure that you don't remove any files accidentally.

The lpr Command

You can request printouts of several files at once by listing them separately or by using an ambiguous file name in the **lpr** command. The files are printed in sequence when the print request is processed by the queue. If you use the **-m** option, you won't be notified until all the files are printed.

Unix System Exercise 2.3

Purpose: Create file names and use ambiguous names in commands.

1. Log on to Unix if necessary.
2. Create a new directory with any name at the level of the **machine** directory, and then change to the new directory.

continued on following page. . .

Exercise 2.3 continued. . .

3. Create three files containing the current date in this directory; provide a name for each file so that you can use an ambiguous file name to refer to all three.
4. Copy the three new files to the **machine** directory using their ambiguous file name. Check the **machine** directory listing.
5. Remove all files in your home directory that start with the letter t; use the **-i** option so you see which ones are deleted.
6. Create a file named **year.1901** in the **machine** directory. Then move all files containing **year** in their names to the new directory. Check the directory listing.
7. Use an ambiguous file name with square brackets to print a few files from your home directory. Notice that the print ID lets you know how many files will be printed.

If it doesn't work:

A. If you don't get the effect you want, try **pwd** to be sure where you are. Use **ls** as needed.

B. Don't worry too much if you remove and rearrange the files differently from the ways mentioned in this exercise. Just make sure you can control what happens when you specify ambiguous file names.

SUMMARY

In this chapter you learned to construct directory names and file names as well as create and maintain directory structures. In the process, you learned to do the following:

- Display the current directory path with **pwd**.
- Create a new directory with **mkdir**.
- Change the working directory with **chdir** or **cd**.

- Remove an empty directory with **rmdir** or **rd**.
- Display file names included in an ambiguous reference with **echo.**

You also learned additional features of various file handling commands covered in Chapter 1.

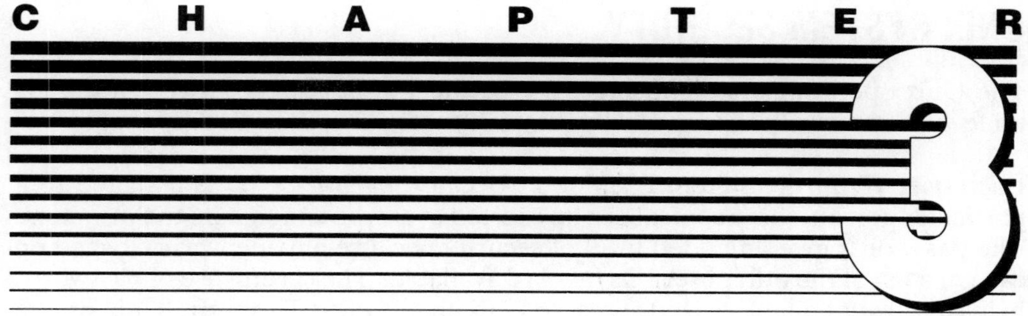

UNIX SECURITY AND ACCESS

So far, you have been working in directories created for you or that you created. You have full access to these directories. There is much more to any Unix system, and security and control are a large part of the system administrator's job. You need to know enough about security so that you understand what you can accomplish within the Unix system. You must know enough about access to arrange the permissions you need and to provide or prevent access to your files for others in your work group.

In this chapter, you will examine the overall security structure and see how your password is just the tip of the iceberg. You'll also see how each user is a member of a group, which allows for limited access. You will learn to determine and change access for any file listed in any of your own directories. You'll also learn to establish links to your files from other locations, which may be other directories in your own structure or in some other user's directory structure.

UNIX SYSTEM SECURITY

The Unix operating system includes a great deal of built-in security. At the log on level, the security is achieved by requiring user ID codes and passwords.

Each user ID in the system is unique. Because each user ID is assigned to a particular person, some control can be exerted over who can sign on to the system. The passwords give an added level of security because anyone who is logged on can get a list of the other user IDs that are available. The careful use of passwords helps to prevent unauthorized access to Unix and its files. The entire Unix system can find out your user ID, but no one can find out your password from within the system.

Password Rules

Once you receive your password, you enter it whenever you log on to Unix. You should keep this password in a safe place (if you write it down) and change it regularly. If you forget your password, you aren't quite out of luck. The system administrator can't find out what your password is, but he or she can issue you a new one. You can then change it to one you will not forget. In this section, you'll learn to change your password.

Like Unix commands and file names, passwords are case sensitive. They can be composed of any printable characters; they should be at least six characters long. Your password should be memorable to you, but not easy to guess; don't use your first name, your user ID, your telephone number, or anything quite so obvious. You can help make it harder to guess your password by mixing upper and lowercase letters; you could use **shOoteRs** rather than **shooters**, for example. The password should also be somewhat easy to type. While **%c!0-2D** would be just dandy to Unix, it would be difficult to type, as well as to remember. Remember that you never see the password on the screen, so you don't want to get lost while you are typing it.

Changing the Password

When you are logged in, you can change your password with the **passwd** command. Here is how the screen looks after you have changed your password:

```
$ passwd
Changing password for carson
Old password:
Type new password:
Re-enter new password:
$ _
```

Unix responds to the command by displaying your user name (**carson** in the example) and then requesting the old password. You type it and press **Return** (remember that passwords never appear on the screen). If it is correct, you are asked to type your new password. This new password must be longer than the minimum length for your installation (you'll be asked to enter a longer one if it isn't) and can be as much longer as you please; however, Unix uses only the first eight characters. Once you've typed a valid new password, you are asked to confirm it by retyping the same new password. If you type it just as you did before, the password is changed. The next time you log on, you must use the new password.

If you type the old password incorrectly, you'll see a brief message, and then the shell prompt will return. Type the **passwd** command again, and type more carefully. If you had trouble with the old password, give some extra care to specifying a new one that is easy for you to type.

If you retype the new password incorrectly, you'll be notified of a mismatch and informed that the password is not changed. You can enter the **passwd** command once more to try changing your password again.

Trying the New Password

Once you have the password changed, you should log off immediately and log back on, using the new password. If you have trouble, see your system administrator immediately.

Unix System Exercise 3.1

Purpose: Change your password

1. Log on to Unix if necessary.
2. Change your password.
3. Log off and back on to see if it works.

If it doesn't work:

A. Be sure you type the new password the same way when you first enter it and when you confirm it.

B. If you have trouble, see the system administrator. Changing the password should not cause any problems.

FILE AND DIRECTORY SECURITY

Just as Unix has passwords for preventing unauthorized system access, it also has security to prevent unauthorized access to files and directories. Different types of users need different types of access. In this section, you'll learn about the general types of users and the types of access. You'll learn to use **ls -l** to check the access various groups have to your files and directories. Later, you'll learn to change the access other user types have to your files. While there is a certain default setup at each installation, you can change the accesses of files and directories that you own.

Types of Users

As far as file access is concerned, there are three types of users. The first type is the **owner**, the creator of the file or directory. If you used **mkdir** to create a directory and created the files in it yourself, you own them. The second user type is the **group**. Each user is a member of a defined group that has one or more members. Often the members of a group work on the same project, are in the same department, or need to run the same programs. All the members in a group may have access to any member's files by default, although you can change this in many cases with special commands. The third type of user includes everyone outside the owner's group. These people generally need less access to a user's files.

Actually, there is one more type of user; that's the **superuser**. The system administrator may be the only superuser, but often several people have access to the superuser password. Anyone logged in as the superuser has total access to every file and directory in the system. You can't change or affect superuser access. Your system administrator has the responsibility of ensuring that only reliable people can access your data.

Types of Access

Just as there are three types of users you are concerned with, there are three types of file access: read, write, and execute. **Read** access lets you read (including listing and printing) the contents of files; you can even copy files to which you have read access into your own directory. You automatically have read access to your own files; you probably have read access to the files of others in your group; in some systems, you may have read access to even more files. Other users in your group may have read access to your files as well.

When you have **write** access, you can change, move, or delete files. You automatically have write access to your own files, but you may not have write access to anyone else's files. And you may not want anyone else, even in your own work group, having write access to your files. **Execute** access means you can execute a file; this is only meaningful with programs or script files. Many systems don't automatically give execute access to files. But you'll have execute access to many Unix utility programs that you run every day.

Having a type of access is referred to as having **access permission**. You can change the access permissions for your own files. For example, if you don't want anyone else to read a file, you can remove read access for anyone but you. If you want other users in your group to be able to write to a group of your files, you can extend write permission to the group. Even though you always have write access to your own files, you may want to change this so that you don't accidentally erase or change a file. Some Unix installations don't give execute access to a user's files automatically. Most files aren't executable, so this doesn't really matter. If you want to execute a file you own, you can always assign yourself the required execute permission.

The execute access type is not appropriate for directories, so Unix gives it a different meaning; for a directory file, execute access gives users the right to perform some advanced functions that affect directory listings, such as establishing file links. You can read directory listings with only read access. If you create a directory you don't want others to check out, you have to remove their read access. If you can list the root and **/usr** directories, you have read access permission to them. You probably won't have execute permission to system directories automatically.

Each of the three user types (the owner, the group, and others) can have any combination of the three access types (read, write, and execute) for each file or directory. For example a file's owner may have read, write, and execute permissions for his or her home directory; other group members may have read and execute permissions; and everybody else may have no access to the directory at all.

Default Access

Your installation has defaults set up for all newly created files and directories. It may give all access permissions to the owner, just read and write permissions to the group, and just read permission to everyone else. It may give read and write access permissions to the owner as well as the group and no access to anyone else. You can check your default access through the **-l** option of the **ls** command.

Figure 3.1 shows how the first set of characters in each line of the long listing represents the access permissions. As you know, the first character indicates whether the file is a directory (*d*) or not (-). The next nine specify the permissions; the first set of three indicate the owner access, the next set of three indicate the group access, and the final set of three indicate the access for everybody else. The maximum access is represented by *rwx*, indicating read, write, and execute. Wherever a dash appears, an access permission has not been given.

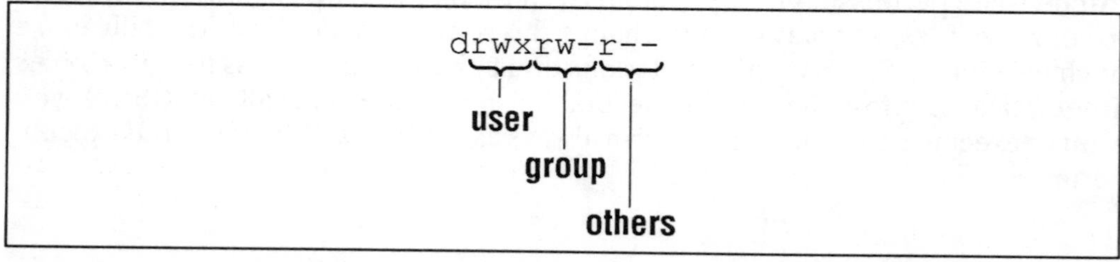

Figure 3.1 Access specifications

Checking Access

The result of **ls -l** for three files is shown below. Note that the first character is **d** for the first file listed, which indicates that it is a directory file. The file names appear on the right.

```
drwxrwxr-- 2  carson   784 May 15  08:53 processing
-rw-rw-r-- 1  carson  1128 May 17  10:14 realty.data
-rw-rw-r-- 1  carson  9176 May 15  11:12 weather.data
```

In the example, the owner has **rwx** access for the directory, which allows reading, writing, and advanced operations. By default, the owner doesn't have execute permission for the ordinary files. The owner's group also has read and write access permissions for all the files, indicated by **rw**. The group member can't execute any programs, but they can search the directory because the listing for **processing** includes an **x**, indicating execute permission. Everybody else has only read access (**r--**); they can't make changes to the files or search the directory.

You can check the access permissions in any directory you can search. If you can change to the directory of another user in your group, you can check the permissions there. If you try to change to a directory of a user in another group, you probably won't be able to. A message such as *bad directory* or *access denied* means that the directory doesn't exist or you don't have execute permission for that directory.

Changing Access Permissions

You can change access permissions for any files or directories you own. You must do it by user type, though; you can't give some members of your group access that you don't want others to have. If you want more access to a file you don't own, you must work that out with the file's owner. Some of your files and directories may be required by others in your group, so don't try to restrict legitimate access.

Access changing is done with the **chmod** command. Figure 3.2 (see following page) shows the format. When you use this command, you change the access for yourself as owner, for all members of your group, for everybody else, or for some combination of the three user types. You can't change access for a single user this way, or even for a group that you don't belong to, without affecting the rest of "everybody else."

Command: chmod

Purpose: Change access permission for one or more files.

Format: **chmod** *user-types[operation]*[*permission*] *file-list*

user types

u	User or owner of file.
g	Group owner belongs to.
o	All other users.
a	All three user types.

operations

+	Add the permission.
–	Remove the permission.
=	Set permission; all other permissions reset.

permissions

r	Read permission.
w	Write permission.
x	Execute permission.
s	Set ID to owner during execution.

Examples:

1. `chmod u-w finances.data`
2. `chmod go+r newyork.1990`
3. `chmod o+r newyork/*`
4. `chmod g-x $home/miscel`

Results:

1. Write permission for owner removed for one file; probably done to prevent changes by accident.
2. Group and "other" users get read access for file **newyork.1990**.
3. Read access given to "other" users for all files in the **newyork** directory.
4. Execute permission removed for group from **$home/miscel** directory, which means the group members can't display the directory listing.

Figure 3.2 The **chmod** *command*

You specify four items in most **chmod** commands; the type of user you are dealing with, the particular operation, the particular access, and the file(s) to be affected. The user type can be yourself (**u**), your group (**g**), other users (**o**), or all three (**a**). You can combine these if you like, using **ug** to represent yourself and your group or **go** to represent every user except yourself.

The operation can be to add an access permission (+), to remove an access permission (–), or to add a particular permission while removing all others (=).

The permissions you specify are the same ones that appear in the directory listing (**r** for read, **w** for write, and **x** for execute) as well as a new one. The code **s** gives execute access permission, but also resets the ID of the other user to that of the owner while the program is being executed. This allows temporary access to data files and other programs that program may need to access while the specified program is being run but doesn't allow general access to those files.

The command **chmod u+x newprog** adds execute access to the file named **newprog**. The command **chmod a=r newfile** provides read access permission for **newfile** for all three user types, and removes any write or execute access permission. The command **chmod ug+x newprogs/*** gives execute permission to the owner and its group to all files in the newprogs directory. If you use the = operation, you can omit the access if you wish; the effect is to remove all accesses for the user-type, as shown below:

```
$ ls -l exam
-rw-rw-rw- 0  carson   4567 May 18  12:50 exam
$ chmod go= exam
$ ls -l exam
-rw------- 0  carson   4567 May 18  12:50 exam
$ _
```

Notice that the user type specified is **go**, which includes both the group and all others but not the owner **carson**. The = operation includes no permission types, so all the permissions are removed. In the second expanded directory entry, all access permissions for the group and other users are gone.

After you use a **chmod** command, it is a good idea to check the directory entry to make sure you entered the command correctly and produced what you intended, as in the previous example.

Limitations of the chmod Command

As previously mentioned, the **chmod** command doesn't let you change permissions for a particular individual (other than yourself) or subset of users. If you decide to let one member of your group have write access to your directories, you must give write access to the entire group. Similarly, if you want to shut a particular member of your group out of one of your files, you'll have to exclude the entire group.

Unix System Exercise 3.2

Purpose: Change access permissions.

1. Log on to Unix, if necessary.
2. Examine your extended listing to see your default access permissions. If you can, check the access permissions in the root directory.
3. List your **machine** directory, and then remove your own read and execute access permissions and try to list it again. Restore the read access and try it. Then restore the execute access.
4. Remove the write permission for file **my.address** in your home directory, then try to add the date line to the file. Restore the write permission and try listing it again.
5. If your files have read permissions for the group, remove it for a few files. Get another group member to try to read those files. Restore the permissions if you want.
6. Remove your group's permission to search the **machine** directory. Now you can put private files there!
7. If you know the user ID of another user in your group, try to display (with **cat**) a file you don't have read access to. Try to add a date line to a file you don't have write access to.

If it doesn't work:

A. Check your access regularly as you perform these exercises. Every time you use **chmod**, follow it with **ls -l**.

B. If you don't have access to anyone else's files or directories, try changing your own access to your files. Be sure to restore it before going on.

FILE LINKS

When you create a file on disk, Unix places the file name in the appropriate directory and creates a link or pointer that points to the physical file. When you remove a file with **rm**, the link is broken and the pointer is removed from the directory. One of the values you see in the **ls -l** listing is the number of **links** to the file. In the partial directory listing that follows, the directory entry has two links (standard for directories) – one for the directory entry and one for a link to the parent directory. If the directory has subdirectories, you'll see a higher number of links. Each ordinary file has a single link; you'll never see a file without any links because the directory entry itself represents a link.

```
drwxrwxr-- 2  carson    784 May 15  08:53 processing
-rwxrw-r-- 1  carson   1128 May 17  10:14 realty.data
-rwxrw-r-- 1  carson   9176 May 15  11:12 weather.data
```

Creating New Links

Suppose you and another member of your group use a single file in which both of you list your scheduled meetings, so that you can tell at a glance when you are both free. This file belongs to one or the other of you and is stored in that user's directory; the other needs read and write access to the file and must use a path to access the file.

Unix lets you put file names pointing to a single file in more than one directory by using **links**; all links will point to the same physical file. The file names that constitute the links need not all be the same, but when the file can be reached directly by several directories, the process of reaching it is simplified for all the users. You can create a new link from the file to the other person's directory, causing a pointer to the same file to be placed in the other directory. Both directory entries will show two links instead of one.

In order to set up multiple links to a file, you must have execute access to the second directory; each user must change his or her own accesses, however.

Again, suppose you have a file in which you keep error data from activities you pursue while working in three different directories, **$HOME/projects/os_2**, **$HOME/projects/dos4**, and **$HOME/research/troy/britain**. Wherever you store your file, it seems you always have to use a path name to access it. You can solve the problem by having the exact same file (not a copy of it) appear in all three directories so you can use a simple file name in all cases.

When you create a new link to a file, Unix places the name you provide in the target directory, and establishes a new pointer to the file. The entry in the extended directory listing showing the number of links to the file is incremented by 1. Both file names point to the same file and, in fact, actually refer to the exact same file. The file can be referenced without a path from any directory it appears in, even if it has a different name in each directory. You can access your error data from any of three locations without a path.

When you use **rm** to delete a file, it removes a single link. If a file has more than one link, you can remove one file name and still access the file from the other link. Once a file has more than one link, Unix doesn't remember which link came first, so you can remove links independently. Once a file is down to a single link, however, the next time you specify it in an **rm** command, you'll lose the physical file.

The ln Command

You can use the **ln** command to create a new link for a file. Figure 3.3 shows the format. The source file or new link can include the appropriate path. You must have execute access to any directories affected. The specified source file is the file that already exists and from which a new link is created. If the new link specification is omitted, a link to the specified file is placed in the working directory, which means you must specify a path with the source file. If you do specify a new link, it must include a file name that will appear in the target directory. If you just specify a directory or omit the new link specification, the original file name is used. If you use two links to the same physical file in the same directory, you must use different names for the two links.

Command: **ln**

Purpose: Create a new link to an ordinary file.

Format: **ln** *source-file* [*new link*]
ln *source-file directory*

Examples:

1. `ln /usr/ashley/theatre.data`
2. `ln team.schedule /usr/carson/team.dates`
3. `ln team.schedule /usr/davis`

Results:

1. The file name **theatre.data** appears in the current working directory; it links to the specified source file.
2. The file name **team.dates** appears in the **/usr/carson** directory; it refers to the same file as does **team.schedule** in the working directory.
3. The file name **team.schedules** appears in the **/usr/davis** directory referring to the source file.

Figure 3.3 The **ln** *command*

Once new links to a file are established, the number of total links appears in each directory listing. When you remove a file that has multiple links, it can still be accessed through any of the others. Only when the final link is broken is the physical file lost.

Unix System Exercise 3.3

Purpose: Establish new links to a file.

1. Log on to Unix if necessary.
2. Make the file **$HOME/machine/year.1900** appear as **link.1900** in the **$HOME/exercise** directory.
3. Do a long listing of either directory and note the number of links for the file.

continued on following page. . .

Exercise 3.3 continued. . .

4. To verify that both file names point to the same file, use **date > >** to add the date line to the end of one of the file names. Then display the file under the other name to see if the date line appears at the end of the file.
5. Create another link to the same file from your home directory. Note that the directory shows three links.
6. Remove the original file name from the **machine** directory. Check the **exercise** directory listing and note that the link total is down to two. Remove the pointer in **exercise**.
7. Check the listing in the home directory. Note that there is one link; leave the file here for now.
8. If you have write access to another user's directory, create a link to one of your files there. Ask that user to try it out.

If it doesn't work:

A. Be very specific in the command; some systems require a target file name even if you aren't actually changing the file name.

SUMMARY

This chapter has focused on security and access in a Unix system. Of all the material you've learned so far, these topics are most likely to be somewhat different from system to system because each installation determines how to implement the security measures. You have learned to do the following:

- Change your password with **passwd** .
- Modify other users' access to your files and directories with **chmod**.
- Create additional links to files with **ln**.

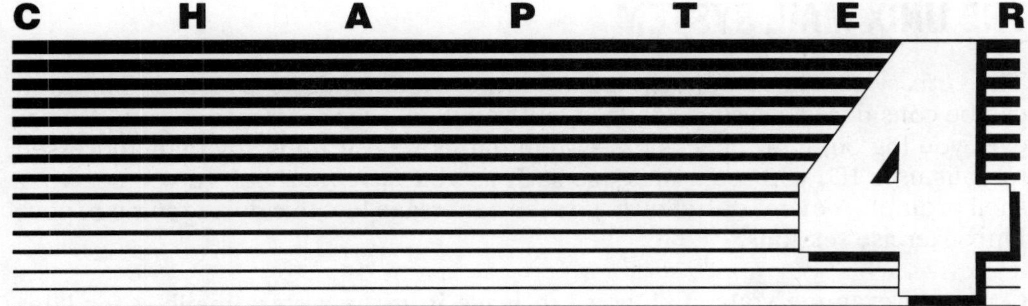

UNIX COMMUNICATIONS

Unix provides an extensive electronic mail system that lets you send letters and messages to other Unix users and receive them in return. The Unix system administrator and various Unix processes can also send mail to you. You can send mail to other users, including the system administrator, whether or not they are actually online at the same time. Whenever someone logs on, Unix displays a message if any mail is waiting. Some versions of Unix even notify you if mail arrives while you are online. In this chapter you'll learn to manage the messages you receive as well as to send mail to other users.

Most versions of Unix also provide commands that let online users communicate directly with each other without going through the mail system. You will learn to use those commands later in this chapter.

THE UNIX MAIL SYSTEM

The Unix system has a system mail area where mail to users is stored. This area can be considered a system mailbox, but you'll only see messages to you. Whenever you log on, Unix checks the system mailbox. If it finds any mail addressed to your user ID, you see a message such as *You have mail* before you see your shell prompt. You may already have seen a message like this during some of your Unix exercise sessions.

Once you examine your mail, you can leave it in the system mailbox for later processing, delete it from the system, or save it in a file or in your personal mailbox. You'll learn to handle all these options in this chapter.

Reading Your Mail

Suppose you log on and discover that you have some mail. While it isn't a requirement, you may want to read it immediately. To do that, just type **mail**. The exact result depends on your version of Unix. You might see a message displayed immediately, somewhat as shown in Figure 4.1. If so, just read it, and then press **Return**. If there is another message, you'll see it; if not, you'll be back at the shell prompt. For most Unix systems, the message will still be in the system mailbox, so if you type **mail** again, you'll see it again. For other Unix systems, the messages are automatically transferred to a personal mailbox in your home directory.

```
$ mail
From carson  Sun Nov 16  15:08:42   1990
Hi Steve -- today's meeting with her eloquence has been
rescheduled for 4:30.  We'd better not plan to meet at
the spa until 6 or later.          Mike

? _
```

Figure 4.1 Reading Unix mail

The result of typing **mail** may be a message stating that you have messages and perhaps a list of message numbers and the senders. This message will be followed by a prompt, much as shown in Figure 4.2. The prompt may be just a cursor on a new line, as in the figure, or a question mark on a new line. Press **Return** and you'll see the first message. Press **Return** again and you'll see the next message if there is one. If there are no more messages, you will see either the shell prompt or a message that you can't go beyond the last message. If you see the message, type **Ctrl-D** or **q** to quit the mail system and return to the shell prompt.

```
$ _
mail version x.x  January 28, 1987.  Type ? for help.
5 messages
   5 carson   Fri   May 26  16:14   10/382  "sorting"
   4 monty    Fri   May 26  13:22    2/94   "urgent"
   3 george   Thu   May 25  12:41   35/834
   2 monty    Thu   May 25  11:54    6/248  "schedule"
   1 alice    Thu   May 25   8:32    4/137  "benefit change"
_
```

Figure 4.2 Listing of Unix mail messages

Some Unix versions use the Berkeley mail system (regardless of which prompt you see). The electronic mail works similarly, but in the Berkeley mail system you must start it with **Mail**, using an uppercase "M." And when you press **Return** to see the next message, the previous one is removed from the system mailbox and stored in a special personal mailbox (**mbox**) in your home directory. You may have to type **q** to exit the Berkeley mail system.

Sending Mail

Sending mail is generally very simple. You send it by specifying the user ID of the person (or persons) you want to receive the mail in the **mail** command. You can even send mail to yourself. To send a message, you type **mail** *userID*, inserting your own user ID or a colleague's user ID, and press **Return**; the message you prepare is sent to the user you specify. To send the same message to several users, just include all the user IDs in the command line. Once you press **Return**, the mail system enters **compose mode** and lets you type the message.

For example, suppose you want to send a message to users named Davis, Monty, and Smithson. You would use this command:

```
mail davis monty smithson
```

Unix places you in the mail system's compose mode, in which you can compose a message directly from the keyboard. You may be prompted for additional information that your version of Unix uses; the most common prompt asks for the subject of the message. Just type a few words to indicate what the message is about. For example, if you are scheduling a meeting, you could use the meeting date or topic as the subject. You may be prompted for carbon copies (CC:); then enter the user IDs of any others to receive the message. Many people like to send themselves a copy of each message they mail, just for documentation. Eventually, you'll see a line containing only the cursor at the left margin.

When you see a line containing only the cursor at the left margin, start typing the message. Use **Backspace** or **DeleteLine** (if you have this feature) to make corrections, and press **Return** at the end of each completed line. Once you've pressed **Return**, the line is sent, just as with command lines. When you reach the end of the message, press **Return** again, and then place a period on the next line as the first character. After the next **Return**, you'll be returned to the shell prompt and the message will have been sent. Some Unix systems don't respond to the period on a separate line. If you try this and don't see the shell prompt, press **Ctrl-D**. You'll see a message such as *(end of message)* or *EOF*, and the shell prompt will be back. You can use **Ctrl-D** to end any message and terminate compose mode. If you press your break key (it may require **Ctrl-Break**) before the message is ended, the message won't be sent.

After you have composed the message, your screen might show something like this:

```
$ mail davis monty smithson
Subject: Board meeting
Don't forget we have a special meeting Friday afternoon
at the Blarney Stone.  The agenda includes ethnic heritage
and extensive non-prime time activities.  I'll be there by
5:15.
Thanks.    BB
.
$ _
```

Sending Prepared Files

Many times you won't want to type the mail at the keyboard but will want to either use your editor to compose the message or send a file that already exists. You can send a file that already exists by using **<** to redirect the command input, so it uses a file instead of the standard input device. If your user ID is **carson**, for example, the command **mail carson < test.message** sends the contents of the file named **test.message** to you as a mail message. You can also send a prepared file to multiple users. For example, suppose you have already prepared the previous message and stored it in a file named **blarney**. You can send it to the same people with this command:

```
$ mail davis monty smithson < blarney
$ _
```

You can prepare messages of any length in advance and send them by using redirection. This method has the added advantage of keeping a copy of the message in your directory for documentation without cluttering up the system mailbox. If you leave too much mail in the system mailbox, you may get a message from your system administrator asking you to clean it out.

Using a Prepared List of Users (alias)

If you frequently send mail to the same list of users, you may want to create an alias to refer to a list of users with a single name. For example, the command **alias buddies davis monty smithson** means that you can use **mail buddies < blarney** and Unix will expand the operand **buddies** into the defined names. If your Unix version permits, you can define as many aliases as you want to refer to different groups of names. The **alias** command is discussed further in Chapter 11.

Undelivered Mail

If you send mail to an invalid user ID, it generally ends up in a file in your home directory named **dead.letter**. Any time this file appears in your directory, check it out on screen. If you used an incorrect user ID, you can resend the contents with the correct one.

Unix System Exercise 4.1

Purpose: Read your mail. *You may find some slight differences in how your mail system works. If* **mail** *doesn't get you in, try* **Mail**. *If pressing* **Return** *doesn't restore the shell prompt after the last message, try typing* **q** *or pressing* **Ctrl-D**. *If your system doesn't recognize the* **alias** *command, you won't be able to use it.*

1. Log on to Unix if necessary.
2. If you have mail, type **mail** and press **Return**. Read any messages you have, pressing **Return** after each.
3. If you don't get your shell prompt after the last message, type **q** or **Ctrl-D**.
4. Now use compose mode to prepare a message to yourself, including about four lines of text. If typing a period as the only character on the last line doesn't restore the shell prompt, type **Ctrl-D**.
5. Send the contents of **many.years** to yourself as mail.
6. Send the contents of **my.address** to yourself as mail.
7. Send yourself a fourth message to ensure a sizable collection next time you check your mail.
8. If you have any colleagues who use the same Unix system, send a message to one or two of them for practice. Ask for a reply.
9. Send a message to a user ID that doesn't exist, such as **ggggg**. You'll see a message that it was sent to **dead.letter**. Try **cat dead.letter** to examine it there.
10. Check your mail again. When the first message is displayed, press **Ctrl-D** to exit the mail system and restore your shell prompt.

If it doesn't work:

A. If you get no valid response from **mail**, try **Mail**.

B. If pressing **Return** doesn't display any messages, you may not have any. Wait until your mail arrives. Send yourself some more messages.

C. If you get messages that indicate mail is not sent when you try, get help. Be sure you use the user ID and not the name or password in the command.

PROCESSING MAIL

You've seen how to read mail and let the default action take place. In most mail systems, the mail remains in the system mail box and will be shown to you again the next time you enter **mail**. In practice, you must manage your correspondence. You must delete some messages, save some in files or in your personal mailbox, look at them again, send other mail from within the mail system, and so forth. In this section, you'll learn much more about basic mail processing. Many versions of Unix have additional commands to process mail, but the commands you'll learn here will meet most of your needs. Figure 4.3 (see following page) shows the basic commands you can use in **mail** command mode. You can find any additional commands supported by your Unix version through the documentation, either in reference manuals or online. Once you can handle the basic processes, check to find out what more you can do.

Mail Command Mode

You've already seen the basics of using compose mode of the Unix mail system to prepare and send mail to other users. When you process mail you have received, you use command mode. Here you can enter commands to manage the mail. You've already seen that pressing **Return** results in displaying the next message on the screen. You've also seen the mail system prompt. In many Unix versions, the mail prompt is a question mark (?); in others you'll just see a blank line with the cursor at the left.

Mail Processing Commands

Mail system commands vary a bit among different Unix systems, but the basic ones are quite similar. Most of them affect the message just displayed by default; when the mail prompt appears following the message, you enter a command to affect that message. If the mail system assigns numbers to the messages, you can often specify the number with a command to affect that particular message without first displaying it.

Command: **mail**

Purpose: Send or manage mail.

Format: **mail** [*user-ID-list*]
mail *file-name*

Commands within Mail System:

d	Delete message just displayed.
p	Show message just displayed again.
s [*file-name*]	Save message just dispayed with header to *file-name*; if *file-name* omitted, save to personal mail box.
w [*file-name*]	Write message just displayed to *file-name*, without header; if *file-name* omitted, save to personal mail box.
mb	Save to personal mailbox **mbox** (only if it doesn't occur automatically).
q	Exit mail system; process deletions (**Ctrl-D**).
x	Exit mail system; cancel deletions.

Examples:

1. `mail`
2. `mail mbox`
3. `mail monty james`

Results:

1. Enter mail command mode to view messages.
2. Enter mail command mode to view messages in personal mailbox.
3. Enter mail compose mode to prepare message to **monty** and **james**.

Figure 4.3 The **mail** *command*

Leaving the Mail System

Some versions of Unix automatically return you to the shell prompt after you read the last message. You can also leave the mail system at any time by typing the appropriate command.

Typing **q** quits the mail system, returns you to the shell prompt, and processes any deletions you requested during the mail session. It has exactly the same effect as pressing **Ctrl-D**. This is the usual way to get out of the mail system when just pressing **Return** repeatedly doesn't do it.

Typing **x** exits the mail system, returns you to the shell prompt, and cancels any deletions that resulted during the mail session. You'll use **x** when you change your mind about message processing or when something seems to be going wrong during a session. When you return to the mail system, all the messages terminated by typing **x** that you may have deleted or saved during the session will appear again in the message listing.

Deleting a Message

After a message is displayed, you can type **d** to delete it from the list of mail. If a list of numbered messages is displayed, the command **d3** deletes message number 3. Mail deletions aren't final until you leave the mail system normally or press **q**. They are reversed if you use **x** to exit the mail system.

Saving a Message

Messages can be saved with or without any **header** information generated by the Unix system. The header may include such information as who the message is from, when it was sent, a subject line, and who received the message.

The command to save the message just displayed, along with any header information, is **s** followed by a file name. Unix saves the message in the named file, creating the file if necessary or appending the message to the end of it if the file already exists. Then Unix deletes the message from the system mailbox. The deletion is finalized when you leave the mail system normally. The deletion is reversed if you use **x** to exit the mail system. In either case, the message is safely stored in the specified file.

Some Unix mail systems save messages to your personal mailbox file if you use **s** without a file name. The message is then written to a file named **mbox** in your home directory and removed from the system mailbox so you won't be shown it again. If **mbox** already contains text, the new message is appended to it; if **mbox** doesn't yet exist, Unix creates it for you. You can examine messages in **mbox** later by specifying **mailbox**.

The command to save a message without header information is **w** followed by a file name. It has the same general effects as the **s** command, but doesn't include the header in the result. The deletion is finalized when you leave the mail system normally. As with the **s** command, the deletion is reversed if you use **x** to exit the mail system. In either case, the message is safely stored in the specified file.

Transferring a Message to a Mailbox

The Unix systems that don't let you use **s** or **w** without a file name to send mail to your own mailbox provide a special command to let you send mail to your mailbox. When you type **mb**, the message just displayed is transferred to your **mbox** file and deleted from the system mailbox. Using **x** to exit the mail system restores the message to the system mailbox. You can find out how to send messages to your own **mbox** file by experimentation in Exercise 4.2 (later in this chapter).

To examine messages you've saved in **mbox**, use the command **mail mbox**. All the command mode **mail** commands will work just as they do in the system mailbox.

Viewing a Message Again

When paging through a list of messages, you may want to see the one you just viewed again, especially if it is a long message that just scrolled off the screen. Just type **p** and the previous message is shown again, even if you just asked for it to be deleted with a **d**, **s**, or **w** command. Because the message isn't actually deleted until you leave the mail system with **Return** or **q**, it can be redisplayed. If you have changed your mind about deleting the message, you can use **x** to leave the mail system and cancel the deletion.

You can use **p** whenever appropriate to view the same message again. When you press **Return**, the system continues with the next message. If you see a list of numbered messages, you can use a command such as **p4** to display message number 4.

Sending Mail from within the Mail System

You may want to respond to a message immediately without leaving the mail system. To do this, you can use the **m** command. When you type **m** *userID-list* at the mail system prompt, Unix puts you into the mail compose mode and you type your message at the keyboard just as with the **mail** command. When you end the message with a period on the last line or press **Ctrl-D**, it will be sent and you will be back in the mail system command mode again. As with the **mail** command, you can use aliases and redirection if appropriate. In most Unix versions, you can't send mail from an existing file from within the mail system. You must return to the shell to do that.

Some versions of Unix let you use the **r** command to reply to a message; you type it as a message processing command, and the message is automatically sent to the sender of the message just displayed.

Using Unix Commands within the Mail System

Sometimes you want to use a standard Unix command while you are in command mode within the mail system. You may want to check the calendar, list a directory, or check the current date. Unix offers a way to issue a single command, and then return to the same point within the mail system.

To issue a command from within the mail system, precede the command with an exclamation point (!). If you type **!cal 4 1990**, you'll see the calendar for the requested month on the screen, and then you'll see the mail prompt again. Unix remembers the last message you viewed, and you can process it again. You can use **p** to display the current message if you aren't exactly sure which one it was.

You can use this technique to execute any single Unix command. Figure 4.4 shows the result of typing **!ls** in a mail session. Notice that the exclamation point appears again at the end of the listing just prior to the Unix prompt.

```
and let me know if the time is alrite with you.
Mike
!ls
first.one
grep.rules
hollenstein
l.sten
proj.A
!
_
```

Figure 4.4 Using Unix commands within **mail**

Online Help in the Mail System

Most versions of Unix offer online help while you are in the mail system. For example, you can get a list of the commands for Unix V by typing an asterisk (*) at the mail prompt; for other Unix versions, type a question mark (?) at the prompt. The resulting screen provides many more options and commands than those covered here. After you are comfortable with the basic mail management commands, you may want to try some of these options.

Special Mail Considerations

Long mail messages can present a problem. The primary difficulty to the recipient is that they are awkward to read on screen. You can use your keyboard's pause key (often **Ctrl-S**), but this requires a great deal of concentration and coordination. If you receive mail that takes more than one screen, the easiest way to handle it is to save it to a file, then use **more** or the **vi** editor (see Chapter 7) to let you read it at your leisure. If you must send long messages, include the message length in the subject line, if you have one. That alerts the recipient that the message might as well be saved to a file and read later.

By default, most versions of Unix present you with your most recent mail first. Most versions of Unix allow you to reverse the order if you prefer. The basic way to reverse the order is to include a **switch** on the command; **mail -r** requests a reverse order. It doesn't work in all Unix versions, however. If you keep your system mailbox cleaned out, you won't have as many messages to deal with at any one time, so the sequence won't be critical.

Unix System Exercise 4.2

Purpose: Manage mail in the system mailbox.

1. Log on to Unix if necessary.
2. Send yourself at least four messages specifying how the weather looks today (or concerning anything else you want).
3. Now check your mail. Look at the first message, then press **d** to delete it.

continued on following page...

Exercise 4.2 continued. . .

4. Look at the second message, then type **s savemail** to save it in your home directory.
5. Exit the mail system with **x**; this cancels your deletions, so the two messages should still be there.
6. List the file **savemail** on the screen (use **cat**).
7. Enter the mail system again. Note that the message list is the same. Delete the first message again.
8. When the second message is displayed, press **p** to show it again. Then delete it.
9. Save the third message to your mailbox **mbox** with **s** or **mb**, then check your directory while still in the mail system to see if the **mbox** file is there (don't worry if it doesn't appear yet).
10. Leave the mail system with **q**, and check the directory again; notice that **mbox** is present now. Then reenter the mail system. Notice that the former first three messages are gone.
11. Check the mail system online help.
12. Send yourself a message from within mail; use the **m** command, and type several lines. Use **Ctrl-D** to end the message.
13. Examine the rest of the mail, disposing of it as you like.

If it doesn't work:

A. If you can't get into the mail system, try **Mail** as the command.

B. If you don't have any mail, and you sent yourself some earlier, try **cat mbox**. Some systems automatically send viewed mail to **mbox**, so if you used **Return** to page through the messages earlier they may have been transferred already. Just send yourself four or five short messages and try the exercise again.

C. If the commands have slightly different effects, check your documentation or online help.

REAL-TIME COMMUNICATION

If the Unix mail system is similar to standard mail, then Unix real-time communication is similar to a phone call or CB radio. You can send a message in real time to someone else who is on line at the same time you are. The recipient can respond to you with another message. This system is entirely separate from the mail system. No permanent copy is kept of real-time messages. This section covers the details of real-time communication.

Just as telephone calls can interrupt a person's work and cause irritations, so can real-time messages over a terminal. Restrict your use of real-time messages to really urgent information or to colleagues who are agreeable to it.

A Sample Session

Before getting into the details of how you start and manage a real-time conversation, it will help to look at what happens. You need two users logged in at two different terminals at the same time. The two users send messages back and forth. Suppose you are online. How do you know who else is logged on? Just ask Unix. type **who** and you'll see a list similar to the following:

```
davis       console  May 25   09:40
carson      tty01    May 25   08:13
smithers    tty04    May 24   23:30
monty       tty09    May 25   10:22
```

The result of the **who** command is a list of the user IDs of all the currently logged in users. Because you must be logged in to send commands to Unix, you will always see your own user ID in the list. Notice that the listing also gives the terminal number for each user, along with the date and time of login. You can communicate with any of the listed users except yourself, unless they have specifically requested not to receive messages. Suppose for this example that you are Carson and you have arranged to communicate with Monty this afternoon.

To start the session, you type **write monty** at your shell prompt now that you know he is logged in. A message appears on Monty's sreen indicating that he has a message from you. At the same time, the cursor on your screen moves to a new line. You type your message, pressing **Return** at the end of each line. As you press **Return**, each line appears on Monty's screen. At the end of your message, you type **o** (for "over") on a new line, and then press **Return**. Each line appears on Monty's terminal. The line containing **o** tells him that's the end of this part of the message and you are waiting for a response. Figure 4.5 shows how both screens would look at this point. Bold type indicates what was actually typed by the user at that terminal.

Carson's screen

```
zyindex
$ write monty
Have you got a few for me?
I need info about her royal
eloquence.
o
_
```

Monty's screen

```
$
$ Message from carson  tty01
Have you got a few for me?
I need info about her royal
eloquence.
o
$ _
```

Figure 4.5 First steps in real-time conversation

Now the ball is in Monty's court. Monty enters the command **write carson** and presses **Return**; a message appears on your screen. As Monty presses **Return** at the end of each line, it appears on your screen. On his last line, Monty types **o** and then presses **Return**. You see the message and know it's your turn. Figure 4.6 (see following page) shows how the two terminals look at this point. Again, bold type indicates what was actually typed by the user at that terminal.

Carson's screen

```
zyindex
$ write monty
Have you got a few for me?
I need info about her royal
eloquence.
o
Message from monty  tty09
Why not? I understand she's
off for four days starting
tomorrow. "Marital" leave.
o

_
```

Monty's screen

```
$
$ Message from carson  tty01
Have you got a few for me?
I need info about her royal
eloquence.
o
$ write carson
Why not? I understand she's
off for four days starting
tomorrow. "Marital" leave.
o

_
```

Figure 4.6 Next step in real-time conversation

It's your turn again. You don't need to type **write** again because the **write** command is still in effect. (You can tell because there is no shell prompt.) Just type the response lines as needed, ending with **o** on a separate line so Monty knows when you're finished. Then Monty responds, again ending with **o**. Now you're ready to send your final message and end the conversation. At this time, you use **oo** as the last line, then press **Return**, and finally press **Ctrl-D**. Following the **oo** line on Monty's screen will be a message such as *(end of message)* or *EOF* to notify him that you are finished. You are now back at the shell prompt. Monty, however, is not. He must press **Ctrl-D** to terminate the effect of the **write** command from his terminal. If he doesn't, whatever he types will continue to be sent to you. Figure 4.7 shows how the screens look when you have ended the conversation and Monty has not. Again, bold indicates where the data was typed. Notice that the shell prompt has returned to Carson's screen, but not to Monty's. Once Monty presses **Ctrl-D**, the shell prompt will return there too and you (Carson) will be notified of the end of the message.

The use of **o** to indicate the end of a statement and **oo** to indicate the end of the conversation are conventions rather than Unix requirements. You can use any signal you want. Without some signal, however, you never know when the other person is finished "speaking" and it's your turn again. When **Ctrl-D** ends the **write** command, a message appears on the other screen signifying the end. Some versions of Unix allow the remaining participant to sign off by just pressing **Return** when the final message appears. If pressing **Return** restores the shell prompt, that method works in your system. If not, use **Ctrl-D**.

Carson's screen

```
zyindex
$ write monty
Have you got a few for me?
I need info about her royal
eloquence.
o
Message from monty  tty09
Why not? I understand she's
off for four days starting
tomorrow. "Marital" leave.
o
Should be "martial". I guess
it may be worth it! Can we
get together at lunch?
o
Sure.  The grapevine's hot.
o
See you later.
oo
^d
$ _
```

Monty's screen

```
$
$ Message from carson  tty01
Have you got a few for me?
I need info about her royal
eloquence.
o
$ write carson
Why not? I understand she's
off for four days starting
tomorrow. "Marital" leave.
o
Should be "martial". I guess
it may be worth it! Can we
get together at lunch?
o
Sure.  The grapevine's hot.
o
See you later.
oo
(end of message)
_
```

Figure 4.7   End of conversation

Using the write Command

To send a message to another logged-in user in real time, you use the **write** command; its format is shown in Figure 4.8 (see following page). Notice that the terminal ID is optional. You would need to include the terminal ID if the user you specify is currently logged in to more than one terminal because your message can be sent to only one terminal. The **who** command output provides terminal IDs as well as multiple log on information.

Command: **write**

Purpose: Send real-time message to another online user; if you both use this command, you can have two-way communication.

Format: **write** *target-user-ID* [*terminal-ID*]

Examples:

1. `write davis`
2. `write davis tty03`

Results: Message appears on Davis's screen. Whatever you type appears there as well until you press **Ctrl-D** to terminate the write command.

Figure 4.8 The **write** *command*

As you saw in the sample session, **write** sends a line at a time to the terminal of the target user. After you enter **write**, the cursor moves to the next line, much as in compose mode for **mail**, and you can type your message. Each time you press **Return**, the line is sent to the other terminal. In between lines, another user can send messages to you, after the **write** command has been entered at his or her terminal. Each **write** command is independent. To make the conversation clear, one of you pauses while the other sends data. If two users write to each other at the same time, you get a real mess on the screen; this mess won't confuse Unix, but it will probably confuse you and the other user. Some signal at the end of a transmission, when you intend to wait for a response, is required to alleviate this problem; many people use the letter **o** on a new line as such a signal and **oo** on a new line to signal the very end.

Unix Commands under the write Command

While your screen is under the control of **write**, for example while you are waiting for a response, you might want to issue some other Unix command. If you just type another command, it is sent as text to the target user terminal. For example, if **ls -l** appears on your screen, your conversant may have typed that command. To send the command to Unix instead of to the other user, precede it with an exclamation point (!), just as you would in the mail system. If you type **!ls -l**, you'll see the command output on your screen and the other user won't know what you are doing.

Avoiding write Communications

In most Unix systems, you are allowed to get real-time messages via the **write** command by default. If you want to prevent them, you can use the **mesg** command. Figure 4.9 shows the format. You can prevent all messages or allow all of them; you can't be selective about which users can **write** to you.

Command: **mesg**

Purpose: Prevent or allow others to use **write** command to send you real-time messages.

Format: **mesg [y/n]**

Examples:

1. `mesg n`
2. `mesg`

Results:

1. Any user who addresses you in **write** receives a message saying *Access denied*. To allow messages again, use **mesg y**.
2. Displays current status of mesg, as in **is y**.

Figure 4.9 The **mesg** *command*

To prevent any real-time messages, use **mesg n** to say "no" to the **write** command. To allow messages again, type **mesg y** at the shell prompt. If you aren't sure what your message status is, type **mesg** by itself. You'll see a response such as the following:

```
$ mesg
is y
$ _
```

The response tells you if you can receive messages (**y**) or not (**n**); you can reset it with another **mesg** command if you want.

Unix System Exercise 4.3

Purpose: Use real-time communications.

1. Log on to Unix, if necessary, and handle any mail.
2. Check what other users are logged on. Do you know any of them?
3. Check whether you can receive messages or not. Set it so you can receive them if necessary.

For the rest of this exercise, arrange in advance with another user. Alternatively, you could log in at two adjacent terminals if they are available. The exercise refers to the other user or terminal as USERB.

4a. Send a message to USERB asking if she has a moment. Use **o** as the last line. Wait for a response.

4b. USERB should use **write** at her terminal and send you a short answer, followed by **o** on the last line, then wait.

5a. Respond by typing a two-line answer, followed by **o** on the next line. While you wait for a response, try **!date** to see the result.

5b. USERB should type a line or two, following it with **o** on the last line, then wait.

6a. Type "Good bye, now. End the session." followed by **oo** on the last line. Then press **Return** again and press **Ctrl-D**.

6b. USERB should see the message you sent, followed by a message such as *EOF* or *end of message* on the screen. She should press **Ctrl-D** to end it.

7. Try another conversation if you want.

If it doesn't work:

A. If you get the message "permission denied" when you use the **write** command, send mail to the other user asking him or her to use the **mesg y** command to allow messages.

B. If you get strange messages on your screen after you have the shell prompt again, use **write** again to remind USERB to press **Ctrl-D** to sign off.

SUMMARY

In this chapter, you have learned to use the following Unix commands to handle communications while you are online:

- Send mail using the compose mode of **mail**.
- Manage your mail in command mode, including deleting (**d**), redisplaying (**p**), saving (**s**), and sending it to your personal mailbox (**mb**).
- Exit mail command mode with **q**, **x**, or **Ctrl-D**.
- Establish a group of users to receive the same mail from you with **alias**.
- Determine what users are logged in with **who**.
- Send a real-time message with **write**.
- Determine and change your ability to receive messages with **mesg.**

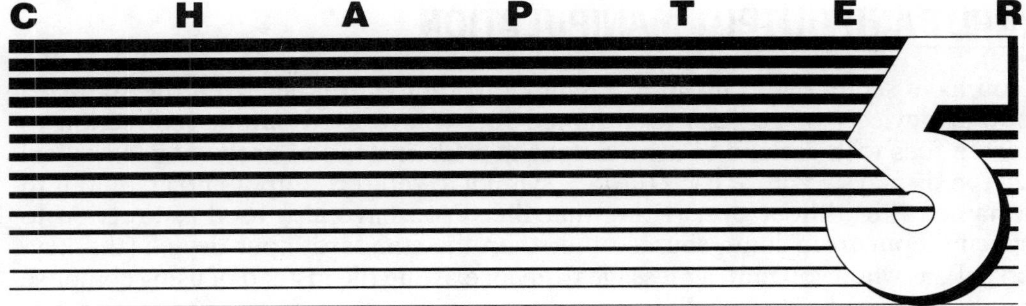

ADDITIONAL UNIX COMMANDS AND TECHNIQUES

Unix offers many more commands you can use to affect the files in your directories and their contents. In this chapter, you will learn to control what happens to output and input when you use pipes and filters, which are logical extensions of redirection. You will also learn to sort lines in a file in the sequence you need, based on any part of the line. Sorting allows you to rearrange lines to create a new file from one or more existing ones. Other commands let you identify the unique lines in a file, lines common to two files, or the lines that differ in two files.

You'll also learn to determine the general classification of a file and discover the number of characters, words, or lines in a file.

INPUT AND OUTPUT MANIPULATION

You have seen how to use the > symbol to redirect output from the standard output device (the screen) to a named file; you've used output redirection to create files with **cat** and to send output to a file instead of producing **ls** and **cal** screen displays. You've used the > > symbol to redirect output and append it to a named file without overwriting that file. You have also used redirection to specify input from some source other than the standard input device (the keyboard), as when you **mail** a message from an existing file instead of using compose mode. In this chapter, you'll learn more commands that can use redirection.

Using Pipes

Redirection is often very handy, but it is even more useful if you use other Unix facilities such as filters and pipes as well. A **pipe** requests two redirections with a single symbol; it redirects the standard output of one command to the standard input of another. Suppose you want a printed copy of your extended directory. You could use these two commands:

```
ls -l > catchit
lpr -r catchit
```

As you can see, you redirect the directory listing output to a temporary file and then send the temporary file to the printer with the option **-r** to erase it after printing.

If you try to redirect standard output, it creates a file on your disk; you can't redirect it to a device. Whenever you want to take the standard output of the first command and send it directly to the second command as input, you can use a pipe to accomplish the same thing in a single command, as in this example:

```
ls -l | lpr
```

The pipe symbol is a vertical bar (|). It can have a space on either side or not, whichever is more convenient.

You can pipe many different things. Any output that normally comes to the screen can be piped to a file on disk or to the printer. One command that is very useful with piping is **tee**, which works much like a tee joint in plumbing to send output in two directions. The **tee** command copies the standard input to the standard output and also stores it in a named file, so it is often the target of a pipe. Suppose you want to see your directory listing and also store it in a file named **savedir**. You could do it with individual commands as in this example:

```
ls -l
ls -l > savedir
```

Or you could use a single command, such as the following:

```
ls -l | tee savedir
```

In this case the standard output (screen listing) of the **ls** command is sent to the screen and also saved in the named file.

Figure 5.1 (see following page) shows the format of the **tee** command. This command is almost always used as the target of a pipe, so you won't enter it alone.

You can specify as many files as you want to hold the output; the same information that is displayed is written to each named file. If any of the listed files already exist, they are overwritten by the new output unless you include the **-a** switch in the **tee** command to cause the new output to be appended. You can use the **-i** switch if you want to prevent the command from responding to interrupts that might bring messages to your screen during its operation.

Command: **tee**

Purpose: Copy standard input to standard output device and to specified files.

Format: **tee** [*options*] *file-list*

Options:

-i No interrupts.
-a Append to an existing file.

Examples:

1. `ls -lt | tee save.list`
2. `who | tee -a whos_on savedir/savewho`

Results: The standard output produced by the first command is piped to the second command as standard input, where the **tee** command sends it to the standard output device as well as to the named file(s).

Figure 5.1 The **tee** *command*

Using Filters

You have seen how to use redirection to send standard output somewhere else or get standard input from another source. You've also seen how to use a pipe to transfer output from one command for use as direct input for a different command. Still another technique uses a **filter**. A filter is a program that manipulates the output of one command before passing it on to another command. Figure 5.2 shows how a filter differs from a pipe. A filter may use standard redirection or a pipe for its input and/or output.

Many different programs can function as filters. The most common Unix filter is **sort**, which sorts input lines producing sorted output lines. The **sort** command has many options and features we'll cover later in this chapter. For now, you will use the basic **sort** effect; if you use it without any options or arguments, it takes standard input from the keyboard, sorts it, and sends it to the standard output device.

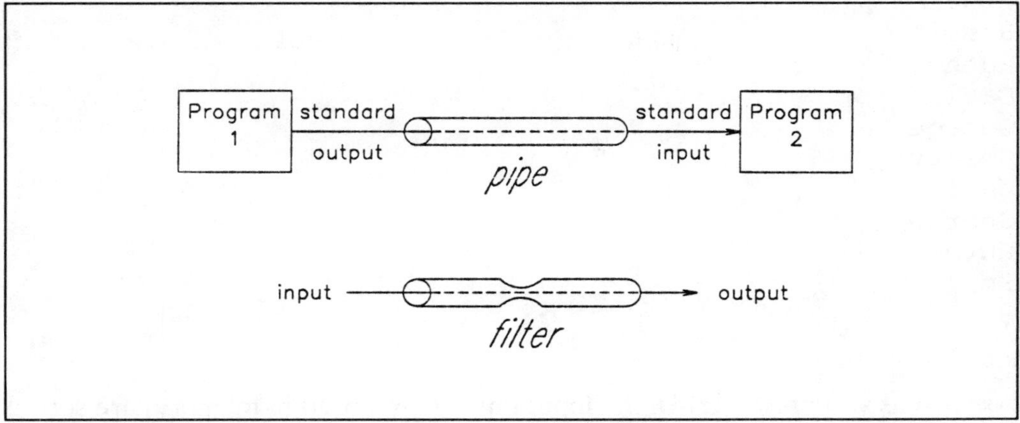

Figure 5.2 Pipes and filters

THE BASIC sort COMMAND

When you type **sort** at the shell prompt, the cursor moves to the next line and waits for input. Suppose you type a list of several names, pressing **Return** after each. For this example, assume the screen now displays the following lines:

```
$ sort
Ruth
David
George
Smitty
_
```

You have been providing data through the standard input device. You press **Ctrl-D** to terminate the input. The **sort** command takes over, sorts the input lines, and returns the data to the standard output device, so the screen now contains the following lines:

```
$ sort
Ruth
David
George
Smitty
David
George
Ruth
Smitty
$ _
```

As soon as you press **Ctrl-D**, the input lines (now stored in memory) are sorted and sent back to the screen; then the shell prompt is restored. Sorting from the screen to the screen is not a very common procedure. Luckily, you can use redirection with **sort**. For example, if you use the command **sort < phone.list**, the named file is used as input and all the lines in the file are sorted in ascending ASCII sequence and sent to the standard output device. If you redirect the output too, as in the command **sort < phone.list > sorted_list**, the sorted output is sent to the **sorted_list** file.

Suppose the **supply.list** file contains these lines:

```
44463 barbecue,sm 122
10203 Hammer 800
44465 patio-umbrella 11
44464 barbecue,lg 110
12222 Hammer 210
33333 Saw 24
88888 Apron 42
20022 Nail,ten-p 233
44444 patio-chair 48
21099 Screw,flat 244
21098 Screw,phil 321
44455 patio-table 12
44462 hibachi,table 16
44460 hibachi,stand 5
```

You can use the command **sort < supply.list**. The following is displayed on the screen:

```
10203 Hammer 800
12222 Hammer 210
20022 Nail,ten-p 233
21098 Screw,phil 321
21099 Screw,flat 244
33333 Saw 24
44444 patio-chair 48
44455 patio-table 12
44460 hibachi,stand 5
44462 hibachi,table 16
44463 barbecue,sm 122
44464 barbecue,lg 110
44465 patio-umbrella 11
88888 Apron 42
```

You can store the sorted output in a file instead by redirecting the output as in **sort < supply.list > sorted.supps** or **sort < supply.list | tee sorted.supps**.

You can use **sort** to sort the output of any command that produces screen output. For example, you could use **who | sort** to cause the alphabetically sorted list of logged-in users to appear on your screen. Without the **sort** command, the list is in terminal ID order.

You can also use **sort** as just one step in a process. For example, **who | sort | lpr** sends the sorted output to the printer instead of the screen. The command **who | sort | tee -a keep.all** sends the output to the screen and appends it to the **keep.all** file as well.

Unix System Exercise 5.1

Purpose: Use basic pipes and filters.

1. Log on to Unix if necessary.
2. Use **tee** to send a long listing of your home directory to **keep.home**. Generate another extended listing and append it to the same file. Examine **keep.home** on the screen.
3. Create a long listing on the screen and pipe it to the printer.
4. Use **sort** to arrange four or five words you type at the keyboard in order on the screen. Try it again to produce a sorted file of six or seven names; call it **sort.names**. Examine **sort.names** on screen.
5. Use **sort** to produce a sorted listing of all logged on users and send a copy to the printer.
6. Sort **keep.home** to the screen. Notice that it is sorted by the entire line, beginning with the access permissions, rather than by the file names. Sort it again and store the result in **sorted.keep**.
7. Use **cat > forsorting** to create a file containing these lines:

```
8  Michael M'Sweeney
12  Carla Martinson
9  Ruth Ashley
6  Judi Fernandez
4   (any name)
10  (any name)
```

8. Sort **forsorting** to the screen. Note that the lines that start with 10 and 12 are first, before the one that starts with 4; this is ASCII sequence. Save this file; you'll use it again in the next exercise.

If it doesn't work:

A. If you have trouble with **tee**, try a simple example, such as **ls | tee hold.dir** to see if it works (use **cat hold.dir**).

B. Try accomplishing the effect with a series of separate commands and simple redirection; remember to use < for input and > for output.

THE COMPLETE sort COMMAND

You have seen how to use the **sort** command to sort complete lines in a file, treating the entire line as one entity. Actually, **sort** has many more features and capabilities. With it, you can sort several files at once, producing a single output file. You can change the order, sort by specific fields in each line, and otherwise modify the sort. Figure 5.3 (see following page) shows the format of the **sort** command. Your version of Unix may have additional options you can use. You have already seen the effect of using no options and no arguments.

The final argument in the command format specifies input files to be sorted; you don't really need to specify input redirection for these files. If you use a command such as **sort supply.list**, the lines in the specified file are sorted, and the output is sent to the screen. If you use a command such as **sort supply.list on.order**, the contents of both files will be sorted together and sent to the screen.

You can use redirection for the output file, or you can use the **-o** option. The command **sort supplies.jan supplies.feb supplies.mar > first.quarter** sorts the records in all three files together in ascending sequence by line and sends the resulting collection of sorted lines to **first.quarter**. If you omit the redirection, the output is sent to the screen.

Specifying the Output File

One of the **sort** options is **-o***file-name*, which lets you specify the output file in the standard command line. The option letter **o** must be followed by the output file name; you may include a space between the option and the file name. Any of the following commands has the same effect:

```
sort supply.list > sorted.supps
sort -osorted.supps supply.list
sort -o sorted.supps supply.list
```

If you want to sorted output appended to another file, you must use redirection with the **> >** symbol.

Command: sort

Purpose: Sort files and produce new output.

Format: **sort** [*options*] [*sort-field-info*] [*file-list*]

Options:

-b	Ignore leading blanks in a field.
-c	Check sequence only; no output.
-d	Dictionary order; ignore non-alphanumeric.
-f	Fold cases together; uppercase = lowercase.
-m	Merge files; input files are presorted.
-n	Numeric sort; signs and points count.
-o*file-name*	Output *file-name*.
-r	Reverse order; descending sequence.
-t*x*	Change field separator from blanks to *x*.
-u	Unique lines only in output.

Sort field info:

[+*f*.*c* -*f*.*c*]
Specifies where to begin and end sort, according to field and character locations; can be repeated as needed.

Examples:

1. `sort suppliers.89`
2. `sort -rosuppliers.sort +2 -3 suppliers.*`
3. `sort -t; -u -oinventory.out +1 -2 +4 -5 inventory.*`

Results:

1. Sends sorted output to screen.
2. Sorts files based on the third field and sends output (reversed) to the named file.
3. Sorts files based on the second field and then the fifth field, delimited by semicolons; then puts only unique lines in the output file.

Figure 5.3 The **sort** *command*

Modifying the Sort Sequence

Leading blanks in a line, or indeed in any field, are sorted first. So if some lines in the input start with blanks, they'll appear first in the default output. You can specify the **-b** option to cause leading blanks to be ignored. The command **sort -b -osorted.supps supply.list** will ignore leading blanks on each line in preparing the sorted output. You can combine options in a single command without including the hyphen before each one, as in **-fd** or **-bd**.

Several options let you modify the sort sequence from the standard ASCII sequence. You can use **-d** to sort in dictionary order; in that case, any characters that aren't letters, digits, or blanks will be ignored. If your data includes symbols, you probably won't want to use the **-d** option. On the other hand, if your data includes names such as "O'Brien," you might want to ignore the apostrophe and sort based only on alphanumeric characters. Your data determines whether or not you should use this option.

Sometimes you want uppercase and lowercase letters to be significant in a sort and sometimes you don't. In the standard ASCII sort, they are critical, and the letter *A* comes before *a*. If you want the name *O'Brien* to appear after *Oberlin* in a sorted listing, you'd need to use the **-f** option in addition to **-d**. The **-f** option folds the upper- and lowercase letters together, so that *B* is the same as *b* and *L* is the same as *l*.

If you want your sorted output in reverse order, that is, so that lines starting with *9* precede lines starting with *8* and lines starting with *Z* precede lines starting with *Y*, use the **-r** option. If you want the output to contain only unique lines, use the **-u** option; in this case, the **sort** program discards any duplicate lines so that each line in the sorted output is unique.

If your input contains values you want sorted as numbers rather than as ASCII characters, include the **-n** option. This causes the sorting to be done algebraically; that is, plus and minus signs have an effect, as do decimal points. If the field includes ASCII characters other than numbers, you'll get an ASCII sort. Suppose the lines to be sorted in **ratings** are as follows:

```
-40
14.8
-12.6
0
0.00
-9
```

A sort in ASCII sequence results in the following output:

```
-12.6
-40
-9
0
0.00
14.8
```

The command **sort -n ratings** results in this sequence:

```
-40
-12.6
-9
0
0.00
14.8
```

The command **sort -nu ratings** eliminates the 0 value because it is arithmetically equal to 0.00. As you can see, you use the options that are required by the data you are trying to sort.

Merging Files

Sometimes you want to combine the contents of several files into one sorted file. Because sorting takes quite a bit of time, Unix provides options that you can use if part of the work is already done. For example, you can use the **-c** option to check and see if a file is already in sequence; you'll get a message if it isn't. No sorting is done when you use the **-c** option.

If you have several files that are already sorted, you can use the **-m** option to merge them so they won't be resorted. If the input files aren't sorted when you use the **-m** option, the output won't be in a valid sequence. All files to be merged must previously be sorted with the same set of options; that is, they must be in the same type of order. If you used **-d**, **-r**, **-n**, or some combination with any of the files, you must use the same options with all of the files, as well as in the final **sort** command that does the actual merge operation. Suppose you have already sorted **supplies.jan** and **supplies.feb** in sequence with the **-f** option to fold upper-

and lowercase letters together. Suppose you aren't sure if **supplies.mar** has been sorted, but you think it has and that you then want all three files merged into **first.quarter** with duplicate lines dropped. You could use these commands:

```
sort -cf supplies.mar
sort -fum supplies.jan supplies.feb supplies.mar -o first.quarter
```

If any error message results from the sequence checking command, you would sort the **supplies.mar** file, using the **-f** option before merging the three files. In each of these commands some options are combined; you need only a single hyphen when you group the options, just as in other Unix commands.

Sort Fields

Many times you don't want to sort lines by the entire line. You may not want to use the first character in a line as the key to sorting. Unix offers a way to select a different field for sorting. You can even specify several different fields, called **sort keys**, in which case lines are sorted first on the first specified key. Lines that match on the first key are then sorted according the contents of the next specified sort key, and so on. In order to use field specification, you first must know how the **sort** command identifies a field. Then you'll see how you can specify particular fields or parts of fields as sort keys to achieve the sort results you need.

By default, line fields are separated by spaces. Figure 5.4 shows several lines with the fields marked in each. In a sequence of spaces, the first space starts the next field. All spaces are considered to be part of the field that follows them. You can see that if you are sorting based on the fourth field, the **-b** option to ignore spaces can be very useful.

```
7777   Michael Smith   619  555-3172    CA

8888   John Patrick Foley     616  555-4130   MI

6689, Mary T. Smith, 555 Terrace Way, Baton Rouge, LA, 70777
```

Figure 5.4   Line field identification

To make sense out of sorted output, each line in the file must have the same number of fields. If some lines have three fields, some four, and some five, you can sort safely only on the first three fields. The first two lines in Figure 5.4 (see previous page) contain similar information, but the first line contains six fields and the second line contains seven. To cause each of those two lines to sort adequately based on any field other than the first, you have to modify the structure of one or the other. You could add a field to the first line like this:

```
7777  Michael nmi Smith       619 555-3172  CA
7777  Michael - Smith         619 555-3172  CA
```

Either alternative contains seven fields. You would arrange the sort so that the second field is ignored and doesn't affect the sequence. The other option is to modify shorter lines so they contain one less field, as in the following :

```
8888  JohnPatrick Foley       616 555-4130  MI
8888  J.Patrick Foley         616 555-4130  MI
8888  John Foley              616 555-4130  MI
```

If you try to sort on a field that doesn't exist in all the lines being sorted, such as field four or five when one of the lines being sorted contains only three fields, the line that doesn't contain that field will sort first because its sort field is null. If each line to be sorted contains a name, you'll need to do some planning. As you have seen, names frequently contain different numbers of fields. If the names are all in the same file, you may have trouble sorting them if you don't want to sort based on the first field, as in this example:

```
Mary Smith                        (2 fields)
Mr. David Johnson                 (3 fields)
Dr. Alfred P.  Steigfried         (4 fields)
Mrs. Maria Elena Gustavo         (4 fields)
Mr. M. Craig Stockwell, Sr.       (5 fields)
```

If you can't manage to have the same number of pieces in each name, you may be able to specify a different field separator with the **-t** option. This is a character other than a space that you tell the **sort** program to use to separate fields. You should choose a character that isn't used for any other purpose in the file. The last line in Figure 5.4 (earlier in this chapter) includes commas to separate logical fields. If you use the option **-t,** in the **sort** command, a comma instead of a space marks the beginning of the next field, and spaces that occur between commas are ignored or treated as standard text.

A mailing file with names and addresses could probably use the semicolon (;) as a separator at the end of each field that should appear on a separate line of the address. A file with no commas as data could use a comma (,) as a separator. You might use a slash (/), a caret (^), or an ampersand (&) instead, depending on the data. When you do, all characters between the beginning of the line and the first separator are one field; all characters between any two separator characters are another field; and all characters between the last separator character and the end of the line form another. Suppose you created a file with lines such as the following:

```
Mary;Smith;555-8888;555-8989
Mr. David;Johnson;555-1111;555-3232
Dr. Alfred P.;Steigfried;;555-6767
Mrs. Maria Elena;Gustavo;555-1212;555-2123
Mr. M. Craig;Stockwell, Sr.;;
```

If you sort the file using **-t;** each line contains four fields. The first field contains the first name, including a title sometimes. The second field contains the last name. The third and fourth fields each contain a telephone number. Wherever two separators are adjacent, the field is empty. Notice that the last line is missing two fields, one between the two semicolons and one between the last semicolon and the end of the line. It's much easier to keep track of separators and missing fields when you use a character other than the space as a separator. With the file structured as it is, you can sort based on any field in the file.

Specifying Sort Fields

By default, **sort** uses the entire line to sort by. Suppose you want to sort by some other field, or by the first field then the third. To do this, you need to specify sort field information, as indicated earlier in Figure 5.3. A field specification for a sort key isn't the same as a line field. However, you specify where the sort key is and how long it is in terms of where line fields are, based on spaces or an alternate separator. Each sort field specification can have two parts, one giving the starting position (+) of the key and one giving the end (–). If you give only the starting position, the key extends to the end of the line. If you use both the starting and ending position, it takes the following form: *+f. c–f. .c*

The *f* position gives the number of fields to skip over. For example, to use the first field in each line as a sort key, use **+0 –1**, which means skip over no fields and start at the beginning of the next field (which is the first), and then skip over one field and stop at the beginning of the next. To specify the second field as a key, use **+1 –2**. To sort on the fifth field, specify **+4 –5**. If you don't specify an ending position, the key is assumed to go to the end of the line. **sort –b +1 supplies.list** sorts based on the values from the beginning of the second field (after leading spaces) to the end of the line.

The *c* position gives the number of characters to skip over after skipping fields. If you want to start at the beginning of a field, **c** is 0, in which case you can omit the *c* position as previously shown. To limit the sort to the first five characters of the third field, you could use a command like **sort -osorted.out +2 –3.5 input.data**. The sort key now starts at the beginning of the third field and ends at a point five characters beyond that. To limit a sort key to the last six characters of a ten-character long ninth field, you could use **+8.4 –9**.

You can use several sets of sort field specifiers to name a series of sort keys. For example, suppose you want to sort based on the third field. If the values in the third field match, you want it sorted based on the first three characters of the first field as well. You could use this command:

```
sort -bosorted.out +2 -3 +0 -0.3 input.data.
```

When you use a series of sort keys, you may still have lines that match in all the keys. If this happens, the lines with matching keys are sorted based on the rest of the line. Ideally, you'll specify enough keys to ensure an adequate sort. Specifying the **-u** option results in dropping only completely duplicate lines, not lines that match in all the specified key fields.

Combining Options with Sort Keys

You have seen that you can specify various options in the **sort** command to affect the order and operation of the sort. When you specify an option with a hyphen, it affects the entire sort. If you want to limit an option to a particular sort key, you can attach it to the *+f. c* operand. If you use this command,

```
sort -r -osorted.out +2 -3 +0 -0.3 input.data
```

the reverse sequence applies to both sort keys. To sort the first key in normal sequence and the second in reverse, code the command this way:

```
sort -osorted.out +2 -3 +0r -0.3 input.data
```

Notice that no hyphen is needed when you attach the option to a sort key. You can attach **b**, **d**, **f**, **n**, or **r** to a particular key as needed; those options then apply only to any sorting done with that key.

Sort Command Examples

Suppose you have a file containing lines in the following form:

```
Davis, Michael, 405, 555-3333
Smithers, Steven J., 405, 555-2222
Washington, George, 409, 555-1111
Lincoln, Abraham, 202, 598-0909
MacArthur, James, 505, 555-9090
Macadam, Jennifer, 505, 555-6576
Fernandez Sr., Judson, 619, 444-0900
Lincoln, Alexander, 212, 333-2222
Smithson, Institute, 202, 444-9999
```

Even though spaces separate the fields in most of the lines, the comma forms a more useful division because some fields contain extra spaces. To sort the records in order of area code, you would use this command:

```
sort -t, +2.2 -3 +0df -1 telephone.tree
```

+2.2 was used to start at the beginning of the third field and skip the first two characters; you don't really want the sort to include the comma and space, although it won't affect the result. The **-3** stops this sort key at the beginning of the fourth field. If two lines have the same area code, you want them sorted by last name, the first field. The options attached to the sort specifier cause it to use the dictionary sequence and consider uppercase and lowercase letters equivalent.

Unix System Exercise 5.2

Purpose: Sort lines based on field contents.

1. Log on to Unix if necessary.
2. List **forsorting** on the screen. Sort it in order of the first names.
3. Sort it in order by last name.
4. Sort the file in numeric sequence by the first field.
5. Sort your **keep.home** file in order by time of day. (Use +7; don't use the **-n** option.)
6. Try some more sorts if you like. Try a reverse one. Try combining two similarly organized files into a single sorted output file. Use **cat** to create a new file using another character besides space to separate the fields, and then sort that new file with the **-tx** option.

If it doesn't work:

A. Try a simple sort with no options, just redirection. Add one option at a time, starting with **-o** to name an output file.

B. If a sort doesn't seem to produce the sequence you expect, try again. Check your options and try them on the same input one at a time until you spot the problem.

ADDITIONAL FILE PROCESSING COMMANDS

Unix has several more commands you may want to use to identify what is in various files. For example, you may want to know the number of characters, words, or lines in a file. You may need to know the general classification of a file, what type of data it contains. You may want to know what is common between two files or what is in one that is not in the other. You may want to know what must be done to convert one file into another. You may want to find out whether lines or fields are repeated in a file.

In this section, you'll learn to use the basic form of several Unix commands to locate and display (or redirect, tee, or pipe) the output.

File Classifications

The **file** command lists the general classification of a file. The command output lets you know if the file contains ASCII text, English text, or masm (assembler) or C program text, for example. It also lets you know if a file is a directory. If you don't have access to the file, you'll be told so. You specify one or more files in the **file** command. Following is an example:

```
file sort*
sort           ascii text
sort.address   English text
sort.temp      directory
sortdir        masm program text
```

The classifications you see in the output are Unix's best guess; for some reason it thinks a redirected directory listing is masm language text. But at least you know the file is text, and thus printable. A directory is never printable as such.

Counting File Elements

You can use the **wc** command to display the number of characters, words, and lines in a file. Figure 5.5 (see following page) shows the command format. Notice that the command displays all three counts if you don't specify any options. It determines a word as any set of characters bounded by space, tab, and the beginning or the end of the line. You can use the appropriate options to display just one or two counts.

Command: **wc**

Purpose: Count lines, words, and characters in the specified files.

Format: **wc** [*options*] *file-list*

Options:

-c	Display character count.
-w	Display word count.
-l	Display line count.

Examples:

1. `wc members.old`
2. `wc -l f*`

Results:

1.
```
48    193   1297  members.old
```
2.
```
52 filemess
   14 f_meetings.stf
   22 fight7
   88 total
```

Figure 5.5 The **wc** *command*

Suppose you want to count the elements of the file **phone.list**. Here is how the output looks:

```
$ wc phone.list
    25      112     480  phone.list
$ _
```

If you get results on a list of files, you get a set of values for each individual file plus a total, as in the following example:

```
$ wc f*
      9      34     181  firstmon
      4      25     108  fixmix
     14      53     384  forsort
      7      30     256  forsort.1
     34     142     929  total
$ _
```

You can specify only one or any two counts if you want. Following is the result of asking for a word count only:

```
$ wc -w f*
    34 firstmon
    25 fixmix
    53 forsort
    30 forsort.1
   142 total
$ _
```

Identifying Repeated Lines in a File

Unix provides the **uniq** command to identify repeated lines in a file and display the file with only one copy of those lines. If the file has been sorted, any identical lines will be together in the file. If not, identical lines may not be in sequence. The **uniq** command locates only identical lines that are adjacent to each other in the file. It won't locate the same line at a different point. Figure 5.6 (see following page) shows the format of the **uniq** command. Like many other commands, it doesn't alter the input file. First you will see how it works when you specify files without any of the other elements.

Command: **uniq**

Purpose: Display file with only one copy of repeated lines.

Format: **uniq** [*options*] [*-field*] [+*char*] [*input-file*] [*output-file*]

Options:

- **-c** Show how many occurrences.
- **-d** Display only repeated lines.
- **-u** Display only lines not repeated.

Examples:

1. `uniq inventory`
2. `uniq -d -1 inventory inventory.one`

Results:

1. Sends unique lines in file to screen.
2. Sends repeated lines to named file, starting the comparison for uniqueness in the second field.

Figure 5.6 The **uniq** *command*

When you use the **uniq** command and include only an input file, Unix processes the file, dropping any repeated lines. Then, the remaining lines are displayed—you can redirect the output to a file if you prefer. Suppose file **members.old** is a file that regularly has lapsed members appended to it and that it now contains the following lines:

```
John Davidson
Mary Smith
Mary Smith
John Carroll
David Newcorn
John Davidson
Michael Washington
Michael Washington
Michael Washington
John Carroll
Eleanor Carroll
Judi Fernandez
Davida Fernandez
```

If you use the command **uniq members.old**, you will see this display:

```
John Davidson
Mary Smith
John Carroll
David Newcorn
John Davidson
Michael Washington
John Carroll
Eleanor Carroll
Judi Fernandez
Davida Fernandez
```

Notice that no two adjacent lines are identical in this listing. To get a complete removal of repeated lines you could use a command such as **sort +1 members.old | uniq**. Then the output is as follows:

```
Eleanor Carroll
John Carroll
John Davidson
Davida Fernandez
Judi Fernandez
David Newcorn
Mary Smith
Michael Washington
```

Now you can tell how many unique lines are in the file. If you want to know how often a line has been repeated, use the -c option. The command **uniq -c members.old** gives this output:

```
1 John Davidson
2 Mary Smith
1 John Carroll
1 David Newcorn
1 John Davidson
3 Michael Washington
1 John Carroll
1 Eleanor Carroll
1 Judi Fernandez
1 Davida Fernandez
```

The command **sort +1 members.old | uniq -c** gives this result:

```
1 Eleanor Carroll
2 John Carroll
2 John Davidson
1 Davida Fernandez
1 Judi Fernandez
1 David Newcorn
2 Mary Smith
3 Michael Washington
```

The **-d** option displays one copy each of every line in the file that Unix identifies as repeated. The **-u** option displays every line in the file that Unix does not identify as repeated; it doesn't show even one copy of repeated lines. These two options are mutually exclusive; Unix will use the first one it encounters if you put both **-d** and **-u** in the same **uniq** command.

So far you've seen that **uniq** works with the entire line. You can specify a particular place in the line to start the comparison, causing the rest of the line to then be used. The *-field* value refers to the starting point; you specify the number of fields to skip over. A "field" here is the same as a "word" in the **wc** command or a default field in the **sort** command—a set of characters bounded by spaces, tabs, or the beginning or end of a line. To compare based on the second field, you would use a command such as **uniq -c -1 members.old**. Options can be included before the field specifier. Following is the result:

```
1 John Davidson
2 Mary Smith
1 John Carroll
1 David Newcorn
1 John Davidson
3 Michael Washington
2 John Carroll
2 Judi Fernandez
```

Notice that the last line shows a count of **2** for Judi Fernandez. This really means there were two adjacent lines that matched starting with the second field. The fact that the first field differed does not affect the output. If you want a more specific position from which to start the comparison, you can use the **+char** specification. Used without **-field**, it measures a specific number of character positions from the beginning of the line. The command **sort members.old | uniq -d +8** results in the following output:

```
John Carroll
John Davidson
Mary Smith
Michael Washington
```

If you use both **-field** and **+char** in the same **uniq** command, the characters are counted from the beginning of the comparison field.

Identifying Lines Common to Two Files

Another command, **comm**, lets you compare two sorted files to identify lines common to both files, those that appear just in the first file, and those that appear just in the second file. You type the command, giving the names of the two files. Suppose **suppliers.89** and **suppliers.90** are to be compared and that the first six lines of each file contain the following information:

```
suppliers.89                  suppliers.90

AT&T                          American Express
Blue Cross Insurance          AT&T
Bullinger's                   Bell Implements
Classified Consultants        Blue Cross Insurance
Croatan Croissants            California Dreamin'
Cycles Unlimited              Croatan Croissants
```

You use the command **comm suppliers.89 suppliers.90** to compare the two files. The output appears on screen in three columns (you will want to use redirection for the output in most cases). The first column contains the lines that appear only in the first file. The second column contains the lines that appear only in the second file. The third column contains lines that are common to both. The output appears as follows:

```
              American Express
                            AT&T
              Bell Implements
                            Blue Cross Insurance
Bullinger's
              California Dreamin'
Classified Consultants
                            Croatan Croissants
Cycles Unlimited
```

Notice that the information in the columns overlaps on screen, which can be a real problem if the file contains longer lines. You have no control over the placement of the columns. One solution is to use options of the **comm** command to generate just one column at a time; this produces more readable output. Figure 5.7 shows the **comm** command's format.

When you use **comm** with no options, the standard output listing has three columns, as you saw previously. The columns are offset somewhat on the screen but may be difficult to read. You will find it most useful to redirect the **comm** output to a file and examine the listing there. For example, the command **comm suppliers.89 suppliers.90 > save.comm.out** puts the output from the **comm** command in the **save.comm.out** file.

The input files must be sorted if **comm** is to have a valid result. The **comm** program causes the lines to be compared and identified as common or included in only one file. If you want to identify only the lines that are different in a particular file, use the options to exclude the other columns from the listing. For example, use **-23** to produce only a listing of the lines in *file1* that are not in *file2* or **-13** to produce a listing of the lines in *file2* that are not in *file1*. Using **-12** produces a listing of the lines the two files have in common, but it does not identify lines that are different in either file. If you request two listings by specifying a single option, those listings are offset in the output. If you request a single listing by specifying two options, that listing appears at the left edge of the screen.

Command: **comm**

Purpose: Display lines in common and not in common between two files; output is displayed in three offset columns.

Format: **comm** [*options*] *file1 file2*

Options:

-1	Suppress repeated lines only in *file1.*
-2	Suppress repeated lines only in *file2.*
-3	Suppress lines common to both files.

Examples:

1. `comm members.old members.arch`
2. `comm -3 members.old members.arch`
3. `comm -12 members.old members.arch`

Results:

1. Display three columns, the first with lines only in the first file named, the second with lines only in the second file, and the third with lines that occur in both files.
2. Display two columns, the first with lines only in the first file named, the second with lines only in the second file.
3. Display one column, containing only the lines that occur in both files.

Figure 5.7 The **comm** *command*

If you omit one of the file names when you enter the **comm** command, Unix expects you to use the standard input (keyboard) to provide data for the other file. While you could use this technique to determine what is in a file, you must be careful to enter the data perfectly and in sorted order. Using an editor and a search (see Chapters 7 and 8) is a more effective way to examine file contents.

If a file contains repeated lines, the type that are identified by the **uniq** command, the result of **comm** may show that a record appears only in *file1* but is also in common between the files. Suppose file **index.save** and **index.add** contain the following lines:

```
index.save                  index.add

addendum                    almanac
almanac                     almanac
archival                    Amundsen
asseveration                Appomatox Courthouse
attenuation                 asseveration
attenuation                 auteur
auteur                      axiomatic
```

Following is the result of **comm index.save index.add**:

```
addendum
                                    almanac
                almanac
                Amundsen
                Appomatox Courthouse
archival
                                    asseveration
attenuation
attenuation
                                    auteur
                axiomatic
```

Note that the word *almanac* appears in the common (third) column as well as in the file2-only (second) column because the word appears twice in the **index.add** file. The word *attenuation* appears twice in the first column because it appears twice in the first file and never in the second file. To avoid such duplications, it is a good idea to use **uniq** with the files first, creating new output with only unique lines. Then run the **comm** program to produce the output you need.

Differences between Two Files

Another command you may need occasionally is the **diff** command. This command not only lets you know how two files differ, but it also includes instructions for converting one file to the other. You wouldn't really need to convert one file to the other, but you can pick and choose what to convert. The output of **diff** is in the form of editor commands that use Unix's **vi** editor (see Chapters 7 and 8); you won't understand editor commands yet, so they won't be discussed here in any detail. Figure 5.8 shows the **diff** command format.

Command: **diff**

Purpose: Show differences between two files on a line-by-line basis as instructions you can use to convert one to the other.

Format: **diff** [*option*] *file1 file2*

Option:

-e Produce script file for editor.

Examples:

```
1.  diff members.old members.arch
2.  diff -e members.old members.arch  toedit.mem
```

Results:

1. Produce differences list to screen.
2. Produce script file for use by Unix editor.

Figure 5.8 The **diff** *command*

The output identifies lines that are different. It includes indications of changes (**c**), lines to be added (**a**), and lines to be deleted (**d**) from both files. A less-than symbol (<) precedes references to *file1* and a greater-than symbol (>) precedes references to *file2*. The **diff** program assumes you are going to convert the first file named to the second file named.

The reason to use **diff** is so that you can save only one version of two files that are substantially similar. Once you run **diff**, you can save the command's output and remove *file2* from you disk. If you ever need it again, you can regenerate the file from *file1* using the **diff** output. Be sure to get some help from a colleague to make sure your **diff** output is sufficient before deleting files you may need someday.

Unix System Exercise 5.3

Purpose: Practice using **wc**, **file**, **uniq**, **comm**, and **diff** commands.

1. Log on to Unix if necessary.
2. Check the file type of each file in your directory.
3. Create a file named **forexercise** containing the lines shown below:

```
7  Sylvia Anderson
6  Judi Fernandez
3  Ray Fernandez
2  Ronald MacDonald
9  Ruth Ashley
9  Ruth Ashley
6  Judi Fernandez
3  Ray Fernandez
```

4. Check the number of lines, words, and characters in **forsorting** and **forexercise**. Then check just the number of lines.
5. Check the unique lines in **forexercise**. (You should get 7.)
6. Sort forexercise and store it as **forexer.sorted**. Now how many unique lines are in **forexer.sorted**? Check the number of unique lines based on the third field, just for fun.
7. How many lines occur in both **forsorting** and **forexer.sorted**? (First sort forsorting into **sorted.lines**, and then use the **comm** command on the two sorted files.)
8. Check the differences between the two sorted files, just to see what the output looks like.

continued on following page. . .

Exercise 5.3 continued. . .

If it doesn't work:

A. You won't have to use many options of the **uniq**, **comm**, and **diff** commands here; feel free to experiment if you want.

B. If you typed your files a bit differently from the ones in this example, you may get different answers. As long as you understand the output you get, don't worry about it.

C. In this example, the files have four lines that appear only in **sorted.lines**, six lines that appear in **forexer.sorted**, and two in common between the two.

SUMMARY

This chapter has covered the uses of pipes (|) and filters (such as **sort**) that you can use to manipulate output and input. In addition, you've learned to do the following:

- Sort lines in a file based on any position with **sort**.
- Determine the general class of a file with **file**.
- Count the number of lines, words, and characters in a file with **wc**.
- Identify the adjacent lines in a file that are unique with **uniq**.
- Identify the lines that occur in only one or both files with **comm**.
- Generate a list of the differences between two files and provide editor instructions for making the files match with **diff.**

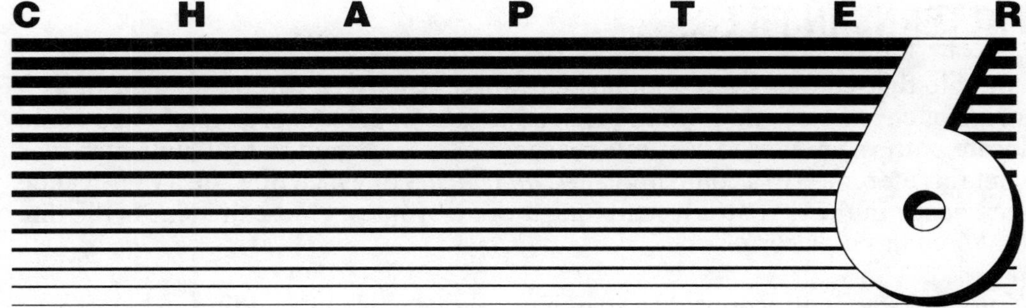

USING EXPRESSIONS AND PATTERNS

Several Unix commands require that you specify expressions or patterns. You may want to search for a particular value in a file or discover which files contain references to a particular item. You may have files containing information that you want to process; for example, Unix can process an inventory file, select the records you want, and calculate the total value represented by those records.

Expressions and patterns are also important in using any editor. The information in the first section of this chapter applies to the Unix editors as well. The second section deals with using a command to locate various types of strings in files. The third section focuses on a command that locates strings in order to select specific lines from the file and then processes those lines according to your instructions.

PATTERNS IN FILES

Any file that contains text contains patterns. A **pattern** can be thought of as a string of characters and is often referred to as a "regular expression." You could locate patterns in files for various reasons. You may want to find out which files contain references to a company called *Imaginetics* or which files use a value called *grexchange* in them. Pattern searching is done by lines; Unix can identify the line that contains a pattern.

You can locate patterns using a search technique while in an editor, of course, or you can use pattern-recognition commands that Unix provides. You can use the pattern-recognition commands from the shell prompt without entering an editor. Before you can learn to use the commands, you must understand patterns. The same rules apply to defining patterns within Unix editors as to defining patterns in standard commands.

Types of Patterns

A pattern can be a simple string or a more complex one. Some applications require a pattern to be enclosed in delimiters to mark the beginning and end of the pattern. The usual delimiter is a slash character (/), like the one you use in paths. Delimiters will be used in this part of the chapter to set the patterns apart from the text, but you may not actually need them when you use patterns in practice. You will need at least the beginning delimiter when you use patterns in the Unix editor, however. A pattern can match one or more strings in a line or in a file; it matches any string defined in the pattern. If you are using a command that replaces a particular string with something else, you must know exactly which one string will be selected to match the pattern.

Pattern matching is case sensitive; that is, it recognizes a difference between uppercase and lowercase letters. If you want to find both uppercase and lowercase versions of a string, you must specify both versions in patterns or use an option within the command that includes both patterns.

Simple Strings

A **simple string** is a series of characters that represent themselves. A pattern of /abc/ is a simple string that matches any occurrence of *abc* in the file. A pattern of /Alabama/ is a simple string that matches any appearance of *Alabama* in the file. A pattern of /ever/ matches the four-letter string *ever* as a separate word, part of *everything*, part of *whenever*, or part of *nevermore*. If you want the pattern to match *ever* only when it occurs as a separate word, you would include a space at the beginning and end of the pattern, within the delimiters.

Special Characters

You can use special characters to cause a pattern to match various strings, in much the same way you use wild card characters in file names to match a variety of file names. The special characters in data patterns are not quite the same, however.

Period The period matches any single character, including the space; the string /.alk/ matches the four-character string in *walk*, *alkaline* (preceded by a space), and *stalking*. If you want to limit this example to match four-letter words ending in *alk*, you could use the string / .alk / (notice that a space begins and ends the pattern). Following are additional patterns that include the period special character. Matches are displayed in italics within the strings in the center column, and no match occurs in the strings in the right column.

Pattern	Matches	Doesn't Match
/chap. /	*chap1* , *chaps*	chap10
/.ing/	*sing*, *sting*y, *ling*er	song

Square Brackets You can use square brackets in patterns just as you can in file names. When you do, to have a match, any single character must match any one of the characters enclosed within the square brackets. For example, /[wt]alk/ matches *walk* or *talk* anywhere the four-letter sequence occurs, but it matches no other string. If you want to allow for any lowercase letter within the brackets, you could use /[a-z]alk/ as the pattern. If you want to allow for any uppercase letter as well, you could use /[A-Za-z]alk/ as the pattern. You can include any characters you want in the square brackets, but each set of square brackets represents a single character in a string. You can also exclude characters with square brackets and the caret symbol. For example the pattern

/[^0-9]alk/ means any single character except a digit or a space is acceptable. Following are additional examples:

Pattern	Matches	Doesn't Match
/s[aiu]m/	*sam*, *sim*, *sum* *sam*e, as*sim*ilate	something, stm skim, scum
/[IN]..../	*Ibbbb*, *I cc*, *Nowis* *Noteb*ooks, *Icicl*e	integer, never
/(...)/	any three-character string between parentheses	(walk), (A)

Asterisk

The asterisk character matches zero or more of the preceding character in the pattern. Unless you tell it not to, Unix locates the longest string in the line that matches the pattern. For example, the pattern /BA*/ matches any string that begins with *B* and is followed by zero or more appearances of *A* immediately after *B*, so it matches *B BAAA*, *BA*, or the first part of *BA*RBARY, but it doesn't find a match in *BBBBCAAAA* or *AAABBB*. The pattern /A.*/ matches any string beginning with the first *A* in the line and extending to the end of the line; if the pattern were /A.*a/, the match would end with the last *a* in the line. A pattern of /a*a/ matches the longest string of consecutive *a* characters in the line. A pattern of /.*/ matches the entire line, if it contains at least one character. A pattern of /(.*)/ matches the longest string in the line that begins with an open parenthesis and ends with a closed parenthesis, even if that encompasses several sets of parentheses. Unix does not check to make sure the parentheses in the line balance.

Remember that you can use the caret (^) to specify a nonmatching character. For example, a pattern of /([^)]*)/ finds the shortest string in the line that is enclosed in parentheses. Note that the pattern starts with an open parenthesis. Within the square brackets, the caret indicates that any character except a close parenthesis can intervene, forcing Unix to use the next close parenthesis as the end of the string. Following are additional examples:

Pattern	Matches	Doesn't Match
/po*t/	*pot, poot, poooooots*	poet, politically
/po.*t/	*poot, pomate poet, politically, spots of gold on the floor.*	pot, pirate
/[A-Za-z]*	*Help me, fourth*	8967, -%$
/(.*)/	*(ab)* and *(cd)* *(18 - (43 + radius))*	
/([^)]*)/	*(18 - (43 + radius)*	

Caret and Dollar Sign

The caret (^) has another use as well as excluding a character or identifying the shortest match in a line. If you begin the pattern or regular expression with a caret, it will match only a string at the beginning of a line. For example, the string /^time/ won't match anything in a line consisting of *Now is the time for* . . . . The dollar sign ($) marks a pattern to be matched only at the end of a line. The pattern /time$/ won't match anything in the line *Now is the time for*. . . ., but it would match a line consisting of *Now is the time* (it won't match if a period or other character follows the string, however). Following are additional examples:

Pattern	Matches	Doesn't Match
^newfig/	*newfig* (at start of line)	newfig (anywhere else)
/100$/	*100* (at end of line)	100 (elsewhere)
^end$/	*end* (as only item on a line)	end (within a line)

Special Characters as Standard Characters

Unix uses the period (.), square brackets ([ ]), asterisk (*), caret (^), and dollar sign ($) as special characters in patterns. It also may use a slash delimiter (/) for each pattern. Sometimes you may need to use one or more of these special characters as standard text in a string. Some commands let you **quote** the entire string using either single or double quotation marks. Others require that you precede the special character with a backslash (\), which forces the special character to be treated as text. If you want to refer to a backslash as itself, you use a double backslash to quote it. (Do not use backslash to quote the parentheses and 0-9 characters because this has special effects you'll learn about when you study the **vi** editor in Chapter 7). Suppose you want a pattern to find every line containing the word end followed by a period. A pattern of /end./ would find this string, but it would also find every line containing end followed by any single character. If you use /end\./ with the backslash before the period, the pattern matches only the four characters you want. Here are some more examples:

Pattern	Matches
/\.*/	.*
/\[4-.\]/	*[4-1]* or *[4-2]* or *[4-3]* (and so on)
/and\/or/	*and/or*
/\^[Cc]/	^*C* or ^*c* (anywhere in line)
/^\^[Cc]/	^*C* or ^*c* (at start of line)
/\$/	*$* (anywhere in line)
/100\$/	*100$* (anywhere in line)
/100\$$/	*100$* (at end of line)

Pattern Matching Rules

The expression that makes up a pattern always matches the longest possible string; it starts as far to the left as possible in the line and extends as far to the right as possible. If you use /g*h/, you'll match every line with a *g* appearing before an *h*; the exact match will use the first g in the line and the last h. If a line contains *while many years ago, a strong wind whistled through the gorge*, the pattern /wh.*go/ matches the string *while many years ago, a strong wind whistled through the go*. To match the shorter phrase *while many years ago*, you could use the pattern /wh.*ago/ to be more specific.

If you want to match a particular parenthetical expression, be as specific as possible in the pattern. If you use /(.*)/, the string starts with the first open parenthesis on the line and ends with the last close parenthesis; Unix doesn't check to see if the parentheses in the match are balanced. You can use /([^(]*)/ to tell Unix to start at one open parenthesis and find the next close parenthesis without another intervening open parenthesis if you want to find the first complete parenthetical expression on the line.

LOCATING PATTERNS IN FILES WITH THE grep COMMAND

Unix provides the **grep** command so you can locate strings in files without having to use an editor. You include any options you need, specify the pattern without delimiters, and name one or more files to be searched. Standard output is produced, which you can redirect to a file if you wish. Suppose you use the command **grep myaddress savedir**, where **savedir** contains a redirected directory listing. The **grep** command takes over, searches through the file for the string *myaddress*, and displays output something like this:

```
myaddress
myaddress.sav
```

If you name several files, the output includes file name headers for each line so you can tell where the match was found. If you use the command **grep add savedir archives**, the output might look like this:

```
savedir:addison
savedir:myaddress
savedir:myaddress.sav
archives:old.addresses
archives:addison.arc
```

Figure 6.1 shows the command format for **grep**. The pattern can be any valid pattern such as those discussed earlier, although the standard slash delimiters are not allowed. You must quote patterns that contain special characters, spaces, or tab characters with a preceding backslash and enclose the entire pattern in single quotes. The *file-list* can be a single file, an ambiguous file name, or a list of several file names. If you don't specify any files, Unix gets data piped in via the standard input device.

Command: **grep**

Purpose: Search files, line by line, for strings that match the pattern; produce standard output, divided by file names if more than one is specified.

Format: **grep** [*options*] *pattern* [*file list*]

Options:

-c	Display the count only.
-e	Use only if pattern starts with -.
-h	Don't include the file name headers.
-l	List only the file names that include the pattern.
-n	Include line numbers in the output.
-s	Provide status code only; no other output.
-v	Reverse; produce lines that don't contain pattern.
-y	Ignore case in matching strings to pattern.

Examples:

1. `grep anderson members.old members.arch`
2. `grep -ny 'anders.n' members.old members.arch`

Results:

1. List of all lines that contain the string "anderson" in either of the two files listed; each is preceded by the appropriate file name.
2. List of all lines that contain any string that matches "anders.n", regardless of case, in either of the two files listed; the line is preceded by the line number.

Figure 6.1 The **grep** *Command*

To see how the **grep** options work, assume your home directory contains the following two files, with the indicated contents:

```
suppliers.89                 suppliers.90

AT&T                         American Express
Blue Cross Insurance         AT&T
Bullinger's                  Bell Implements
Classified Consultants       Blue Cross Insurance
Croatan Croissants           California Dreamin'
Cycles Unlimited             Croatan Croissants
```

The **grep** output includes the entire identified line; the string that matched the pattern is not identified. The interactions below show the output produced by **grep** commands on these files when no options are specified.

```
$ grep C.*C suppliers.89
Classified Consultants
Croatan Croissants
$ grep C.*t suppliers.*
suppliers.89:Classified Consultants
suppliers.89:Croatan Croissants
suppliers.89:Cycles Unlimited
suppliers.90:Croatan Croissants
$ _
```

The -c Option

The **-c** option produces a count of the lines that contain a match rather than displaying the lines themselves. Here is how the output looks on screen:

```
$ grep -c C.*C suppliers.89
2
$ grep-c C.*t suppliers.*
suppliers.89:3
suppliers.90:1
$ _
```

File name headers are provided before each separate count if more than one file is involved.

The -e Option

The **-e** option is needed only in special circumstances. If a pattern you want to specify starts with a hyphen, such as /-fi/, you must prefix the pattern with the **-e** option so that Unix won't think you have specified an invalid option. The command **grep -e-fi inventory.jan** requests a list of all lines in the specified file that contain the string *-fi*. If you include another character in the pattern ahead of the hyphen, you won't need to use the **-e** option.

The -h Option

This option suppresses the file name listing, producing only a list of lines such as the following:

```
$ grep -h C.*t suppliers.*
Classified Consultants
Croatan Croissants
Cycles Unlimited
Croatan Croissants
$ _
```

The result doesn't let you know which file each line came from, but the files are handled in the order in which you name them in the command. You might use the **-h** option when you expect to pipe the output directly to another command. This option has no effect if you use a single file name.

The -l Option

Sometimes you want to know which files contain lines that match the pattern, but you don't really care which lines are involved. In that case, you would use the **-l** option to generate a list of the file names that contain the specified string. This is most useful when you are checking all the files in a directory with *. Following is a sample of how the output looks:

```
$ grep -l ss *
addresses
melrose
suppliers.89
suppliers.90
zyindex
$ _
```

Each file that contains a match is listed only once, no matter how many matches it contains.

The -n Option

If you want to know the numbers of the lines that contain matches, you can include the **-n** option in the command. Each displayed line will be preceded by a line number, as in the following:

```
$ grep -n C.*C suppliers.89
4:Classified Consultants
5:Croatan Croissants
$ grep -n C.*t suppliers.*
suppliers.89:4:Classified Consultants
suppliers.89:5:Croatan Croissants
suppliers.89:6:Cycles Unlimited
suppliers.90:6:Croatan Croissants
$ _
```

The lines in the files need not include line numbers as such; **grep** uses the appropriate line number relative to the beginning of each file.

The -s Option

In some applications, you may not care what the matches are, but instead you simply want to know if there are any. The **grep** command returns a status code that can be used to tell another program whether any matches were found in any of the specified files. A status of 0 means at least one match was located. A status of 1 means no match was found in any of the input files. A status of 2 means an error of some sort interfered and the search was not accomplished. Some versions of Unix treat the **-s** option differently. In those versions, the **-s** option suppresses error messages instead of generating a status code.

The -v Option

Sometimes you may want to produce lines that don't contain a particular pattern instead of those that do. You can do this with the **-v** option. If you combine it with any other option (except for **-s**), you'll get combined output. Following is an example:

```
$ grep -v C.*C suppliers.89
AT&T
Blue Cross Insurance
Bullinger's
Cycles Unlimited
$ grep -vn C.*t suppliers.*
suppliers.89:1:AT&T
suppliers.89:2:Blue Cross Insurance
suppliers.89:3:Bullinger's
suppliers.90:1:American Express
suppliers.90:2:AT&T
suppliers.90:3:Bell Implements
suppliers.90:4:Blue Cross Insurance
suppliers.90:5:California Dreamin'
$ _
```

Note that all lines that do not contain matches for the specified pattern are listed. After the second **grep** command, the lines are numbered as well.

The -y Option

By default, Unix pattern matching is case sensitive. If you want the **grep** command to ignore the case of all characters in the string, you can use the **-y** option in the command. This option doesn't let you ignore the case of only a single character in the string; you must ignore the case of all characters or none. The effect is just what you would expect; more matches will be identified in the search. You can combine the **-y** option with any other option to produce the output you need. Following is an example:

```
$ grep -yn a.*t suppliers.*
suppliers.89:1:AT&T
suppliers.89:4:Classified Consultants
suppliers.89:5:Croatan Croissants
suppliers.90:2:AT&T
suppliers.90:6:Croatan Croissants
$ _
```

Any line containing an *a* or an *A* followed in the same line by a *t* or a *T* matches the pattern.

Using the grep Command

Figure 6.2 shows the first twelve lines of a file containing inventory information. Note that the file is set up so that each line contains information about one item.

```
87877;Hammers,claw;5.98;A-8;B-12;Zimmerman Manufacturing;wood handle
99999;Ripsaw;12.49;A-7;B-14;Zimmerman Manufacturing;steel (wood handle)
54543;Barbeque grill;25.89;A-6;B-1;Schwartz Picnicking Supplies;charcoal
46120;Patio table;45.95;A-8;B-19;Schwartz Picnicking Supplies;plastic (solid)
12324;Picnic Basket;12.50;A-9;B-12;Schwartz Picnicking Supplies;rattan
44331;Nails, ten-p;.05;A-8;C-1;Petersons Hardware;standard (dozens)
33224;Cordless screwdriver;19.00;A-7;B-12;Petersons Hardware;battery
44111;Carburetor head;287;A-1;B-1;Automotive Retailers;no installation
56129;Batteries, car;69.50;A-8;B-12;Caledonia Supplies;12v
21213;Carburetor screw;1.19;A-4;B-3;Cantankerous Automotives;simple
33224;Electric screwdriver;15.00;A-7;B-12;Petersons Hardware;cord (no battery)
54543;Barbeque grill;25.89;A-6;B-1;Schwartz Picnicking Supplies;charcoal
```

Figure 6.2 Inventory data

Suppose you want a file of all items that are stored in aisle 8. You could use this command:

```
grep A-8 inventory > inv.8
```

To see on screen the items that are stored in bin 12 or 17, you could use this command:

```
grep B-1[27] inventory
```

To produce a file containing lines of all items that include parentheses in their descriptions, you could use this command:

```
grep (.*) inventory > annot.out
```

As you can see, you can use the **grep** command to extract lines from the data file based on whatever information you need.

Using the egrep and fgrep Commands

Unix provides two commands that are very similar to **grep** that you may prefer to use. The **fgrep** command is much quicker than **grep**, but it works only on simple strings. The **egrep** command can handle all types of patterns, but it requires considerably more memory; it too is faster than **grep**, however. Most of the **grep** options work with these two programs as well; the only significant difference is that you can't use **-y** to ignore case in **fgrep**. If you search for strings with no special characters, you may find that **fgrep** meets your needs more quickly. If you have more space than time at your disposal, you may want to use **egrep** instead.

Unix System Exercise 6.1

Purpose: Practice using patterns to extract lines.

1. Log on to Unix if necessary.
2. List all the lines in **forsorting** that contain the character *M*.
3. List and number all lines in **forsorting** that contain the character *s* or *S*.

continued on following page. . .

Exercise 6.1 continued. . .

4. List any lines in **new_directory** that contain neither of the characters *e* or *a*.
5. List any lines in **forexercise** that include *and*. Then list to a file the ones that don't include it.
6. Check how many lines in **keep.home** include the character *a* at least once.

If it doesn't work:

A. Try these commands for items 2 through 6 if you have trouble:

```
grep M forsorting
grep -n [sS] forsorting
grep -v [ae] new_directory
grep and forexercise; grep -v and forexercise > not.found
grep -c a keep.home
```

B. Try **fgrep** for simple strings or **egrep** for others if you have trouble.

PROCESSING A MATCHING PATTERN

Unix provides another command that matches patterns in file lines much as **grep** and its related commands do, but this command goes further and lets you specify an action to be taken on the selected lines. In effect, the **awk** command lets you process a text file much as you can with a database language or a programming language. This section won't cover all the possible things you can do with **awk**, but you'll see how the command works and learn enough options to do some useful work with it. If you are going to do much file processing, you probably have specialized software or a programming language at your disposal.

Figure 6.3 (see following page) shows the basic format of the **awk** command. The *file list* can contain one or more files, just as with **grep**. Similarly, you can omit the *file list* if you want to enter data lines at the keyboard or you have redirected or piped the input from another source. The *program* or *program file* specifies the pattern to be matched and the action to be taken on lines that contain matches. Each line of the *program file* works like an IF-THEN command. IF the pattern specification is located, THEN the action is performed. There is no equivalent to an ELSE option. You would use a second line to test the opposite if an alternate action is desired for other lines.

Command: **awk**

Purpose: Search files, line by line, for strings that match the pattern; perform the action associated with each pattern match.

Format: **awk -f** *program-file* [*file-list*]
awk *program* [*file-list*]

Format of program or program file lines:

/pattern/ {*action*}

Examples:

1. `awk /anderson/ {print $1 $2} members.old members.arch`
2. `awk -f fixit.awk members.old members.arch`

   fixit.awk contains the following:

```
$4 + 0 > 1000  {  print $2, $3, $6 }
END { print " Summary of customers with high limits" }
```

Results:

1. The first two fields from each line that contains "anderson" in either file are sent to the standard output device.
2. Three fields are printed from each line in either file in which the fourth field contains a value greater than 1000; following the last data line, a final line is printed.

Figure 6.3 The **awk** *command*

If you have a single pattern-action combination, you can include it as the *program* in the **awk** command. Some versions of Unix require that the pattern-action be enclosed in single quotes to set it apart from the rest of the command line. To use more than one pattern-action, you can include the pattern-action lines in a special *program file* and then use the **-f** option followed by the name of the file that contains the lines in the **awk** command. You can use a program file even for a single pattern-action. The *program file* is simply a text file that contains the pattern-action combinations to be processed. You can create it with an editor or from the console using the **cat** command. If you have more than three lines or so, you'll probably want to use your editor to create the program file.

Suppose you want to identify all lines in file members.old that contain the string /Mac/ and then print them out. You could use this command: **awk /Mac/ { print } members.old**. Notice that the action is enclosed in curly braces. Some versions of Unix require that you code **awk '/Mac/ { print }' members.old**, setting the pattern-action program apart with single quotes. Alternatively, you could create a program file containing the line **/Mac/ { print }**. If you name this program file **getMacs**, you could use the command **awk -f getMacs members.old** to process the file.

When you use the **awk** command, you invoke a special program that processes the files you name in the command, selecting lines that contain matches for the pattern and performing the action you provide on those lines. In the previous example, the program selects lines containing *Mac* and prints them to the standard output device. If you use a program file to specify several sets of patterns and actions, the first line in the first file in the file list is compared to all patterns and the associated actions are performed as the matches are made. The same line could have several actions performed on it before the next line is examined. If you omit the pattern completely, all lines in the files are selected. If you omit the action, the default is to print the line to standard output, just as with the **grep** command. The previous example makes the default action explicit.

Addressing Specific Fields

The **awk** program need not test or print an entire line. You can identify specific fields to be matched or printed, in any order. You can spot line fields just as you do for **sort** because a space or tab is the default input field separator, and a carriage return or newline is the default record or line separator. In the **awk** command, you can specify fields by number. The fields in the record or line are identified as $1, $2, and so forth until the last field in the input line. If you want to print only the first and last (sixth, in this example) field in a selected line, you could use a program line such as the following:

```
/blue/ { print $1, $6 }
```

The pattern to be matched is enclosed in slash delimiters. The action is enclosed in curly braces. Spacing in the action area is not significant, but the comma causes a space to appear between fields in the output. If you omit the comma, the fields are printed without intervening spaces.

Pattern Variations

The pattern in a program line can be used in a comparison to allow the program to select exactly the lines you want. For example, you can specify that the match occur in a specific field. You can use additional special characters to determine the lines to be selected. You can check if the value of a field is greater or less than a specific value. Figure 6.4 shows various operators you can use with patterns, along with examples of each. Notice that only the pattern itself is included within the delimiters. Other operators can precede or follow the pattern, depending on the operation. In a command or program line, the action is enclosed in curly braces, so it doesn't get confused with the pattern.

The most useful characters here are **~** and **!~**. The first (~) specifies that the pattern appears in the field, and the second (!~) specifies that it doesn't. You could use a pattern of **$1 ~ /and/** to select lines in which the string /and/ appears in the first field. A pattern of **$4 !~ /Inc/** selects lines in which the string /Inc/ does not occur in the fourth field. Suppose you want to select lines in which the value in the fifth field starts with the letters *A* through *E*. You could use **$5 ~ /^[A-E]/**. Note that the square brackets have the same effect as with other patterns; any of the characters specified within the brackets will produce a match.

You can use the operators in the action as well. For example, suppose you want to print the contents of the second field with the product of the sixth and seventh fields for all the selected lines. You could code the program line as follows:

```
$2 ~ /Blue/ { print $2, $6 * $7 }
```

For every line in which the second field contains *Blue*, the output will contain the contents of the second field, along with the product of the sixth and seventh fields, separated by a space. Because the action is enclosed in the curly braces, you don't need to quote the asterisk; **awk** knows that you want multiplication here.

You can specify a range of lines by separating two pattern specifications with a comma. The program line **$1 + 0 > = 10000, $1 + 0 < = 20000 { print $1, $3, $6 }** selects the first line containing a value greater than or equal to 10000 and all lines following until the first line that contains a value less than or equal to 20000. The purpose of the **+ 0** here is to ensure that **awk** treats the contents of the first field as numbers.

Basic Operators

Operator	Meaning	Example
~	contains	$1 ~ /USA/
!~	doesn't contain	$1 !~ /USA/
=	equals	$1 + 0 = 90
!=	does not equal	$1 + 0 != 90
>	greater than	$3 + 0 > 1000
<	less than	$3 + 0 < 0
> =	greater than or equal to	$3 + 0 > = 1000
< =	less than or equal to	$3 + 0 < = 0

Note: ***Use + 0 to force field to be treated as numeric.***

Additional Operators

+ – / * %	**for standard arithmetic; use preceding backslash to quote - / or * unless it is included within curly braces**
+ = – = * = / = % =	**for accumulating arithmetic; value is added to former value in field and held there**

Note: ***Temporary variables defined by appearance on right of =***

Figure 6.4 Operators in program lines

Using Program Variables

You have already seen how to use variables to define a specific field for pattern matching on input or printing on output. The **awk** program includes additional program variables that you can use in specifying pattern matching or actions. Figure 6.5 (see following page) lists and defines the program variables.

Variable	Definition
$1 to *$n*	one particular field in line
NR	line or record number
$0	entire line
NF	number of fields in entire line
FS	input field separator; default is space or tab
OFS	output field separator; default is space
RS	input record or line separator; default is carriage return or newline
ORS	output record or line separator; default is carriage return or newline
FILENAME	current file name

Figure 6.5 Program variables for **awk** *program*

You can use the variables in specifying the matching criteria or in the output, as you've seen with the field variables. You can also use them in different ways. For example, you can select a range of lines based on their position in the input file with this specification: **NR= =51, NR= =100**; lines 50 through 100 are selected and the associated action applied to them all. You can change the default value of the separators as part of the pattern. To specify that commas are used instead of spaces as input separators, use **FS** = **","** followed by the rest of the pattern. To cause output fields to be separated by semicolons, use **OFS** = **";"** as the first part of the action.

Multiple-Line Programs

There are two unique patterns you can use to supplement the file processing. One (BEGIN) is handled before the first file listed is processed, and the other (END) is handled after the last file listed is finished. You can include several lines in a program to produce more sophisticated output. For example, you may want a header line if the output will be printed as a report rather than processed by another program. Your program file might include the following lines:

```
BEGIN { print "Summary of Records with High Balances" }
$8 + 0 > 1000  { print $1, $2, $3, $8 }
```

When you use a command such as **awk -f sum.awk outstanding > save.sum**, the heading is prepared, and then lines are selected and the processing takes place; in this case, the output is redirected to **save.sum**. Suppose you want the same effect, but you also want a final total of the values in the eighth field to document how much money is tied up in the high balances. You could expand the program to look like this:

```
BEGIN { print "Summary of Records with High Balances" }
$8 + 0 > 1000  { print $1, $2, $3, $8; total += $8 }
END { print " Total amount in high balances is " total }
```

The second line has been modified to add another action. Notice that a semicolon separates the actions. You could start a new line instead to indicate the end of one action and the start of the next. The second part of the action defines the temporary variable **total** and accumulates the value of the eighth field by adding it to the previous value every time a record is selected. The last line is processed after the last line in the last file is processed; it prints a summary line that includes the final value in the temporary variable.

Suppose you want to accumulate values in several fields and print them all out at the end. You can do this by including several actions in the END action. Here is another example:

```
BEGIN { print "Summary of Records with High Balances" }
$8 + 0 > 1000 { print $1, $2, $3, $8; total += $8; paid += $6}
END    {
       print " "
       print " Total amount in high balances is " total
       print " Amount paid last month is        " paid
       }
```

Notice that the separate actions within the curly braces can be separated by semicolons, as in the second command line, or by carriage returns or newlines, as in the END action. The first print action in END prints a blank line to separate the summary lines from the rest of the report.

Sophisticated Programming

You can get quite sophisticated in programming with **awk**, so that it can act almost as a database handler if you want. For example, you could program it to print information whenever a certain field changes; this would let you handle new dates, new customers, any field where a change signifies a breakpoint. The following command line prints the entire line whenever the contents of field 6 changes:

```
$6 != recall { recall = $6; print }
```

The initial value of all temporary variables is null; therefore, the first time this line is processed, the value of the sixth field will *not* equal the value in recall, so the action *will* be taken. The current value in the sixth field is then stored in the variable and the record is printed. After the line has been processed for the first time, a record is selected only when the value in that field is not the same as the value in **recall**; then the temporary variable (**recall**) is reset and the record is printed.

Some versions of Unix have much more extensive operations you can achieve in **awk** program files. Xenix, for example, has a command language you can use to create more complex decision making and branching within the file. Those techniques, however, are beyond the scope of this book.

Redirecting awk Output

You can redirect the print output by specifying the redirection (or piping) in the **awk** command. Suppose you have a program named **fixlist.awk**, containing these lines:

```
BEGIN { print "Summary of Records with High Balances" }
$8 + 0 > 1000 {print $1, $2, $3, $8; total += $8; paid += $6}
END {
      print " "
      print " Total amount in high balances is " total
      print " Amount paid last month is        " paid
      }
```

You can redirect the output in the command, as in **awk -f fixlist.awk custrecs > save.highs**. All the output produced by the commands is redirected to the same place. If you prefer, you can use > > to append the output or | to pipe it to another program.

Using the awk Command

The file in Figure 6.2 (earlier in this chapter) can be processed effectively using the **awk** command. Because the command is easier to use with program files, it will be shown that way here. Suppose you want to display the item number and storage location for all carburetor parts. The file **carb.awk** contains this line:

```
$2 ~ /arbure/ { print $1, $3, $4, }
```

The command **awk -f carb.awk inventory** causes **awk** to search the file named inventory and select lines containing the string *arbure* in the second field. Three fields from the line are then listed on the screen.

Suppose you want a listing of all items stored in aisle 6, including the name, item number, and bin number in the listing. You could format and display it with this program:

```
BEGIN   {
        print "Items stored in Aisle 6 "
        print "#      item name                    Bin"
        print " "
        }
$3 ~ /A-6/ {
             print $1, $2, $4
           }
```

You might need to rearrange the spacing of the column headings in the BEGIN portion so that they appear above the appropriate values in the data listing.

Unix System Exercise 6.2

Purpose: Process data using **awk** files at a very basic level.

1. Log on to Unix if necessary.
2. List the lines in **forsorting** that are numbered 7 or greater. If your **awk** doesn't work and you can't figure out why, try enclosing the program in single quotes, as in **awk '7 { print }' forsorting**.

continued on following page...

Exercise 6.2 continued...

3. Create a file named **M.awk** that will contain a line to print the third field three times for every line containing the character **M**.

4. Add an END option to **M.awk** that will skip a line, then print a comment.

5. Use **M.awk** to locate lines in **forsorting**.

6. If you expect to use **awk** in your work, practice with it a bit more.

If it doesn't work:

A. With a single line command, you may have to use single quotes; be sure they enclose the pattern as well as the action.

B. The command to use the program file should be **awk -f M.awk forsorting**. Remember to use the append symbol (**> >**) when you add the END option to **M.awk**.

SUMMARY

In this chapter you learned to specify patterns to match strings in an ASCII file. In the process you learned to do the following:

- Define simple and complex patterns for use in various Unix commands and processes.
- Locate a string in one or more files with the **grep** command.
- Locate lines containing a string and process that line with the **awk** command.
- Create a program file for use with the **awk** command.

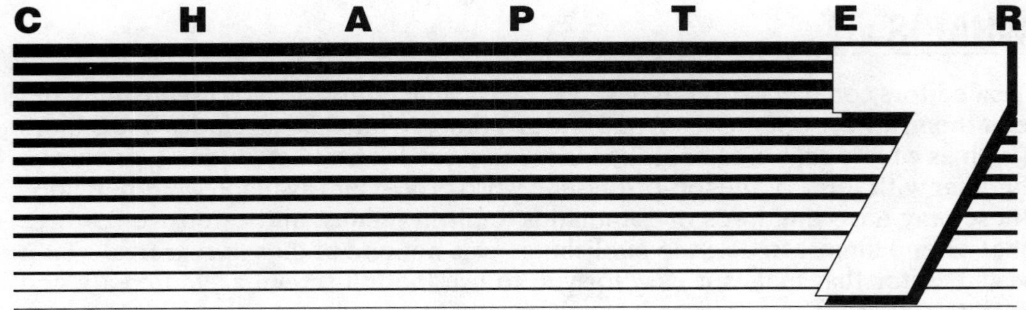

USING THE vi EDITOR

Most Unix installations include several editors, any of which you can use for creating data files, source programs, and standard text. This book focuses on **vi** (pronounced "vee-eye"), a visual full-screen editor that is fairly easy to learn and includes many features you will need. The exercises are especially important in this chapter because using **vi** requires you to keep many things in mind at the same time. If you can't do the exercises as you come to them, do them in sequence when you get a chance. Once you learn the basics of **vi**, you'll need practice to get comfortable with it.

In this chapter, you'll learn to start up **vi**, enter text, move the cursor, make changes using insertion and deletion, and exit **vi**. You'll also learn to undo deletions and combine lines. By the time you finish this chapter, you'll be able to create and modify useful files on disk.

WHAT IS vi?

Text editors come in various types. Very basic line editors let you create lines and edit them, always operating on one line at a time. While Unix includes line editors (such as **ed** and **ex**, for example), **vi** is much more than a line editor. You may be familiar with some of the top-of-the-line word processors available commercially; these may have hundreds of commands, built-in menus, and extensive features that extend almost to desktop publishing. **vi** is not one of those programs. **vi** is a visual editor that makes it easy for you to use the full screen as you create and maintain files. The **vi** editor lets you create ASCII files of any type. You can create data files, source programs in any language, or text files such as documentation, reports, and letters. The basic procedures for using **vi** are the same for any document. It produces standard ASCII output, which is just what is needed for most purposes.

vi is not a word processor, and it is not designed to produce formatted printouts. It is much more than a line editor, however. You can edit anything you can see on the screen. You can move the cursor at will throughout the file and add, change, or delete text as needed. While you can print files you create in **vi** from the disk using the Unix **lpr** command, they will, by default, print just as you see them on the screen when you display them with **cat**. In Chapter 9, you will learn to use **nroff** to format **vi** files for printing.

STARTING vi

You start the **vi** editor by entering the **vi** command at the shell prompt, followed by the name of the file to be edited. If you name a file that doesn't yet exist, you will get to create a new one. If you name a file from your directory, you'll see the beginning of that file on screen, ready for editing. Figure 7.1 shows the screen following the command **vi members.old**. The text from the file appears on the screen. The status line at the bottom of the screen shows the file name and the number of lines and characters in the file. Each line beginning with a tilde (~) is a line following the end of the file. The cursor in the figure follows the last character. When you first enter a file, the cursor is in the upper left corner of the screen, at the first nonblank character.

If you name a file that doesn't yet exist, you'll see a similar screen, but each line except the first and the status line contains only a tilde. The status line contains the file name you entered, with a comment such as *[New file]* or *No such file or directory*. Later you can save the file under the name you entered when you first started the **vi** editor. The cursor is located in the upper left corner, ready for you to enter data.

```
John Davidson
Mary Smith
Mary Smith
Carroll Emerson
Davis Emerson
Davida Fernandez
Marcia Carlyle-Dawes
Jennifer Alderson
Stephen Pouros
Michael Stockwell
Charity Blackstock
William Thackeray
Dorian Gray_
~
~
~
~
~
~
~
~
~
~
~
~
"members.old"   13 lines, 195 characters _
```

Figure 7.1 Beginning **vi** *– existing file*

On some terminals, you may not see an entire screenful of data; if the system is quite slow, it may be set up to show a lesser number of lines. You won't be able to change this, so you'll have to adjust to seeing fewer lines. Whatever number is the maximum shown is treated as a full screen insofar as the commands affect it.

THE WORK BUFFER

When you start up **vi**, the file is read into an area called the **work buffer**. Any changes you make to the file are actually made in the work buffer. If you are editing an existing file, no changes are made to disk until you tell **vi** to do so. If you are editing a new file, that file isn't placed on disk until you tell **vi** to do so. There are several ways to tell **vi** to change the existing file or create a new one. This is generally done when you leave **vi**.

EXITING vi

You can exit **vi** in either of two ways. You can use the **:q!** command to quit and abandon any changes you have made to the file, or you can use the **ZZ** command to save any changes and return to the shell prompt. When you enter **ZZ**, be sure to use uppercase characters. When you include a colon in a command, as in **:q!**, the command appears on the bottom line of the screen. When you finish typing the command, it takes effect.

vi MODES

When you start up **vi**, you are placed in **command mode**. In command mode, you can move the cursor, delete text, change text, perform searches, and exit **vi** to return to the shell prompt, among other things. What you cannot do in command is add text. To add text, you need to use **insert mode**. Several command mode commands switch you to **vi**'s insert mode; each puts the cursor for insertion at a specific location.

Command Mode

While in command mode, you can enter dozens of different commands. Most of them consist of one or two letters and perhaps a number. You don't need to press **Return** unless it is part of the actual command. For example, if you type **ZZ** while in command mode, the file is saved with its changes and you are immediately returned to the shell prompt. Commands that start with a colon (:) require **Return**. If you type **:q!** while in command mode, then press **Return**, the changes are abandoned, any original file is unchanged, and you are returned to the shell prompt.

While you are in command mode, the arrow keys and various cursor movement commands let you move around on the screen and scroll through a file that takes up more than one screen. Additional commands let you perform other operations.

Insert Mode

You enter insert mode by typing certain commands while in command mode. One common way is to type **i** for **i**nsert. You are immediately placed in insert mode with the cursor positioned where it was before, and you can start typing text; characters you type appear to the left of the cursor and push any existing characters to the right. If you start insert mode in a new file with **i**, characters begin in the very first position in the file. If you type commands such as **ZZ** while you are in insert mode, they just become part of the text. If you type **i** while you are insert mode, the character appears on the screen and in the buffer.

Another way to enter insert mode is by typing **a** for **a**ppend. Characters you type next are inserted to the right of the cursor. When you use **a** to begin insert mode, the cursor is placed right after the last character already in the file. Except in new files, the position of the cursor before you enter the insert mode command determines where characters you insert are placed.

To leave insert mode and return to command mode, no matter how you got to insert mode, just press **Escape**. Then you can continue with other commands or leave **vi**.

Command Mode vs. Insert Mode

You generally can't tell by just looking at the **vi** screen display whether you are in command mode or insert mode. One way to find out is to press **Esc**. If you are in insert mode, this puts you in command mode. If you are already in command mode, the machine may beep or flash, but it has no effect on **vi** or your file. So once you press **Esc**, you know you are in command mode. Then you can enter insert mode if that is where you want to be.

If your keyboard has arrow keys, you may be able to use them to determine the mode as well. If you are in command mode, pressing the the arrow keys moves the cursor as indicated on the keys. If you are in insert mode, pressing these keys may cause a beep or have no effect at all.

Most people use command mode as a base mode while working in **vi**, unless they are creating a new file. While entering a great deal of new data, it's easier to just stay in insert mode. Making corrections to any line other than the one currently being typed must be done in command mode, however.

Basic Data Entry

You need to create a file. What do you do? First, decide on a name. You can change the file name later if you want. Then enter the command to start **vi**, following the command name with the file name, as in **vi booklist**. You'll see a screen with the cursor at the upper left, tildes (~) down the left margin, and a status line with the proposed file name at the bottom. First, you must enter insert mode, so press **i**. Then just begin typing lines, pressing **Return** at the end of each. If you don't press **Return**, the line will wrap on your screen, but it will still be considered a single line by **vi**. If you are typing standard English sentences, it is convenient to break them at each major sentence part. At the very least, start each sentence on a new line. This technique makes it easier to change your file later on.

You can make corrections in any line before you press **Return**, just as you can in the command line. Using **Backspace** lets you overtype characters. For example, suppose you have started creating a file. Figure 7.2 shows how the screen looks while you are typing the fourth line. Note the tildes that mark lines that contain no text. Once the screen is filled with text, the status line disappears. You'll see later how to restore it for reference.

```
Salinger, J. D.: Catcher Catcher in the Rye: C
Rand, Ayn: Atlas Shrugged: C
Alcott, Luisa May: Little Men: B
Alcott, Luisa may: _
~
~
~
~
~
~
~
~
~
~
~
~
~
~
~
~
~
~
~
~
"booklist" [New File]
```

Figure 7.2 File being created

While in insert mode, you can't go back and correct the first line or change the spelling of "Luisa" in the third line, for example. You can always make corrections in the current line, however. Just use **Backspace** to move the cursor to the **u** and overtype the rest of the line. (As in command-line editing, you may need to use **Ctrl-H** to get the backspace effect.) Backspacing destroys any characters you back over, but the characters don't disappear immediately. You can overtype them if you want. If you press **Escape** to leave insert mode, the excess characters disappear. You can't just use the arrow keys to move over and insert the **o** while in insert mode. To make corrections like that, you must press **Escape** to return to command mode.

If you want to indent, you can use **Spacebar** or press **Tab**. The arrow keys generally have no effect in insert mode. In some versions of Unix, however, pressing an arrow key while in insert mode puts you into command mode. When you notice errors in lines other than the one you are currently typing, you can correct them later through command mode.

Basic Cursor Movement

Once a file contains data, you'll have to be able to move the cursor within it. The first step is to make sure you are in command mode by pressing **Escape**. Then you must move the cursor to the character to be deleted or to a character at the insertion point. If your keyboard has arrow keys, they undoubtedly work in **vi**. Each moves the cursor one character in the direction indicated by the arrow – up or down, left or right.

You can also use keyboard commands to move the cursor. The arrow key functions can be achieved with these lowercase commands:

Lowercase command	**Arrow key equivalent**
l	right arrow
h	left arrow
j	down arrow
k	up arrow

On your keyboard, notice that **l** is farthest of the four keys to the right; it moves the cursor one character to the right. **h** is the farthest left; it moves the cursor one character to the left. If you think about the shape of the letters, you can see that **j** extends below the line when it appears in text; it moves the cursor one line down. When it appears in text, the letter **k** extends above the line; it moves the cursor one line up. In command mode, the space bar also moves the cursor one character to the right. In insert mode, the space bar inserts a space into the file.

Basic Corrections

The most basic corrections in a **vi** file involve deleting and inserting characters. While there are many more ways to do it, here you will learn how to delete one character at a time, and you'll see the difference between the insert and append commands when making corrections.

While in insert mode, you can delete characters in the current line by backspacing over them. You can delete characters from any line while in command mode. First move the cursor to the first character to be deleted. Then press **x**. The character is gone and the character to the right slides over to take its place. If you want to delete six characters in a row, just position the cursor on the first one and press **x** six times. Or you can position the cursor on the first character and type **6x**. The digit **6** here is a repeat factor; you'll see that you can use a repeat factor before many commands to multiply the effect.

Suppose you are working with the file shown earlier in Figure 7.2. You have noticed some errors, so you press **Escape** to enter command mode.

The word *Catcher* is repeated in the first line and you want to delete one occurrence of it. You can move the cursor to the letter *C* and then press **x** eight times or just type **8x** to delete the seven letters in the word *Catcher* plus the space after it.

Suppose you want to correct the spelling of *Luisa* by making it *Louisa*; to do so, you must insert a character. Move the cursor to *u* and type **i**; then type **o**, and it is inserted before the *u*. To correct the spelling of the other *Luisa*, move the cursor to the *L* and type **a**. This time when you type **o** it is inserted after the current character. You can use either **i** or **a** to insert additional characters; just decide ahead of time where to place the cursor so inserted characters appear where you want them.

Unix System Exercise 7.1

Purpose: Use basic data entry, cursor movement, and editing commands. In this exercise, you'll create a telephone listing file. *Note: In the* **vi** *exercises, you may find that you get the screen messed up. Take your time. If you insert extra characters, just backspace over them or enter command mode and delete them. Whenever you are done typing in insert mode it is a good idea to press* **Escape** *to make sure you enter command mode.*

1. Log on to Unix if necessary.
2. Enter **vi** to create a file named **phone.list**. Use either insert command (**i** or **a**), and type the following lines (be sure to press **Return** at the end of each line):

```
Ruth Ashley       619 555-1111
Judy Fernandez    619 555-0807
Damon Alexander   505 555-7777
Steve McMakin     213 555-8989
```

3. Start another line with your first and last name. Backspace over the last name and spell it differently. Then enter command mode.
4. Move the cursor (using **h**, **j**, **k**, and **l**) within the lines. Try the arrow keys as well so you know if they work or not. Then position the cursor and add your telephone number.
5. Enter command mode, and then save the file by typing **ZZ**; be sure to use uppercase letters here. Notice the shell prompt. Return to **vi** to edit the same file.
6. Change the name of *Damon* to *Michael*.
7. Abandon the file by returning to command mode, and then typing **:q!**.
8. Enter the file with **vi** again. Notice that the change did not take place.
9. Change the spelling of *Judy* to *Judi*. (Delete the *y*, and then insert *i* at that location.)
10. Add five more lines to the file; create any data in the same format.
11. Save the file, including changes. Print or display it from Unix if you want.
12. If you like, create another file and practice with insert mode and the commands you already know how to use.

continued on following page. . .

Exercise 7.1 continued...

If it doesn't work:

A. Pressing **Escape** should put you in command mode any time you aren't in it. Use the keyboard keys for cursor movement. Use **x** to delete the character at the cursor, **a** to insert characters following the character at the cursor, and **i** to insert characters preceding the character at the cursor.

B. If your screen looks a real mess, press **Ctrl-R** or **Ctrl-L** to redraw it. You can abandon the file (**:q!**) and start over if necessary.

C. To add data at the end of the file, move the cursor to the last character you have typed, then type **a**.

Units of Measure

You have seen how to move the cursor one line or one character at a time and how to delete one character at a time. Many **vi** commands operate on larger blocks of data than this. The blocks you can operate on are determined by fixed units of measure. If you understand which units of measure **vi** recognizes, you can be much more efficient in using **vi**.

Characters

A **character** is a single character, whatever is stored in a single byte, whether or not it prints on the screen. The letter *a* is a character, a space is a character, a tab is a character.

Words

A **word** is the equivalent of an English word. It's a string of one or more characters marked on each side by some combination of the following: any punctuation mark, space, tab, digit, or newline. Each group of punctuation marks is also considered a word. Following are some examples:

1 word	`david`
2 words	`david?`
2 words	`david*?!`
4 words	`david? (The`
9 words	`Who is David?  He is the superuser!`

Blank-Delimited Words

A **blank-delimited word** is like a standard **vi** word except that it includes adjacent punctuation marks. They are separated by space, tab, or newline only. Here are the same examples as blank-delimited words:

1 blank-delimited word	`david`
1 blank-delimited word	`david?`
1 blank-delimited word	`david*?!`
2 blank-delimited words	`david? (The`
7 blank-delimited words	`Who is David? He is the superuser!`

Lines

A **line** is a string of characters separated by newlines. It may be more than a line as displayed on your screen if you didn't press **Return** because lines wrap around in the display if necessary. If you work mostly with computer program code, you will want to be sure and press **Return** at the end of each line. If a file contains data lines that take more than 80 characters, you may want to let the lines wrap so you can treat each data line as a separate line in **vi** and as a separate record when processing the data.

If you are writing text to be used in documentation or reports, you will want to press **Return** after each major sentence component to make for easier changes later on. In Chapter 9, you'll learn to format text for output, using **nroff**.

Sentences

To **vi**, a **sentence** is like an English sentence. It is a string of characters that starts at the end of the previous sentence and ends at the next period, exclamation point, or question mark, followed by two spaces or a newline character. If only one space follows the period, exclamation point, or question mark, **vi** doesn't recognize it as the end of a sentence. If a newline follows the punctuation, it does. You'll find that sentence measures are useful only in text, as when you are preparing documentation or reports with **vi**.

Paragraphs

A **paragraph** is a group of one or more lines surrounded by blank lines. Two newline characters in a row create a blank line in the text, which **vi** considers as the division between two paragraphs. A single line or 45 lines can be a paragraph, depending on where the blank lines are placed. You don't need sentences to have paragraphs; **vi** can deal with groups of data or program lines separated into groups with blank lines as paragraphs even if the file doesn't contain any **vi** sentences.

Screen

The **screen** includes the displayed part of the data in the work buffer. You can use scroll and cursor movement commands to see parts of a file that don't fit on the screen.

COMPLETE CURSOR MOVEMENT

You can move the cursor many different ways, using any of the standard units of measurement. Figure 7.3 shows the complete set of commands that move the **vi** cursor in most Unix versions. You have already seen how to use the first five commands. As you know, pressing the arrow keys has the same effect as pressing the letters **h**, **j**, **k**, and **l**.

Command Key	Cursor Movement
Spacebar	Forward one character position.
l	Right (forward) one character position.
h	Left (backward) one character position.
j	Down to same position in line below; moves left to last position.
k	Up to same position in line above; moves left to last position.
w	Forward to first letter of next word.
W	Forward to first letter of next blank-delimited word.
b	Backward to first letter of previous word.
B	Backward to first letter of previous blank-delimited word.
Return	Forward to beginning of next line.
0	Back to beginning of current line.
$	End of current line.
(	Back to beginning of current sentence.
)	Ahead to beginning of next sentence.
{	Back to beginning of current paragraph.
}	Ahead to beginning of next paragraph.
H	Home, or left end of top line on screen.
M	Middle, or left end of middle line on screen.
L	Lower, or left end of lowest line on screen.
G	Last line in work buffer.
***n*G**	Indicated relative line *n* in buffer.
Ctrl-U	Up half screen.
Ctrl-D	Down half screen.
Ctrl-F	Forward (down) almost a full screen.
Ctrl-B	Backward (up) almost a full screen.

Figure 7.3 Cursor movement commands

Moving by Words

The **w** command moves the cursor to the beginning of the next word; it may advance to the next line if necessary. The **W** command moves the cursor to the beginning of the next blank-delimited word. The **b** command moves the cursor to the previous word beginning, while the **B** command moves it to the previous blank-delimited word beginning. The lowercase **w** and **b** and the uppercase **W** and **B** affect words and blank-delimited words in some other commands you'll see later on as well.

Figure 7.4 shows part of a listing from a phone number listing file. When you open the file, the cursor is on the first character of the first line and you are in command mode.

```
Carson Davis  555-7865
Stephen Twohey  555-1000
George Bush  555-2343
Virginia Loveland  555-7777
Christine Wysocki  555-6543
```

Figure 7.4 Phone list file

If you type **w** at this point, the cursor moves to the character *D*; type it again, and the cursor moves to *5*; type it again and the cursor moves to -. Type **w** once more, and the cursor moves to the *7*. If you type **w** one more time, the cursor moves to the first character in the second line. That's how moving the cursor by words goes, using spaces, the line end, and punctuation marks as word boundaries. Now suppose in the second line you type **W**; the cursor moves to *T*. The next press of **W** moves the cursor to *5*. The next press of **W** brings the cursor to the next line because this time the hyphen does not delimit a word.

Moving by Lines

Another set of cursor movement commands moves by lines. **0** (zero) moves the cursor to the beginning of the current line, and **$** moves it to the end of the current line. Pressing **Return** moves the cursor to the beginning of the next line. Remember, these commands work this way only in command mode. In insert mode, pressing **Return** starts a new line in the file.

Moving by Sentences or Paragraphs

You can move back to the beginning of the current or previous sentence by pressing the (key or ahead to the beginning of the next sentence by pressing the) key. You can move back to the beginning of the current or previous paragraph with { or ahead to the beginning of the next paragraph with }. Actually, the brace keys move you to a blank line. If there is a sequence of blank lines, the cursor will rest in the first blank line the cursor encounters. The parenthesis and brace keys affect sentences and paragraphs in additional commands you'll learn to use later as well. Figure 7.5 shows part of a text file that includes sentences and paragraphs. When you open the file with **vi**, the cursor appears in the upper left corner of the document.

```
Michael T. Morrison is learning to use a computer.
This is not difficult.
He starts by learning some of the commands
the computer can understand.
You wouldn't expect to speak directly to a person
who didn't speak your language.
So it is up to you to learn to speak the
computer's language.

Luckily, computers understand very few words.
And they are mostly short.
Here are a few and what they mean:

      ls        List a directory on the screen
      rm        Erase a file from the disk
```

Figure 7.5 Documentation file

When you type), the cursor moves to the *T* at the beginning of the next sentence. It doesn't stop at the *M* because the period preceding this character is followed by a single space. If you type } next, the cursor moves to the first blank line in the file, following the line that contains *computer's language*. Typing } again moves the cursor to the next blank line, and pressing it again moves the cursor to the first line in the next group of blank lines.

Positioning the Cursor on the Screen

You can move the cursor to certain positions on the screen with some uppercase commands. Use **H** to move it to the home position in the upper left corner. Use **M** to move it to the beginning of the middle line on the screen. Use **L** to move the cursor to the beginning of the lowest line on the screen. You can move the cursor to the very last line in the work buffer with **G**. If you use a number before it, as in **19G**, the cursor moves to that line in the file; in this case, the cursor moves to the nineteenth line. You don't actually need to number the lines for this to work; **vi** counts them from the beginning of the file.

Scrolling through the File

You can also move the cursor in such a way as to scroll through the lines in the work buffer, showing other parts of the file on screen. The commands to do this are control commands; they can be either uppercase or lowercase, but you must press the **Ctrl** key as you press them. Use **Ctrl-U** to scroll up about half a screen or **Ctrl-D** to scroll down about half a screen. To move by almost complete screenfuls, use **Ctrl-F** to scroll forward in the file (that's down on the screen) and **Ctrl-B** to scroll backward (that's up on the screen).

Using Repeat Factors

You can specify a repeat factor in many cursor movement commands to cause a multiple effect. For example, the command **7l** causes the cursor to move seven characters to the right. The command **10B** causes the cursor to move backward to the tenth preceding blank-delimited word. You can't use a repeat factor on any control commands (such as **Ctrl-U**) or on any commands to position the cursor at a specific point on the screen (such as **L**).

Unix System Exercise 7.2

Purpose: Practice using units of measurement and cursor movement in **vi**. *Note: Don't worry about perfection here; if you have trouble, practice some more. The techniques and commands are much more important than the contents of the file at this point.*

1. Bring up your **phone.list** file (the one created in Exercise 7.1) in **vi**.
2. Add about 25 lines, so the file takes up more than one screen. Don't worry about the data or the correctness of it, but try to maintain the same format of first name, last name, area code, and phone number. Then save the file with its changes.
3. Bring up the same file and practice using the cursor movement commands for words (**w** and **b**) and blank-delimited words (**W** and **B**) in **phone.list**. Then try pressing **Return** in command mode to move to the next line. Try moving to the ends of the current line with **0** and **$**.

continued on following page. . .

Exercise 7.2 continued...

4. Try the scrolling commands to see all of the file. Then delete an entire line using **x**. Notice that the carriage return is not deleted. Correct (or change) a few of the names in your listing. Then save the file.
5. Create another file named **explain.prac**. Include the following text in it. Be consistent in your typing. If you continue on a line following the sentence end, put two spaces following the period and include an extra blank line between paragraphs.

```
What is vi?
It is an editor,
but it is neither a line editor nor a full-screen editor.
You can insert characters,
and you can delete them.

You can't use the full screen in insert mode,
but you can in command mode.

In insert mode, you can correct only
what you have just typed on the current line.
In command mode,
you can correct whatever you can move the cursor to.

End of Report
Robert P.  Ashley
```

6. Save **explain.prac**, and then bring it into **vi** again.
7. Try moving by words, then try doing it by sentences and paragraphs. Use repeat factors in several of the commands.
8. Remove the word *and* from the fifth line, and then change the first character in *you* in that line to an uppercase letter. Change the comma that ends line 4 to a period. Save the file.
9. Print both files from the shell for future reference.

continued on following page...

Exercise 7.2 continued. . .

If it doesn't work:

A. The cursor movement commands should work. Practice some more until all have the effect you expect. If you put only one space after a period or question mark, **vi** won't recognize it as a sentence. If you didn't leave blank lines, **vi** won't recognize the end of a paragraph.

B. Remember that you must be in command mode to use the commands. Press **Escape** as soon as an insertion is completed.

DELETE COMMANDS

The **vi** editor provides a complete set of delete commands, corresponding to most of the units of measurement already covered. The delete commands covered in this section are all given in command mode, and they leave the file in command mode. While in insert mode, you can delete only in the current line using the **Backspace** key.

You've already seen how to delete the character at the cursor by typing a lowercase **x** while in command mode. You can delete the character following the cursor by typing an uppercase **X** instead. Either can include a repeat factor. Just as the command **10x** deletes ten characters, starting with the character at the cursor, the command **8X** deletes eight characters, starting with the character following the cursor. Figure 7.6 lists the delete commands that are common to all **vi** systems. Later in this chapter, you will learn the command that can undo the most recent deletion.

Deleting by Words

You can delete by standard words or blank-delimited words using commands that start with **d** for **d**elete. The position of the cursor in the word has an effect on what is deleted. No command simply deletes the entire word containing the cursor; you can delete from the cursor to the beginning of the word or from the cursor to the end of the word. To delete the entire word, first position the cursor on the first or last character, and then use the appropriate command.

Command Key	Deletion
x	Character at cursor
X	Character following cursor
dw	To end of word
dW	To end of blank-delimited word
db	To beginning of word
dB	To beginning of blank-delimited word
d then **Return**	Two lines; current and following
dd	Current line
d0	To beginning of line
D	To end of line
d)	To end of sentence
d(	To beginning of sentence
d}	To end of paragraph
d{	To beginning of paragraph

Figure 7.6 Delete commands

To delete a standard word, type **dw** to delete from the cursor to the end of the word or **db** to delete from the beginning of the word to the cursor. Similar deletions based on blank-delimited words are typed as **dW** and **dB**. If the cursor is on the first or last character, whatever marks the end (or beginning) of the word is deleted as well. For example, suppose the cursor is on the *D* in the first line of the file shown earlier in Figure 7.4. If you type **dw**, all characters up to the *5* are deleted. If the cursor is on the *v* in the same line and you type *dw*, the characters *vis* are deleted, without including the following spaces.

You can include a repeat factor in these delete commands to multiply the effect. The number occurs following the **d** but preceding the unit of measurement. The command **d4w** deletes from the cursor through the end of the current word (that's one) and then the next three words. It continues to the next line if necessary.

Deleting by Lines

You can delete the entire line containing the cursor by typing **dd**. If you type **d** followed by **Return**, **vi** deletes the entire current line and the line following it. This is the only delete command that must be followed by **Return**; if you don't press **Return**, **vi** waits for the rest of the delete command. To use the repeat factor and delete more than two lines, precede the first **d** with the number; the command **12dd** deletes twelve lines, starting with the current one.

You can also delete from the cursor to the beginning or end of the line. The command **d0** (that's "zero," not the letter "O") deletes from the beginning of the line to the cursor, while **D** deletes from the cursor to the end of the line.

Note that these are physical lines, ended by **Return** or newline. If the file includes lines that wrap automatically on screen, such lines are considered as a single line, no matter how many lines they take on the screen. If you aren't sure what is a line in the file, move the cursor by line first (by pressing **Return** while in command mode) to see the effect. Then move back into the line and issue the delete command.

Deleting by Sentences or Paragraphs

Just as you can move the cursor by sentence or paragraph, you can also delete by sentence or paragraph. Note that these commands work more like word deletions than line deletions. To delete an entire sentence or paragraph, the cursor must be at the very beginning of that sentence or paragraph or the following sentence or paragraph. Then you can issue the appropriate command to delete the preceding or following sentence or paragraph.

To delete from the beginning of the sentence to the cursor, type **d(**. To delete from the cursor to the end of the sentence, type **d)**. You can use **d3)** to delete the rest of the current sentence and the next two sentences as well.

To delete from the beginning of the paragraph to the cursor, type **d{**. To delete from the cursor to the end of the paragraph (the next blank line), type **d}**. The command **d2{** deletes part or all of the current paragraph, depending on the cursor location, and deletes the entire preceding paragraph.

UNDOING A DELETION

The developers of **vi** realized that people occasionally make a mistake or change their minds, so **vi** provides a command that lets you undo the most recent deletion, change, or insertion. This means you can enter a command that takes the last thing you deleted from the file and puts it back in the same location. The same command can take the last thing you typed during insert mode and remove it from the work buffer.

The command **u** **u**ndoes the most recent change. It affects more than just deletions, as you'll see later. Suppose you typed **d4(** to delete several sentences, but you really wanted to delete lines. Just type **u**, and the deleted sentences are back in the same location. Type **u** again and they're out again. You can toggle back and forth with **u** until you decide how you want it to be. You can move the cursor between the deletion and the "undoing," but don't make any other changes in the meantime. For example, if you delete several sentences and then remove a word, typing **u** only restores the word; the sentences are gone for good unless you retype them. If you want to undo a deletion, you must undo it before you delete or insert anything else.

If you enter insert mode and type seven lines and then change your mind, you can press **Escape** to enter command mode, then type **u** to undo the insertion; the entire text you entered in the latest insert mode is removed. You can toggle **u** until you decide how you want the file to appear; however, once you delete even one other character, that deletion is the only thing you can undo with **u** .

The command **U** restores the current line to the way it was before you started making changes. You could have deleted and inserted several things in the line, but when you press **U**, it is restored to the way it was just before the changes were started.

REPEATING A COMMAND

While in command mode, you can type a period (**.**) to tell **vi** to repeat the command that was just performed. It repeats only commands that caused some change to the file, so cursor movement or scrolling commands will not be repeated. For example, if you had just used **d4w** to delete four words and you then want to delete four more somewhere else, you could move the cursor to the new location and type **.** (period) to repeat the **d4w** command.

If you have just been inserting text, you can use the period to repeat the insertion. Suppose you have just typed four lines in insert mode and you want four more just like them. Press **Escape** to enter command mode, position the cursor where you want the lines to appear, and then type a period. The four lines are repeated. If you want to use five lines that are pretty similar, you could enter insert mode, type the first line and press **Return**. You could then press **Escape** to enter the command mode and type four periods in a row and the insert operation is repeated four times. Then you can edit the lines as needed.

The period repeats only the most recent operation. If you stop and make a change to something you just inserted, you won't be able to insert it again by typing the period. The period will repeat the very last operation only. When you repeat insertions, the entire amount of text entered since you started insert mode is inserted again. To limit what will be repeated, be sure to start insert mode, type what you want repeated, then immediately exit to command mode and repeat it. You can, however, move the cursor to insert the text in another location without affecting what text will be repeated.

CLEANING UP THE SCREEN

Once you start making extensive deletions and insertions, you will find that your screen may get really messy. Sometimes Unix doesn't redraw your screen as often as you want. Deleted lines may still appear, even though **vi** has marked the first characters @, for example. Any time you want the screen brought up to date, you can type **Ctrl-R** or **Ctrl-L** (which command works depends on your system).

Another problem you may have is with lines getting too short. Suppose you have deleted parts of two adjacent text lines and want to combine those text lines. Just place the cursor anywhere on the first line and press **J** (uppercase); **vi** inserts a space and pulls up the contents of the next line; it leaves the cursor on the new space. You can split, or unjoin, two lines by pressing **Return** where you want lines to break.

MORE WAYS TO WRITE FILES

Sometimes you may want to write a file to disk without leaving **vi**. Or you may want to append the contents of the work buffer to another file on disk. If you started entering text in **vi** without providing a file name, you need another way to save the file. This section will show you how to solve these problems.

The :w (write) Command

You can use the **:w** (write) command to send the current contents of the work buffer to a file. The complete command format is as follows:

:[*address*]**w**[**!**] [*file name*]

The optional *address* limits the command to affect only part of the work buffer (you'll see how to use this address in Chapter 8). The colon indicates that the command will appear on the status line, just as when you use **:q!**. Including the exclamation point in the **:w** command allows you to overwrite an existing file; you'll need this option if you are updating a file instead of creating a new one. If you omit the exclamation point and the file exists, you'll get a message from Unix. After the **:w** command, you'll remain in **vi**; to get to the shell, you'll have to use **ZZ** or **:q!**. If you omit the file name from the command, the name you used when you entered **vi** is used. If you use a file name in the command, the lines are written to that file, no matter what file name you used when you started **vi**.

The command **:w** writes the current work buffer to the file you named when you started **vi**; all changes you've made so far become a part of the file on disk. The new file name appears on the status line. The work buffer remains intact, with all the changes you have made in it. The original file, if there is one, has not yet been affected unless you didn't specify a file name in the **:w** command; however, if you use **ZZ**, the changes will be written to the original file; to prevent this, use **:q!** to abandon the changes after they have been written to the desired new file. The command **:w!** has the same effect as **ZZ**; it saves the entire file, overwriting an existing one if necessary, and exits to the shell.

Suppose you want to save your changes to a new file without changing the current file at all. You could use **:w new.version** to save a new file, followed by **:q!** to abandon the work buffer and exit the shell. If you entered **vi** without providing a file name, you can use **:w! savenewstuff** to send the text you entered to a file. If you want to append your new text to an existing file, you can use **:w > > practice**; in fact, you may prefer this if you aren't sure if the file **practice** already exists or not.

Unix System Exercise 7.3

Purpose: Practice deletions, undoing, and writing to other files using **vi**. *Note: As with other* **vi** *exercises, take the time to figure out what is happening. Most problems arise from being in the wrong mode. As before, the file contents are unimportant right now.*

1. Bring **phone.list** into **vi**, and then insert a blank line every five or six lines.
2. Delete a paragraph, and then restore it.

continued on following page...

Exercise 7.3 continued...

3. Delete a blank line with a single command, and then restore it. Delete a line, using repeated delete word commands. Then, try the restore command.
4. Delete two blank lines with a single command. Try the command repeat symbol to delete the next two.
5. Save the file in its current form as **new.files**. Then abandon the changes so the original file is unchanged.
6. Bring **explain.prac** into **vi**. Delete the third paragraph and then restore it.
7. Add a paragraph before *End of Report*; use any text you want, taking about five or six lines. Try removing the insertion with **u**, and then type **u** again to restore it.
8. Append the contents of the work buffer to the file **my.address**, and then save the changed version of **explain.prac**.
9. Bring **my.address** into **vi** and notice that it contains the report.
10. Insert a blank line between the former contents of **my.address** and the new text; then save the file.

If it doesn't work:

A. Take your time. Remember that **u** affects only the very latest deletion or insertion. Only cursor movement commands can occur between the change you want to undo and the undo command.

B. Press **Escape** whenever you aren't sure what mode you are in. If you are already in command mode, you should hear a beep, but that's all right. On some systems, arrow keys put you in command mode as well.

SUMMARY

This chapter has covered the basic commands you'll need to edit files using **vi**. You have learned to do the following:

- Enter the editor with the **vi** command.
- Leave the editor with the **ZZ** or **:q!** command.
- Send text to a file with the **:w** command.
- Use insert mode following the **i** or **a** command.
- Use cursor movement commands in command mode.
- Delete characters with the **x** or **X** command.
- Delete strings of text with variations on the **d** command.
- Use repeat factors and the command repetition command.
- Undo deletions and insertions.

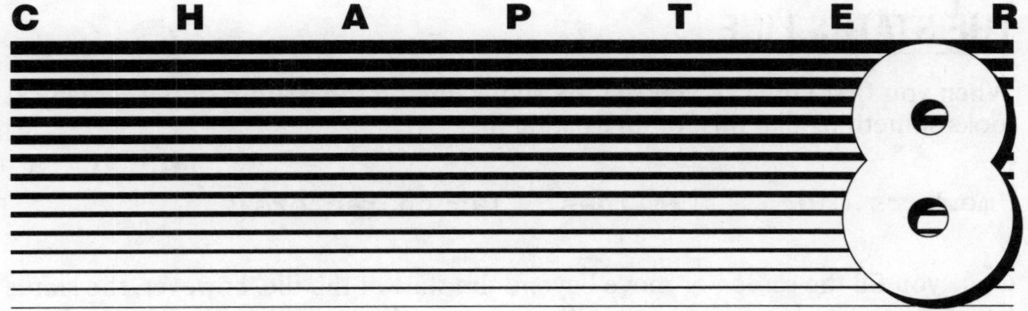

MODIFYING vi FILES

Chapter 7 showed you how to enter **vi**, how to insert and delete text in several different ways, and how to save (or abandon) the changes you make. You also learned to handle cursor movement and clean up the screen when necessary.

You can do a great deal more with **vi**. In this chapter, you'll learn various commands for making changes and searching for text in your files. You'll learn to use other buffers (in addition to the work buffer) in the process of using various commands. You'll also learn to set parameters to modify the default effects of your **vi** sessions.

THE STATUS LINE

When you first enter **vi**, you see the status line on the bottom of the screen. It looks something like this for an existing file:

```
"members.old"    13 lines,  195 characters
```

Once you fill the screen or move beyond the start of the file, however, the status line disappears. Even if you move the cursor to the end of the file, you won't see it. At times, you may forget the name of the file you are editing or you may need to know exactly where you are in a file. You can bring up the status line again by entering **Ctrl-G**. The new status line gives you the file name, the current line number, the total number of lines in the work buffer, and the percent of the file that precedes the current line. You'll be able to use the line numbers in some commands you'll learn later in this chapter. The new status line looks like this:

```
"members.old"   [modified]     line 9 of 27    --- 33% ---
```

USING SHELL COMMANDS IN vi

Normally, you use **vi** commands in **vi** and shell commands when you see the shell prompt. If necessary, however, some versions of Unix let you use a shell command from within **vi**. Just type **!**, and when the shell prompt appears on the bottom line, type the command. Thus, to see a directory, type **!ls**. The directory listing on your screen is also inserted into the work buffer. You can delete the lines if you don't want them to be a permanent part of the file you are editing.

If you want to pull a file into the current file, you can use a special read command.

INSERTING A FILE WITH THE :r (read) COMMAND

The read command lets you pull another text file into the file being edited without otherwise affecting that file. The text contents are inserted following the current line; they don't overwrite any of the work buffer contents. The command format is as follows:

:r [*filename*]

To pull in the file named **new.books**, use the command **:r new.books**. You can use a path preceding the file name if appropriate. As with other commands that begin with a colon, this one appears on the status line as you type it. You'll be able to make corrections in your typing just as with any other command line.

When you enter the **:r** command, if you don't specify a file name, the current file (that is, the one you are editing) is read into the work buffer on the next line. The result is generally that your work buffer contains the current file twice. If you enter a file name that doesn't exist, you will get an error message telling you so. You might want to check your directory listing before using the **:r** command.

REPLACING AND CHANGING TEXT

You can replace or change characters in a file using any of the standard **vi** units of measurement. Figure 8.1 lists the various commands you can use to change text. You'll learn to use them in this chapter.

Command	Change or Replacement
r	Replace character at cursor.
R	Replace characters until **Escape** is pressed.
cw	To end of word.
cW	To end of blank-delimited word.
cb	From beginning of word to cursor.
cB	From beginning of blank-delimited word to cursor.
cc	Current line.
c0	From beginning of line to cursor.
c$	To end of line.
C	To end of line.
c)	To end of sentence.
c(	From beginning of sentence to cursor.
c}	To end of paragraph.
c{	From beginning of paragraph to cursor.

Figure 8.1 Change commands

All the change commands must be entered in command mode. All commands except the replace commands (**r** and **R**) place you in insert mode once they have been executed. You can use **U** to undo changes in a line before you make changes to any other line. When you type **U**, the line is restored to the condition it was in when you started this change or delete operation. As discussed in Chapter 7, any changes to another line in the interim will invalidate the use of **U**.

Replacing Characters

If you want to replace a single character, make sure you are in command mode, place the cursor on the character to be changed, type **r**, and then type the replacement character; the original character is replaced, and you are still in command mode. The **r** operator is very useful for such changes as changing a character from uppercase to lowercase or correcting a mistype. You can use a repeat factor as well. Suppose you typed *MAil* when you meant to type *mail*. Just place the cursor on *M*, type **2r**, and then type **ma**. The two characters are replaced, and you are still in command mode.

If you want to replace several characters and don't want to bother counting them, you can use **R**. When you do, you can overtype characters until you press **Esc** to end the replacement and return to command mode. Note that typing **R** doesn't actually delete or insert characters; it lets you overtype the characters already in the file. If you want to insert rather than replace characters, you should use **a** or **i** instead.

Changing Text Based on Units of Measurement

When you enter a command based on the change operator (**c**), **vi** performs a deletion of the amount requested, and then lets you add a change. It doesn't necessarily delete the characters from the screen immediately; you may see a $ symbol on the screen following the characters to be deleted. When you press **Escape** to complete the change, the deletion takes effect. It may appear on screen that you are overtyping later text, but when you press **Escape**, the old text will be deleted and the new text inserted in the proper location.

The changed text doesn't need to be the same length as the deletion, however; it can be as short as one character or as long as you want for any change command. When you enter the command, **vi** deletes the amount specified, and then puts you in insert mode. The cursor is logically at the same location it would be if you had used a delete command instead. You can enter the text you want; because you are in insert mode, pressing **Return** inserts a new line. Press **Escape** to return to command mode.

The word change commands work from the cursor location to the beginning or end of the word. When you type **cw** or **cb** to change to the end or beginning of the standard or blank-delimited word, you are telling **vi** that you want to delete the rest of the word and replace it with the text to be inserted. You can type as much as you want before pressing **Escape**. The commands **cB** and **cW** cause **vi** to delete the beginning of the standard or blank-delimited word and let you insert text to replace it. As with the cursor movement and delete commands, you can use repeat factors to increase the amount of text deleted; however, the amount of text you delete still has no effect on how much text you can enter to replace the deleted text.

The line change commands work in much the same way, deleting the specified number of lines and then allowing you to enter text until you press **Escape**. The command **cc** deletes the entire current line; **c0** deletes from the beginning of the line to the cursor; **c$** or **C** deletes from the cursor to the end of the line. In all cases, you are then placed in insert mode to insert as much text as you want. If you want to remove a specific number of lines and then insert text, you can use a command such as **8cc**, which deletes eight lines .

You can remove part or all of a sentence or paragraph and be placed automatically in insert mode with commands such as **c(**, **c)**, **c{**, and **c}**; all delete the same characters as if you used the equivalent delete command instead and then place you in insert mode. You can use repeat factors with these commands just as with the corresponding delete commands.

Example: Change Commands in Action

Suppose you want to update a documentation file. To change a line that reads *The delete command always works from the current cursor location* to read *Most of the delete commands work from the current cursor position*, you have several choices. You could do it completely with delete commands and separate insertions. Following is another option, which involves four steps:

Figure 8.2 shows how the line appears at various points in the process. The underscore character (_) indicates the current cursor location.

1. Position cursor at *T*, type **r**, and then type **t**.
2. Type **i**, and then type **Most of,** following it with a space and **Escape**..
3. Position cursor at the *d* in *command*, and then type **c3w** to remove *d always works*, which also places you in insert mode. (Figure 8.2 shows how the screen looks at this point.) Type **ds work** and press **Esc**.
4. Position cursor at the beginning of location, and then type **cw**, followed by **position** and press **Esc**.

As you work, the screen periodically contains $ markers during a change command. Each time you press **Escape**, however, the line resumes its correct appearance at that point.

Original line
The delete command always works from the current cursor location

After part 1
the delete command always works from the current cursor location

After part 2
Most of the delete command always works from the current cursor location

During part 3 – after c3w
Most of the delete command always work$ from the current cursor location

During part 3 – after ds work, but before you press Escape
Most of the delete commands works work$ from the current cursor location

After part 3 – after you press Escape
Most of the delete commands work from the current cursor location

During part 4 – after cw
Most of the delete commands work from the current cursor locatio$

After part 4
Most of the delete commands work from the current cursor position

Figure 8.2 Line appearance during modification

ADDING TEXT

You have already learned several ways to add text to a file. You can use **i** to insert text before the cursor location. You can use **a** to insert text after the cursor location. You can use the various change commands to remove existing text and insert new text at the location of the deletion. If you are starting a new file, you enter the **vi** command line and type **i**, and you're ready to type. If you want to add text to the end of the file, you enter the **vi** command line, type **G** to go to the last line, and type **a** to append text. If you are in the process of editing and changing a file, you can use a change command to delete text and then enter insert mode. Figure 8.3 shows several additional commands you can use to add text.

Key	Insert Location
i	Before cursor
I	Before first nonblank character on line
a	After cursor
A	At end of line
o	On next line down (open a line)
O	On next line up (open a line)

Figure 8.3 Commands for inserting text

Specifying the Insertion Point

The **I** command lets you insert text immediately before the first nonblank character on the current line. While you could move the cursor there and then type **i**, the **I** command saves you several keystrokes.

The **A** command lets you insert text at the end of the current line. You could achieve this by typing **$** to move the cursor to the end of the line and then typing **a**, but using **A** saves time and keystrokes.

Neither of these commands is ever essential, but the more work you do in **vi**, the more useful you will find them.

Inserting New Lines

Any time you are in insert mode, you can press **Return** to insert a new line. If you know you want new empty lines to work in, however, from the command mode, you can use commands that open new lines either before or after the current line. No matter where the cursor is when you use a command to open new lines, the current line remains intact.

When you type **O**, **vi** opens a blank line just above the current line, places the cursor at the beginning of it, and puts you in insert mode. Just press **Return** every time you need another line.

When you type **o**, **vi** opens a blank line just below the current line, and puts you in insert mode at the beginning of that line. Again, just press **Return** to get another new line.

Unix System Exercise 8.1

Purpose: Practice using various change commands and additional insert commands in a **vi** file

1. Bring up **my.address** in **vi**.
2. Move the cursor to the very end of the work buffer and read in the contents of the **phone.list** file you created in Chapter 7. Bring up the status line and examine the information.
3. Use a replace command to change the last character of one phone number to a different digit.
4. Use a change command to replace the full name on one line of the telephone information.
5. Use a change command to replace the date line near the beginning of the file with a line containing your own area code and telephone number.
6. At the very end of the file, insert your current directory listing by running the **ls** command.
7. Between the address information at the beginning and the report which follows, insert two lines to title the report; insert *Using vi* and *a primer* on two separate lines. Save the file as **my.address**.

continued on following page...

Exercise 8.1 continued...

If it doesn't work:

A. The change commands delete the amount of text you specify, put **$** at the end of them, then put you automatically in insert mode. You can type as much as you want, but you have to press **Escape** to return to command mode.

B. Use **:r** to read in a file, **Ctrl-G** to bring up your status line, and **!ls** to get a directory listing. Remember to use the long distance cursor movement commands to move long distances in the work buffer.

LOCATING STRINGS IN A FILE

You will frequently want to search a file to find out if it contains some particular string of characters. You can do this by specifying a pattern or regular expression (discussed in Chapter 5) in a search command. You may want to find all occurrences of a particular word or phrase. You may want to see if the file contains a reference to a particular word or phrase. You'll find that using **vi** is much easier than using the **grep** command to locate strings in files.

Search Commands

Figure 8.4 (see following page) shows the **vi** search commands. When you enter the slash (/) character, the command you enter appears on the bottom line of the screen so you can see and modify the string as you type it. The string can be a simple string of characters or a regular expression using special characters. **vi** locates the first occurrence of the expression in the appropriate direction, if it exists, and positions the cursor on the first character. It leaves you in command mode. If **vi** can't find a match, you'll see a message such as *Pattern not found*, and the cursor remains in its former location.

Command	Description
/string followed by **Return**	Search forward in work buffer
?*/string* followed by **Return**	Search backward in work buffer
n	Find next string in same direction
N	Find next string in opposite direction

Figure 8.4 Search commands

To locate the word *DuoTech* in a file, position the cursor at the beginning of the file, and use the command **/DuoTech** followed by **Return**. **vi** positions the cursor at the first character in the string. If you then type **n**, **vi** locates the next occurrence of the same string. If you start in the middle of the file with the same search command, you can type **N** after the first string is located to reverse the direction of the search. Starting with **?/DuoTech** followed by **Return** causes **vi** to search backward in the file, and using **N** later reverses the direction of the search. Both **n** and **N** wrap around; that is, when they reach the beginning or end of the work buffer, they continue at the other end.

When the expression is a simple string, it can contain any characters except unquoted special characters. Even embedded spaces are acceptable because the string is terminated by **Return**. As in regular expressions, you can use special characters in a search string to limit or expand the strings that match it. Figure 8.5 shows the special characters you can use in a search. If you want to use any of these characters as itself in the basic search string, be sure to quote it (precede it with \) in the string.

Command	Description
^	Beginning of line
$	End of line
.	Matches any character
\>	Match the end of a word
\<	Match beginning of word
[ ]	Match any character within brackets

Figure 8.5 Search string special characters

When you use **/^(** followed by **Return**, **vi** searches forward for the next occurrence of an open parenthesis at the beginning of a line. If you use **?/)$** followed by **Return**, **vi** searches backward (notice the ?) for a close parenthesis at the end of a line. The special character ^ that limits the search to the beginning of the line precedes the string, while the special character **$** that limits the search to the end of the line follows the string. The period represents any character, so, for example, the command **/t..b** followed by **Return** matches the four-letter string starting with *t* and ending with *b* in each of the following: dis*turb*ing, *tarb*aby, ca*t.* *b*erries, and so forth.

If you want to limit the string to a complete word, you can include the space or punctuation within the expression. You can use square brackets to allow a space, period, or comma at the end, and another set of square brackets to allow either uppercase or lowercase at the beginning. The command **/[Mm]ilk[.,]** followed by **Return** should locate the word *milk* wherever and however it appears in normal text. If you want the string to match only at the beginning or end of a word, use the backslash and appropriate angle bracket. Using both special characters lets you specify a complete word. You could use **/\<the\>** followed by **Return** to match the complete word *the*. The command **/\<fil** followed by **Return** locates the string *fil* only at the beginning of words. It would match *fil*e, *fil*eget, and *fil*bert, but it won't match the three-character string in locations such as infiltrate and landfill.

In all cases, **vi** locates the string, positions the cursor at the first character in the string, and remains in command mode. You issue the appropriate command and continue. If you want to delete the located string, you must issue the appropriate command. For example, if you use the command **/[Aa]t this point in time** followed by **Return**, and **vi** locates the string, the cursor is positioned at the *a* or *A*. To delete the entire phrase, you would then enter the command **d5w**. To change it, you could use **c5w**. To insert more text before the phrase, you could type **i**. What you do when a string is located depends on the reason you searched for it in the first place.

Search and Replace

If you want to automatically replace a located string with another string, you use a different command. The command begins with a colon, like the command to exit **vi** without saving changes. After you type the colon, the rest of the command appears on the bottom screen line, where you can correct it as you type just like any other Unix command line. You still specify the search string, but you also specify a string to replace it. The **vi** search-and-replace operation is called

substitution, and you request it with the **:s** command. This particular command can be terminated with either **Return** or **Escape**; there is no difference in effect. Here's the command format:

:[*address*]**s/***search-string***/***replace-string*[**/g**]

The square brackets in the format indicate that the *address* is optional, as is the **/g** (global) parameter. If you use the format without the **/g** parameter, the search is limited to the current line and only the first occurrence of the search string is replaced with the replace string. The cursor remains on the first character of the line. If the line contains another occurrence of the search string that you want replaced, you must re-enter the command. The period does not repeat a substitution command. You can use the search string special characters as needed, but the replace string can include only the backslash to quote an otherwise special character.

Current Line

If you use the basic form of the **:s** command, it substitutes only for the first occurrence of the search string in the current line. For example, the command **:s/duotech/DuoTech** locates the first occurrence of the string *duotech* in the current line and then replaces it with the string *DuoTech*. Similarly, the command **:s/mc/microcomputer** locates the first occurrence of *mc* and replaces it with *microcomputer*.

Global Replacements

If you want to replace all occurrences of the search string on the current line, use **/g** at the end of the command. The slash character (/) terminates the replace string, and the letter **g** asks to make the replacements "global," which means to replace all occurrences of the search string on the current line, not just the first one. For example, the command **:s/mc/microcomputer/g** changes all occurrences of *mc* on the current line to *microcomputer*, even those occurrences that are within a word, such as *emcee*. If you enter the command **:s/\<l\>/limiting/g** followed by **Return**, every occurrence in the current line of the letter *l* as a complete and separate word will be replaced with *limiting*. Any time you want the **:s** command to affect more than the first occurrence on the line, include the **/g** parameter.

Substitution in More than One Line

If you use an address between the colon and the **s** in the **:s** command, you can extend the search to more than one line. This same type of address can also be used in the write command to limit the lines written to a file.

You can request the entire work buffer, from the beginning to the current line, from the current line to the end, or specific line numbers. The file need not be actually numbered because **vi** counts very well. You must be careful not to specify an actual line number greater than the number of lines in the work buffer. If you do, **vi** simply rejects your command. You can use **Ctrl-G** to see the line number at any point. The status line also shows the total number of lines in the work buffer.

Figure 8.6 shows various specifications you might use in the address. A single number requests a particular line in the work buffer. Two numbers separated by a comma specifies a range of numbers. The period represents the current line, that is, the line containing the cursor. The symbol $ represents the end of the work buffer. The symbol % represents the entire work buffer.

Specification	**Example**	**Result**
Single line	`:17s/`	Use line 17.
Range of lines	`:12,48s/`	Use lines 12 through 48.
Beginning to current line	`:1,.s/`	Use lines 1 through current.
Current line to end	`:.,$s/`	Use current line through end.
Use entire work buffer	`:1,$s/`	Use lines 1 through end.
	`:%s/`	Use entire buffer.
Current through *n*	`:.,+12s/`	Use current through next twelve lines.
Current and *n* preceding	`:.,-9s/`	Use current and nine preceding lines.

Figure 8.6 Addressing in substitution commands

If you want to change the word *iifile* to *ifile* everywhere it occurs in the file, you could use this command: **:%s/iifile/ifile/g**. There are other ways to specify it as well, of course. For example, if the string *iifile* might occur as part of another word, you would want to include the beginning and end of word symbols. You could use **:1,$s/\<iifile\>/ifile/g** as the command (note that in this case the first and last lines in the work buffer were specified rather than using the simpler % command).

Unix System Exercise 8.2

Purpose: Practice using search and substitution in **vi**.

1. Bring up **my.address** in **vi**.
2. Search for the string *in*. Use **n** and **N** to see many places it occurs.
3. Search for the string *ed*. Examine several occurrences of it.
4. Substitute the string *IN* for the first occurrence of *in* in each line in the file. Examine the result, and then change them all back to *in*.
5. Substitute the string *HERE IT IS* for every occurrence of *C* in the file. Examine the result, and then change them all back.
6. Within the lines that include the phone number listing, change every occurrence of *555* to *000*.
7. In the part of the text before the phone number listing, replace every *Y* that is the first character on the line with the period character. Then change all the periods in that part of the work buffer to question marks. (You will need to quote the period when it is part of the search string.)
8. Abandon the work buffer at this point. If you want to try some more search and replace operations, bring your file into **vi** again.

If it doesn't work:

A. The search command shouldn't give you any trouble. If it does, type /, then type a string you can see on the screen and press **Return**. If the cursor doesn't stop at the string, type **N** until it does. A search always affects the entire file.

B. The substitution command can be tricky. Try substituting for something you can see. The command **:s/555/000/g** should accomplish the number substitution. To set the numbers back, use **:s/000-/555-/g** so you don't change any occurrences of 000 other than those that were previously 555.

C. If you use an address, put it between the **:** and the **s**. To find out what line number is current, type **Ctrl-G** to bring up the status line. If you need another line number for the address, check its number as well.

CUT AND PASTE

Any editor worth its salt needs a cut-and-paste facility. That means you must be able to mark some text, store it somewhere, and insert it wherever you need it. **vi** does this with buffers. As you know, the entire file you are editing is copied into the work buffer when you start **vi**. All text insertions, deletions, and changes affect only the work buffer. When you are ready, you can tell **vi** to write the contents to a file. If you prefer, you can abandon the contents of the work buffer. **vi** has other buffers as well.

General Purpose Buffer

Whenever you enter insert mode or make a deletion, **vi** stores the text in the **general purpose buffer**. When you enter insert mode, whatever you type into the work buffer goes first into the general purpose buffer as well. When **vi** deletes text, whatever is deleted goes into the general purpose buffer. In either case, you can use **u** to switch the contents of the general purpose buffer into and out of the work buffer.

The catch is that each insertion or deletion that goes into the general purpose buffer replaces completely whatever was in that buffer before. If you use insert mode to enter 27 lines, all 27 are present in the general purpose buffer when you press **Escape** to return to command mode. If you type **u**, the 27 lines are removed from the work buffer and placed into the general purpose buffer. If you delete even a single character, however, that character replaces the 27 lines in the general purpose buffer, and entering the **u** command simply restores that character.

The **u** and **U** commands always use the general purpose buffer as their source. Because so many commands use this buffer, you may have problems using it for your own purposes. You'll learn to use other buffers shortly.

"Yanking" Data into the General Purpose Buffer

Sometimes you want to put some text directly in the general purpose buffer without deleting it or putting it into the work buffer. To do that, you can use the **yank** commands. They are just like the delete commands in form, as shown in Figure 8.7 (see following page), but they don't delete anything from the work buffer. Each yank command merely puts the specified text into the general purpose buffer. Nothing is confirmed on screen. You are left in command mode, and the cursor doesn't move.

Command	Text "yanked"
yw	To end of word
yW	To end of blank-delimited word
yb	To beginning of word
yB	To beginning of blank-delimited word
y followed by **Return**	Two lines; current and following
yy	Current line
y0	To beginning of line
Y	To end of line
y)	To end of sentence
y(	To beginning of sentence
y}	To end of paragraph
y{	To beginning of paragraph

Figure 8.7 Yank commands

Notice that a single **y** followed by **Return** yanks two lines; use **yy** to yank a single line into the buffer. Once you know what is in the buffer, you can position the cursor and insert the contents into the work buffer with **u** in as many locations as you want.

Named Buffers

You can establish up to 26 buffers of your own named **a** through **z**. These buffers hold deleted or changed text, but their contents aren't overwritten unless you specifically request it. That means you can set up several different buffers to hold text that you want to save for later use. You can specify that text go into the named buffer by including a double quotation mark (") and the name of the buffer before the yank, delete, or change command. For example, the command **"zd3)** deletes three sentences and stores them into buffer **z** rather than in the general purpose buffer. If you then use the **u** command, however, the contents of the general purpose buffer rather than the named buffer is used.

You can specify a named buffer before any delete or yank command. If you use the lowercase version of the buffer's name (**z**), the current text replaces any previous contents of the buffer. If you use the uppercase version of the buffer's name (**Z**), the current text is appended to the buffer. You can use this technique to collect separate lines from various places in your work buffer and use the uppercase name to place them together in a named buffer.

Retrieving Text from Buffers

When you have text stored in any buffer, you most likely want to get it back into the work buffer at some point. If the text is in the general purpose buffer, you can use an undo command to put it back in its original location. But you probably want it somewhere else. For example, you may have a comment line you want to place in several different locations. Or you may be using a named buffer to move text from one location in your work buffer to another. These problems can be solved with the put commands.

The put commands are specified as **p** and **P**. If you use either command by itself, the current contents of the general purpose buffer is placed in the work buffer. If the buffer contains characters or words, typing **p** puts the contents of the general purpose buffer after the current character (much like **a** in insert mode) and typing **P** puts it before the current character (much like **i** in insert mode). If the buffer contains lines, sentences, or paragraphs, **p** inserts the contents after the current line and **P** inserts it before the current line.

You can specify a named buffer before the put command just as in a delete or yank command. The command **"zp** puts the contents of the named buffer **z** before the current cursor location.

Using Buffers

Suppose you want to move two paragraphs from one location to another in your document. Position the cursor at the beginning of the paragraph, use **"rd2}** to delete the two paragraphs and store them in buffer **r**. Then position the cursor when you are ready at the new location and type **"rp** to insert the paragraphs there. If you want to leave them at the original location but repeat them elsewhere, use a yank command instead of delete command. And remember, once the text is stored in the named buffer, it stays there until you replace it or end the session.

Suppose you are working with a file that contains inventory information. You want to rearrange it so that a certain group of lines is repeated together at the end of the file. You make the first line to be saved current, and type **"myy**; this yanks the line into buffer **m**, destroying what was there before. You make the next line to be saved current and notice that the following line is to be saved as well, so you type "**My** followed by **Return**; the two lines are appended to the line already in buffer **m**. You repeat the process, using the uppercase buffer name so the lines are appended. When you have gathered all the lines into the buffer, type **G** to move the cursor to the last line. Then type "**mp** to put the entire contents of the named buffer in the work buffer. Because the contents of the named buffer consists of full lines, they will be placed after the current line.

Unix System Exercise 8.3

Purpose: Practice using buffers to copy and move text.

1. Bring up **my.address** in **vi**.
2. Delete four lines from your phone number listing and place them in buffer **y**. Then delete another line and restore that line with **u**.
3. Place two lines without deleting them into buffer **w**.
4. Move to the end of the file, and put the contents of buffer **y** here. Without moving the cursor, put the contents of buffer **w** into the file.
5. Move the cursor to the beginning of the phone number listing and insert the contents of buffer **w** at that point. Notice that it is still the same.
6. Place the current directory listing (use **!ls**) into the file, then delete it from there and add it to buffer **w**. Then insert buffer **w** at the end of the file.
7. Practice using the named buffers some more if you want.
8. Save the file in its current state as **buffer.stuff**, and then abandon any changes you made to **my.address**.

If it doesn't work:

A. You won't see any indication on the screen when something is placed in a buffer. The only way you can examine a buffer is to put it (using **p** or **P**) into the file. If you put extra lines into a file to check buffer contents, you can just delete them from the file; they will stay safely in the buffer.

vi DEFAULT PARAMETERS

So far, you have been working with **vi**'s defaults. You can change how **vi** reacts by setting various parameters within **vi**. Many of the parameters can also be set within your login file. Many parameters are available; however, this section will cover only the most common ones.

Display Parameters

One useful parameter specifies that line numbers be shown when text is displayed. Use the command **:set number** to cause numbering. If you want to restore an unnumbered display without leaving **vi**, use **:set nonumber**. When you leave **vi**, the default of showing no line numbers is restored.

By default, **vi** wraps to a new line at a specific location on your screen (usually at the right edge). If you want it to wrap at a different point, you can set the **wrapmargin** parameter. To set the **wrapmargin** parameter, you specify the number of characters in from the right edge in the command, rather than the number of characters to fit on the screen. The command **:set wrapmargin=10** causes lines to wrap starting ten character positions in from the right edge of the screen. To restore the default within a **vi** session, use **:set wrapmargin=0**.

Search Parameters

Normally, a **vi** search is case sensitive. If you want **vi** to ignore the case in searches, you can set a parameter to do so. The command **:set ignorecase** turns off the case-sensitive nature of searches. You can use **:set noignorecase** to restore case sensitivity without leaving **vi**.

If you want to be able to use special characters in searches without quoting them, you can use the **:set nomagic** command. This causes the characters **.**, **\<**, **\>**, **[**, and **]** to have their ASCII meanings. The characters **^** and **$** always have special meanings in strings, no matter what you do. You can reset the special characters to have their special effects in search strings with the **:set magic** command.

Normally, when a **vi** search (with **/**) reaches the end or beginning of the file, it wraps around to continue until it reaches the point where you entered the command. If you want to cause it to stop at whichever end it reaches and not wrap around, you can use the **:set nowrapscan** command. You can restore the normal parameter without leaving **vi** with **:set wrapscan**.

Automatic Indentation

When you type outlines or programs in insert mode, you often have to indent lines a great deal so that the structure of the outline or source code reflects the logic of the text or program, respectively. With automatic indentation, you set a standard amount of indentation, such as 4 or 8; each time you press a special key to indent, the cursor moves in that many spaces; these are entirely separate from tab stops.

The indentation positions must be equally spaced; you can't have indents at 4, 12, and 16, for example, but you could have them every four characters across the line. Once the indent amount (called a shiftwidth) is set, you can use **Ctrl-T** and **Ctrl-D** to move between the indent positions, but only when no text is yet on a line. This helps you to position the cursor before you type each line in a program.

Before you can use automatic indentation, you have to set two parameters: shiftwidth and autoindent. If you want to use a four character indent, you can use **:set shiftwidth=4** to establish it. Then you turn on automatic indentation with **:set autoindent** (or **:set ai**). You can change the shiftwidth at any time by specifying a different value. You can turn off automatic indentation with **:set noautoindent** or **:set noai**.

Once these two parameters are set and you are in insert mode on a new line, you can use **Ctrl-T** to move the cursor right to the next indentation point or **Ctrl-D** to back it up to the left. Whenever you press **Return** while autoindent is on, the cursor goes to the next line directly below where the previous line began, saving you from having to indent again. You can use **Ctrl-T** and **Ctrl-D** to move the cursor if necessary. These two commands work much like **Tab** and **BackTab**, but they work only while the line is empty. If you must change indentation later, you'll have to do it manually by inserting or deleting spaces.

Specifying Permanent Parameters

You might want to use certain parameter settings every time you are in **vi**. In that case, you can put the parameters in a special file. In your directory, you have a hidden startup file that sets various parameters for your user ID. If you use the Bourne shell, the file is named **.profile**; if you use the C shell, it is named **.login**. If you examine your home directory with **ls -a** you'll see a hidden file with one of these names. You can edit the file under **vi** to add (or change) various parameters there.

Suppose you want to display line numbers and ignore the case in all searches every time you enter **vi**.

If you use the Bourne shell, add these statements to the end of the **.profile** file:

```
EXINIT='set number ignorecase'
export EXINIT
```

You can list any number of parameters in the EXINIT line.

If you use the C Shell, add the following line to your **.login** file:

```
setenv EXINIT 'set number ignorecase'
```

You can list any number of parameters in the line.

For either shell, notice that single quotes enclose the list. This sets up the variable EXINIT that **vi** will look for next time it is opened. You can change the status of a parameter within **vi** if you want to change it temporarily.

If you specify parameters in your **.profile** or **.login** file, be sure to save the file after editing. If your file already sets EXINIT to some parameters, just add your new ones to the list. If you notice some strange effects or messages when you use **vi**, you can edit the **.profile** or **.login** file again and remove the lines you added. The parameters you set in the startup file don't take effect until the next time you log in.

MORE WAYS TO ENTER vi

Now that you know much more about using **vi**, you may want to enter it differently. Figure 8.8 shows additional ways you can enter **vi**. Notice that you can cause **vi** to position the cursor at a particular line, at the end of the file, or at the first occurrence of a string for the start of your editing.

Command	Result
vi *file-name*	Edit named file.
vi +*n file-name*	Edit named file starting at line n.
vi + *file-name*	Edit named file starting at last line.
vi +/*string file-name*	Edit named file starting at first occurrence of string.
vi -r *file-name*	Edit named file after system crash.

Figure 8.8 Entering **vi**

TROUBLESHOOTING

Once in a very great while (you hope), the Unix system will have some difficulties. The worst case is a system crash while you are editing a file. If that happens, you must wait until the system is restored and available, and then use the last option shown in Figure 8.8. In most cases, the **-r** option recovers the data that was in the work buffer at the time of the crash. However, you can avoid many problems by saving your data regularly with the **:w** command.

Another problem you may encounter is a screen with lots of extraneous characters or a frozen screen, when other Unix users are experiencing no difficulty, but your terminal seems dead. Do not panic. *And do not just randomly press keys.* Try pressing your **Delete** key a few times; this should put you in command mode. If your problem is a garbled screen, type **Ctrl-L**; this should clean up a screen with extraneous characters. If not, try **u** to see what you did last; many times, **vi** just did what you told it to do.

If the screen is still frozen after a few presses of the **Delete** key, try **Ctrl-Q**. If any commands work, try writing the work buffer to another file to rescue it. If that doesn't work, you may have to abandon it. If nothing works, you'll have to contact the system administrator.

If your system is responding to commands but acting strangely, you have to try something else. One common problem is inadvertently pressing **Shift-Lock** or **CapsLock**. That causes commands to be sent in uppercase, which causes them to have very different effects.

Unix System Exercise 8.4

Purpose: Practice setting parameters.

1. Check your home directory for hidden files; notice whether you have **.profile** or **.login**.
2. Bring up **my.address** in **vi**.
3. Turn line numbering on.
4. Set **vi** to ignore the case, then search for the letter *y*. Repeat with **n**. Notice that it finds both *y* and *Y*.
5. Save or abandon **my.address**, and then bring up your hidden file. Search for EXINIT. If it is present, add the number parameter to it. If not, add the commands that define EXINIT and turn line numbering on.
6. Save the file and log off. Then log back on and bring the file up again. Notice the line numbers. Remove the changes you made to it, and save your hidden file again.

   If you are a programmer, you will find the rest of the exercise useful. If you can't imagine any use for autoindent, you are finished with this chapter.
7. Enter **vi** to edit the new file **demoprog.c**.
8. Set shiftwidth to 4 and turn autoindent on.
9. Type the following program, using **Ctrl-T** to indent and **Ctrl-D** to outdent:

```
/* very simple C program */
#include <stdio.h>
main()
    {
    char response;
    printf("\nType one character.\n");
    response=getchar();
    printf("\nYou typed a %c\n",response);
    }
/* end of program */
```

10. Type some more program lines to practice with autoindent. When you've finished, delete the extra lines, but save the file as it appears in item 9 for use later.

continued on following page...

Exercise 8.4 continued...

If it doesn't work:

A. If you can't locate a hidden file in your home directory, you probably don't have access to your own parameters. Don't worry about it; you can always set them in **vi**.

B. The number and ignorecase parameters should work with no trouble. If they don't, make sure your command looks like **:set number**.

C. If you have trouble with autoindent, you may just need more practice. Many systems let you put autoindent in the hidden file but don't allow shiftwidth there.

SUMMARY

This chapter has covered many advanced **vi** features. You have learned to do the following:

- Access the status line and command output while in **vi**.
- Retrieve another file into the one being edited with the **:r** command.
- Make replacements and changes in text with the **r** command and various **c** commands.
- Insert text with the **A**, **I**, **O**, and **o** commands.
- Search for strings in the work buffer with the **/** command.
- Substitute or perform search-and-replace operations with the **:s** command.
- Use addresses and line numbers to expand and limit the effects of some commands.
- Put text in buffers without deleting it from the file with the **y** command.
- Use named buffers.
- Pull text from other buffers into the work buffer with the **p** and **P** commands.
- Set various parameters to override **vi**'s defaults with the **:set** command.

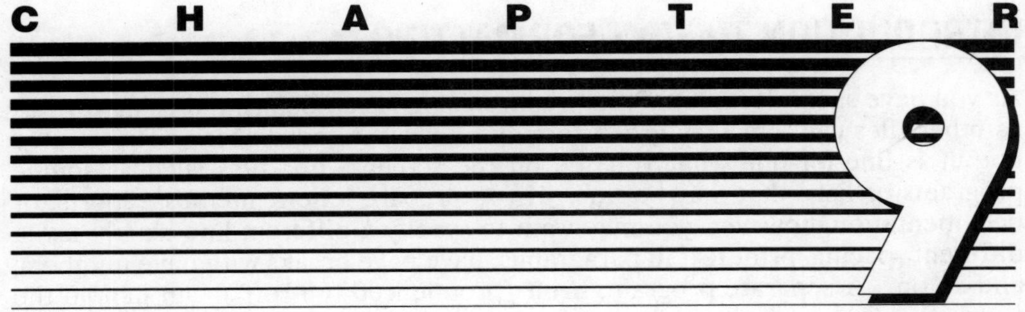

TEXT FORMATTING WITH nroff

You have learned to use **vi** to create and modify a file. You can print the file exactly as it appears on the screen using **lpr**. In addition, Unix provides a separate program to format files for printing. In this chapter, you'll learn to use **nroff** to turn your edited documents into attractive and informative reports.

Some versions of Unix also support a formatting program called **troff**, which prepares documents for a typesetting machine. Most **nroff** commands can also be used with **troff**. However, this chapter will focus on basic formatting for line printers.

INTRODUCTION TO TEXT FORMATTING

As you have seen, documents you prepare using **vi** can be printed using **lpr** just as other files can, but they aren't formatted at all in the process. The printed output is line-for-line what you see on the screen. For files such as source programs or lists, that may be fine. If you prepare letters, memos, reports, or documentation, however, you may want to specify a different line length, use a different spacing, print text in paragraphs, have page breaks with page numbers, and so on. A separate program, **nroff** (pronounced "en-roff"), can handle the formatting for you.

The **nroff** program can handle basic and specialized formatting. Basic commands control spacing, justification, hyphenation, line lengths, and headings. In addition, **nroff** has sets of macros, special commands that combine basic commands to perform more sophisticated formatting, including such techniques as font control. Your system will have at least one, and possibly more, of these **nroff** macro sets available for you to use.

The two most common macro sets are **ms** and **mm**. Virtually all Unix installations include the **ms** set. Xenix prefers that you use the **mm** set but allows you to specify **ms** instead if you want. You can use the **nroff** basic commands even if you don't have either macro set. But you can't use commands from both macro sets in the same file; you must select a macro set for formatting in advance.

Text Formatting Specifics

What can you accomplish with text formatting? In addition to the basics, you can specify that a block of text is to be kept together rather than split over a page, specify that a series of lines be printed unchanged in the midst of a formatted document, or specify footnotes to appear on the bottom of the page. Using macros, you can even produce automatically numbered lists and outlines, as well as manipulate any fonts and type sizes available on your printer.

HOW nroff WORKS

nroff is a filter. It takes your input and produces formatted output on the standard output device. You can redirect the output to a file or pipe it to the printer via **lpr**. Figure 9.1 shows the format of the **nroff** command. There are many more options than those listed in Figure 9.1, some of which you'll learn as you continue in this chapter. When you are able to do basic text formatting with **nroff**, you may want to refer to your installation's documentation to see what else you can do.

Command: **nroff**

Purpose: Format text prepared by **vi** for printing.

Format: **nroff** [*options*] *file*

Options:

-ms	Use the **ms** macro set.
-mm	Use the **mm** macro set.

Examples:

```
1.  nroff document
2.  nroff -ms document > document.form
3.  nroff -mm document | lpr
4.  nroff -ms document | lpr
```

Results:

1. Format input file document and send formatted result to screen.
2. Format input file document using the **ms** macro set and send the formatted result to a new file named **document.form**.
3. Format input file document using the **mm** macro set and pipe the output to the printer.
4. Format input file document using the **ms** macro set and pipe the output to the printer.

Figure 9.1 *The* **nroff** *command*

If you name several files in the **nroff** command, those files are printed in the same document, one after another. To print them as separate files, you must name each file in a separate **nroff** command.

When you prepare a file to be formatted by **nroff**, you insert formatting commands into it. You can use just basic commands or a combination of basic commands and commands from a particular macro set. These tell **nroff** what spacing you want, where indentations occur, and how long each line should be. While the file is being formatted, these commands are interpreted. The embedded commands don't appear in your output, but their effects will.

Line Fill

nroff generally ignores where you pressed **Return** in the text file. It formats by filling the lines to its default line length. Each formatted line is filled with words from the next input line until the next word won't fit, then the next formatted line is started and filled in the same way. Line fill continues, regardless of where you originally pressed **Return**, until **nroff** encounters something that it recognizes as a line break; for example, a space in the first position of a line has this effect. At that time, **nroff** stops filling the current line and starts the next line at the left margin. Basic **nroff** and the **ms** macro set also justify the text; that is, they insert extra spaces in each filled line so that the right margin is straight, rather than ragged. When you use the **mm** macro set, the text has a ragged right margin by default. Some systems even hyphenate by default, but you will usually have to request hyphenation if you want it.

Effects of Spaces

When a line in a file begins with at least one space, line fill stops there. That means that the end of the previous line marks the end of a formatted line. The current line (the one that starts with a space) starts a new line and is printed without formatting. You can get strange effects if you aren't careful with spaces, but you can use them to your advantage if you pay attention to detail. If you leave an entirely blank line in your file, say between paragraphs, it stops line fill and inserts a blank line in the formatted output. If you have a list that you don't want formed into a paragraph, you can start each line in the list with a space, and **nroff** won't fill or justify the lines.

Using Macro Sets

Each macro set has different page layout defaults. Figure 9.2 shows the first part of a sample file called **Gettysburg**, as printed by the command **lpr Gettysburg**. Notice that the line lengths are different. And notice where the blank line occurs in this basic, unformatted file.

```
Four score and seven years ago,
our fathers brought forth on this continent a new nation,
conceived in liberty and dedicated to the proposition
that all men are created equal.

Now we are engaged in a great civil war.
We are met on a great battlefield of that war,
testing whether that nation or any nation
so conceived and so dedicated can long endure.
```

Figure 9.2. Result of **lpr**

Figure 9.3 shows the same part of the file after being printed with **nroff Gettysburg | lpr**. Notice now that the lines are filled and justified. Where a blank line appeared in the original text, a blank line appears in the printed output.

```
Four score and seven years ago, our fathers brought forth on  this
continent a new nation, conceived in liberty and dedicated to  the
proposition that all men are created equal.

Now  we are engaged in a great civil war.  We are met on  a  great
battlefield  of  that war, testing  whether  that  nation  or  any
nation so conceived and so dedicated can long endure.
```

Figure 9.3 Result of standard **nroff** *formatting*

Figure 9.4 shows the same part of the same file after being printed with **nroff -ms Gettysburg | lpr**. Note that it is still filled and justified, but now there is more space in the top margin and the line length is shorter. When you use **ms**, the date is printed in the center of the bottom of the page as a footer. The page number appears at the top of all pages except the first.

```
Four score and seven years ago, our fathers brought forth on
this  continent  a  new  nation,  conceived  in  liberty and
dedicated to the proposition that all men are created equal.

Now we are engaged in a great civil war.  We are  met  on  a
great  battlefield  of that war, testing whether that nation
or any nation so conceived and so dedicated can long endure.



                    ( rest of page)




                           June 13, 1990
```

Figure 9.4   Result of specifying the **ms** *macro set*

Figure 9.5 shows the same part of the same file after being printed with **nroff -mm Gettysburg | lpr**. This time the lines aren't justified. There is more space in the left margin, and the page number appears as a header. There is no default footer with **mm**.

```
                    - 1 -

Four score and seven years ago, our fathers brought forth on
this continent a new nation, conceived in liberty and
dedicated to the proposition that all men are created equal.

Now we are engaged in a great civil war.  We are met on a
great battlefield of that war, testing whether that nation
or any nation so conceived and so dedicated can long endure.
```

Figure 9.5 Result of specifying the **mm** *macro set*

Note: *Once you decide which macro set you are going to use, you can ignore any reference in this book to the other one. If you use Xenix, you'll probably want to stick with* **mm**; *otherwise go with* **ms**. *With either macro set or with none, you can use the basic* **nroff** *commands covered in the next section in any file you intend to format with* **nroff**.

Unix System Exercise 9.1

Purpose: Prepare sample files and try out basic printing with **nroff** and macro sets.

1. Log on to Unix if necessary.
2. Create a file named **sample.let** in **vi** for formatting in this chapter. Use a standard letter heading with a return address and date. In the body of the letter use at least three paragraphs for a total of from 20 to 40 lines. Keep some lines short and extend some almost to the right edge of the screen so that it looks very uneven. Leave a blank line between paragraphs, and wherever else you might eventually want one or more blank lines to appear in the output, but don't start any other lines with a space. Use two spaces following a sentence-ending period unless you press **Return** immediately following the period. Save the file.
3. Create a longer file named **format.doc**. Use a single line title at the beginning of the file, and then type paragraphs, extending most lines close to the right margin. Start each sentence on a new line. Leave a blank line between paragraphs, but don't start any other lines with a space. If you don't have any favorite material to type, feel free to type a few paragraphs from this book. If you don't care to type very much, type a paragraph or two, then use yank and put commands to repeat them at the end of the file until you have about 70 or 75 lines. Save the file and exit **vi**.
4. Print both files using **lpr**. Label the output as "basic lpr" so you can identify it later.
5. Print both files using **nroff file | lpr**. Be sure to use two separate commands. Label the output as "nroff".
6. Print both files using **nroff -ms file | lpr**. Label the output as "nroff -ms."
7. Print both files using **nroff -mm file | lpr**. Label the output as "nroff -mm."
8. Compare the various printouts to see how they differ.

continued on following page. . .

Exercise 9.1 continued. . .

If it doesn't work:

A. You shouldn't have any trouble using **vi** to create the files. You'll use the files you create in this exercise extensively in later exercises in this chapter. If you already have unformatted files of the type requested, feel free to use them instead.

B. If your system rejects either macro set request, you know your version of Unix doesn't support it. If it rejects both, see if you can find out from the system administrator what macros it accepts. You'll be able to use the basic **nroff** commands in any case.

C. If your system rejects the **nroff** command, see your system administrator to find out what text formatting is available. Print your files using that system. If your system is not compatible with **nroff**, there is no point in your completing this chapter.

BASIC FORMATTING COMMANDS

All **nroff** commands must be embedded in the text, which means you must insert them into the file using **vi** or some other ASCII editor. The basic commands always start with a period and begin at the left edge of the line; many commands include an argument, which may be a number or a string of text. The argument must be separated from the command name by a single space. The command (including its argument, if it has one) occupies an entire line by itself; no other text may occur on the same line. The basic commands themselves consist of two lowercase characters. Macro commands are usually in uppercase.

When you run **nroff**, any embedded commands take effect. The commands themselves aren't included in the output, but you'll see the effects. If you use the **lpr** command to print the file containing the embedded commands, you'll see the commands themselves.

Specifying Line Spacing

Single spacing is the default for all **nroff** formatted text. If you want double or triple spacing, you specify it in the **.ls** command. If you want the spacing to affect the entire file, the command must appear before any text in the file. You would enter the command and text as follows:

```
.ls 2
Four score and seven years ago,
our fathers brought forth on this continent a new nation,
conceived in liberty and dedicated to the proposition
that all men are created equal.
```

The command begins at the left edge; the argument (in this case, 2) gives the spacing you want. You can use 1, 2, or 3, although some printers support other values. A space must separate the command name from the argument. When the file shown above is run with **nroff**, the output is double spaced.

To change spacing within the file, place an **.ls** command where you want the change to take effect. The command must be on a separate line each time it appears. It controls spacing for all following text until another command changes it. The **.ls** command doesn't end a paragraph; you still need a special paragraph command (you'll learn about those later) or a line starting with spaces to mark the end. If you want a file to be printed in double spacing with one paragraph in single spacing, you would use **.ls 2** at the beginning of the file, and then just before the paragraph to be single spaced, use **.ls 1** on a separate line. After the single spaced paragraph, include **.ls 2** on a separate line to set up double spacing for the rest of the file. You would enter the commands and text as follows:

```
.ls 2
Four score and seven years ago,
our fathers brought forth on this continent a new nation,
conceived in liberty and dedicated to the proposition
that all men are created equal.

.ls1
Now we are engaged in a great civil war.
We are met on a great battlefield of that war,
testing whether that nation or any nation so conceived and
so dedicated can long endure.
```

When formatted with **nroff**, the text appears as follows:

```
Four score and seven years ago, our fathers brought forth on this

continent a new nation, conceived in liberty and dedicated to the

proposition that all men are created equal.

Now  we are engaged in a great civil war.  We are met on  a  great
battlefield  of  that war, testing  whether that  nation  or  any
nation so conceived and so dedicated can long endure.
```

Vertical Spacing

You may want to insert line spaces between paragraphs, between the heading and the text, between the return address and the salutation of a letter, or between items in a list. You could, of course, just insert all the blank lines you need directly into the file, but this takes up space and can limit your options later. **nroff** provides the **.sp** command to insert line spaces for you. It looks much like the line spacing command, but can take any number as an argument, rather than just 1, 2, or 3. It inserts blank lines in the formatted output at the location of the command. For example, if you specify **.sp 5**, five blank lines are inserted when the file is formatted. If you specify **.sp 2**, two blank lines are inserted.

Like the blank line, the **.sp** command marks the end of a paragraph. **nroff** stops filling lines and begins a new line.

Changing the Line Length

Setting the right margin is done in terms of line length. You can change the default line length with the **.ll** command. If you use **.ll 5.5i**, printed lines from that point on in the file will be 5.5 inches long. You can adjust the line length relatively if you want. For example, the command **.ll -5n** means to make the line length smaller by five character positions; **.ll -.5i** shortens it by one half inch. If you use a plus sign, you get a longer line length. Notice that the character **i** indicates inches, while **n** indicates character positions. In many commands you can specify a length or indentation in terms of either inches or characters. If you omit the measurement indicator, **nroff** generally uses character positions.

Breaking Lines and Pages

You can use **nroff** commands to cause a line break or a page break. The **.br** command specifies a line break. You can insert it wherever you want a new line to start. For example, suppose you want to show an example on a separate line. You could use the command like this:

```
If you use the command
.br
nroff chapter.1 >> save.all
.br
the formatted output is appended to the current contents of
```

Note that the command line will be on a separate line from the text before it and after it.

If you use **nroff** without a macro set, the pages will not be broken; if you examine your printout from when you used **nroff** without a macro set, you'll see that it prints across the perforation. All macro sets automatically handle paging, but you may want to format without using a macro set or to force a page break at an earlier point. Wherever **nroff** encounters the **.bp** command, it begins a new page immediately. If you put in begin page commands throughout your file, it may format beautifully at first. But if you later add several lines to the first page, all the page breaks would have to be moved. In most cases, you'll want to let the macro set do the paging. You can force a blank page by using two **.bp** commands in a row—on separate lines, of course.

Centering

You can tell **nroff** to center lines with a simple command. If you place the command **.ce** before a line, the next line is centered. If you use **.ce 3**, it causes a line break and the next three lines are centered. You can specify as many lines as necessary. They are centered within the current line length; the page width is not considered. If you have a file with a title and author as the first two lines, the beginning of the file in **vi** might appear as follows:

```
.ls2
.sp2
.ce2
Evidence of Emerging Eccentricities
.br
Carson Davison
.sp3
As a result of extensive excavation into the ever-increasing
body of knowledge concerning the elevation of the imminent
```

The **nroff** commands request double spacing, skipping two lines before the title, centering the title and the author lines (the **.br** command keeps them from being combined on one line), and then skipping three more lines before beginning the text.

Filling and Justifying Text

You may be satisfied with the default status of filling and justifying of text. But more likely you will want to change it occasionally. For example, you may want letters to be unjustified so they look more personal, but reports to be justified to look more professional. You may want filling most of the time, but where you have a list, you'd rather not type **.br** before each item to occur on a new line. **nroff** provides commands you can use to turn filling and justifying off and on.

Filling is the more basic of the two processes, because justification is not possible if the lines aren't filled. You turn fill on with **.fi** and off with **.nf**. You turn justification on with **.ad** and off with **.na**. If you use the same process in the entire file, put the appropriate command at the beginning. You won't need to turn fill on, of course, because that's always the default, but you may want to use the nondefault status of justification. If you want a portion of the file to be different from the rest, remember to reset the format with the appropriate command at the end of the text that is to be formatted differently.

When you examine output, you may find that you don't like the way some justified lines look; they may have too much space between words, for example. There isn't a great deal you can do about this. You may be able to turn hyphenation on with **.hy**, but not all Unix systems support hyphenation. You may be able to modify the contents of the annoying line in a way that produces better spacing. If you find you don't care for the quality of justification your system produces, check to see if any other printers are available to you. If not, turn justification off and see if you like the output any better.

Unix System Exercise 9.2

Purpose: Use basic **nroff** commands in your files. *As you do this exercise, be cautious. Make sure you are in insert mode before typing* **nroff** *commands; use* **O** *or* **o** *to insert a line before or after the current line and put the cursor at the beginning of that line. Press* **Escape** *as soon as you complete each bit of input. The period repeats the last command in command mode, so if you aren't in insert mode when you type a period to start an embedded command, it may just repeat the last command. As before, don't worry too much about the contents of your files at this point.*

1. Bring up **sample.let**. Insert commands to set the line length to 5 inches, turn off fill, center the return address information, and then skip six lines before printing the next part.
2. Insert a command to turn fill back on following the greeting (e.g., "Dear John") and then skip four lines following the salutation (e.g., "Sincerely yours") to allow room for a signature. Save the file.
3. Format the file with **nroff sample.let > sample.1**, and then bring up the output in **vi** and examine it. Notice the effect of each command you entered. Print it if you want.
4. Bring up **format.doc**. Insert commands to double-space the output, change the line length to 5.5 inches, start the first line four lines down, center the title, and skip four more lines between the title and the text.
5. Set the third paragraph for no filling; be sure to turn filling back on at the end of it.
6. Set the fourth paragraph for no justification; be sure to turn it back on at the end of the paragraph.
7. Figure out (use **Ctrl-G**) where the 60th line is, and insert a page break command at the end of a paragraph before that point. Then save the file.
8. Format it with **nroff format.doc > format.1**. Examine the output in **vi** or with **more format.1**. Notice the effect of each command you entered.
9. Now that you've formatted the file, edit it again and insert page break commands so the document is paged correctly. Save the file again. Use **nroff** once more to see the effect.

continued on following page. . .

Exercise 9.2 continued. . .

If it doesn't work:

A. Check the commands. Be sure each command starts with a period at the left edge of the screen and is on a line by itself. Be sure you have a space before any number in the command. **sample.1** should start out with a series of commands such as the following:

```
.ll 5i
.nf
.ce 4
the lines of centered information
.sp 6
more stuff
.fi
the body of the letter
.sp 2
Sincerely Yours,
.sp 4
```

Make any changes you want. Make a copy of the file and practice with it if you want to see more effects.

B. Check the effect of each command. The beginning of **format.1** should include these commands:

```
.ls 2
.ll 5.5i
.sp 4
.ce
title line
.sp 4
text starts here
```

The third paragraph should start with **.nf** and end with **.fi**. The fourth paragraph should start with **.na** and end with **.ad**. A page break should occur at the **.bp** command.

The Left Margin

The **.po** command sets the page offset from the left edge, specifying where text shall begin in each line of the output. In other words, it sets the effective left margin. If you use the command **.po 12**, the page offset is set at 12 character positions from the leftmost position of your printer's print head. You can specify the page offset in inches with a command such as **.po 1.5i**. The line length for the file begins at the page offset position and extends to the right. The **.po** command doesn't always work reliably in combination with a macro set, but the macro sets include other ways of setting the left margin.

Indentation

Suppose you want to indent a single line. For example, you may want to indent the first line in each paragraph by five spaces. **nroff** has the **.ti** command to set up a temporary indentation. To cause a paragraph to be indented five spaces, you could use **.ti 5** on the line before the paragraph. The **.ti** command interrupts line fill, starts a new line, indents it as specified, and begins line fill again. It doesn't insert a blank line; if you place the **.ti 5** command on a separate line before each paragraph, the first line of each paragraph will be indented, but no blank lines will appear. Following is an example of how the first part of **Gettysburg** might appear in **vi** with commands inserted:

```
.ll 5i
.po 12
.ce
The Gettysburg Address
.sp 4
.ls 2
.ti 5
Four score and seven years ago,
our fathers brought forth on this continent a new nation,
conceived in liberty and dedicated to the proposition
that all men are created equal.
.ti 5
Now we are engaged in a great civil war.
We are met on a great battlefield of that war,
testing whether that nation or any nation so conceived and
so dedicated can long endure.
```

Once you **nroff** the file, it should resemble the following:

```
                    The Gettysburg Address


     Four score and seven years ago, our fathers brought forth on this

continent a new nation, conceived in liberty and dedicated to the

proposition that all men are created equal.

     Now we are engaged in a great civil war.  We are met on a great

battlefield of that war, testing whether  that nation or any nation so

conceived and so dedicated can long endure.
```

You can specify any amount of single line indentation with **.ti**. You can use relative increments such as **.ti +.5i** and **.ti -.5i** to move in and out a specified amount of space (in this case, .5 of an inch) relative to the current indent location.

If you want to indent an entire block of text, use the **.in** command with the amount of indentation desired. You can use an absolute indentation amount such as one inch (**.in 1i**) or 2.5 inches (**.ti 2.5i**) to indent from the left edge or page offset position, whichever is in effect. You can also specify a relative amount of indentation with a plus or minus sign; this amount is added (or subtracted) from the current indent location. When you change the indentation, the line length doesn't change—the right margin is maintained in the same position.

All lines following the **.in** command are indented until **nroff** encounters another **.in** command. For example, suppose you want to indent a complete paragraph one inch from the current left margin. You could precede the paragraph with **.in +1i**. After the paragraph, you would end the indentation with **.in -1i**. If you want to cause other effects on the block, you can use multiple commands. Suppose a document is double-spaced and justified, and you want to format a specific paragraph within it to be single spaced, not justified, indented .5 of an inch from each margin, and with the first line indented an additional .5 of an inch. The commands in the file would appear as follows:

```
.ls 1
.na
.in +0.5i
.ll -0.5i
.ti .5i
```
(*text of special paragraph*)
```
.ls 2
.ad
.in -0.5i
.ll +0.5i
```
(*resume document*)

You can even create a hanging indentation by using the **.in** and **.ti** commands. For example, suppose you use **.in 10** near the beginning of the file. Then you use **.ti 5** to start each paragraph. Most text lines will begin ten spaces in from the left margin, but the line following each **.ti** command will begin five spaces in. If you really want the paragraphs indented an extra five spaces, use **.ti +5** instead.

As you can see, it can take many commands to set up what you want. You can define macros to issue a series of separate commands. The macro sets also greatly simplify your formatting because they include predefined macros that allow you to issue an entire sequence of formatting commands by entering only a few keystrokes.

Defining Macros

If you expect to use the same sequence of **nroff** commands several times in a file, you can simplify your work by defining macros of your own. You do this by assigning a name to a series of commands. Then just use the name you have defined as a command to apply the entire series. To define a macro, you start with the **.de** command to specify a name, followed by the commands to be included in the macro; then you terminate the list with **..** (two periods). Following is an example of how you might define the two sets of commands used earlier as macros and use them in the file:

```
.de SQ
.ls 1
.na
.in +0.5i
.ll -0.5i
.ti .5i
..
.de EQ
.ls 2
.ad
.in -0.5i
.ll +0.5i
..
.SQ
(text of special paragraph)
.EQ
(resume document)
```

The first macro defined is named **SQ** (for **Start Quote**); it includes five commands. The next macro, **EQ** (for **End Quote**), includes four commands. Each paragraph to be treated as a single spaced, indented quote in the text is preceded by the macro **.SQ** and followed by **.EQ**. Note that the period doesn't precede the macro name being defined in the **.de** command; you use the period only when the command or macro is actually being invoked.

You can define as many macros as you need. Be sure to use a unique name for each. If you aren't using a supplied macro set, any uppercase letters create unique names. If you are using a macro set, check to see what names are already defined and use a different one. If you create your own set of macros to use in many documents, you can define them in a separate file, then read that file in with an **:r** command in **vi**. They will be available whenever you need to use them.

BASIC nroff COMMAND SUMMARY

There are many more basic **nroff** commands, but many are difficult to use or accomplish only a very small change. Figure 9.6 shows the commands covered here, with additional examples. You can refer to Figure 9.6 whenever necessary.

Command	Effect	Examples	Explanation
.ls *n*	Set spacing *n* = 1, 2, or 3	`.ls 1` `.ls 2`	set single spacing set double spacing
.sp *n*	Insert blank lines *n* = any integer	`.sp 2` `.sp 8`	insert 2 line spaces insert 8 line spaces

.po *nx*	Print offset from left edge
	n = measure
	x = units
		`.po 12n`
		`.po 1i`
		`.po 1.5i`
			offset 12 characters
			offset 1 inch
			offset 1.5 inches

.in [*s*]*nx*	Indent following lines
	s = + or –
	n = amount
	x = units
		`.in 5`
		`.in +.5i`
		`.in -1.5i`
		`.in 6n`
			indent 5 spaces
			indent .5 inches
			outdent 1.5 inches
			indent 6 spaces

.ce [*n*]	center following lines	`.ce` `.ce 4`	center next line center next 4 lines

.ll [*s*]*nx*	line length
	s = + or –
	n = amount
	x = units
		`.ll 6i`
		`.ll 60`
		`.ll4.5i`
		`.ll -.5i`
			line length 6 inches
			line length 60 characters
			line length 4.5 inches
			line length .5 inches shorter

.br	break line	`.br`	stop fill, start new line
.bp	begin page	`.bp`	end page, start new page
.fi	begin fill	`.fi`	turn on line fill
.nf	stop fill	`.nf`	turn off line fill
.ad	begin justify	`.ad`	turn on justification
.na	stop justify	`.na`	turn off justification
.de *name*	start macro definition	`.de QQ`	Begin definition of macro QQ
..	end macro definition	`..`	End definition of current macro

Figure 9.6 Basic **nroff** *commands*

For more complex operations, you'll want to use macros from one of the standard macro sets. In the rest of this chapter, you'll learn some useful macros from the **ms** and **mm** sets.

Unix System Exercise 9.3

Purpose: Practice using the page offset and indentation commands.

1. Bring up **sample.let**. Change the formatting so that the entire letter begins 1.5 inches or 12 spaces further in. Then change it so that the return address and date are indented 3.5 inches from the left margin instead of being centered.
2. Indent the closing and signature lines 2.5 inches in from the left margin.
3. Save the modified file. Format or print it and examine the result. Note the effect of each command.
4. Bring up **format.doc**. Set the left margin 1 inch in from the page edge.
5. Define macros to start (**AS**) and end (**AE**) a special paragraph. It is to have both margins indented 1 inch, have the first line indented an extra half inch, and be single spaced. Use the macro instead of the current formatting for the third and fourth paragraphs.
6. Indent every remaining paragraph .5 of an inch, without any extra spaces between paragraphs. (Remember, in command mode, the period repeats the previous command.)
7. Save the file and format it. Examine the formatted output on paper or on screen. Note the effect of each command.
8. In preparation for Exercise 9.5, remove the definitions and references to macros **.AS** and **.AE**. Then make a copy of **format.doc** named **format.ms** or **format.mm** to use with the appropriate macro set.

continued on following page. . .

Exercise 9.3 continued. . .

If it doesn't work:

A. If you tried **.po** and don't get a wider left margin, try using **.in** to set up a major indentation. If you can't make it work consistently, you'll have to use one of the macro sets for margin setting.

B. Check the examples in the preceding section if you have trouble defining a macro. You may have accidentally used a name that already exists if you get strange effects. If the defined macro doesn't work, try entering all the commands into the file and see if the effects work without the macro definition.

USING MACRO SETS

When you use a macro set, you specify it in the **nroff** command. In order for **nroff** to use the specialized macros for the set, however, you need to use an initializing macro before any text appears in the file. The initializing macro can be any of several, but the standard paragraph command, which requests a paragraph with a standard indentation, is generally used. For **ms**, start the file with **.PP**; for **mm**, start the file with **.P 1**. Then continue with the commands and text you need.

You can use the basic **nroff** commands interspersed with ones from the macro set you are using. But you can't use macros from two different macro sets in the same file. By this time, you should have decided which macro set you will be using.

COMPLEX FORMATTING

Several effects you may want to accomplish in text formatting are much better done through the predefined macro sets. For example, specifying a paragraph indentation is required before each paragraph; each macro set has special commands for requesting different types of paragraphs. Automatic paging is one of the major effects of all macro sets. You may want a certain group of lines or text to be kept together rather than split across a page break. Or you may want a group of lines to be printed just as they display on screen. You might want headers or footers for each page. Another useful effect is footnotes. In this section, you'll learn to accomplish all these effects for both **ms** and **mm** macro sets.

Both of these macro sets have many additional commands that perform more functions. Once you can use the ones covered in this book, you may want to check the documentation you have to see what else you can accomplish.

Setting the Left Margin

If you use the **ms** macro set, you can use the **.RS** macro to indent five spaces from the left margin. Every time you use **.RS**, the indentation moves in another five spaces. You can use **.RE** to move the indentation back five spaces. These indentations work in conjunction with any **.in** and **.ti** commands you have in the file. Be sure to use plus and minus signs with indentation commands so that any changes within the file are relative to the current left margin.

If you use the **mm** macro set, you can set the left margin (page offset) in the command line when you format and print the file. Add the option **-rO***n* following the macro set indication, replacing *n* with the number of spaces to be indented. For example, to set a left margin of 12 spaces, you would use the command **nroff -mm -rO12 Gettysburg | lpr**.

Headers and Footers

The macro sets put default header and footer information on pages, as you saw in your early printouts. When you run **nroff** with **ms**, you get the page number as the top center header, except on the first page, and the current date as the bottom center footer. When you run it with **mm** you get a centered page number as a header on each page and no footer. But you can specify whatever headers and footers you want. If you do, the header takes effect on the next page; if you want the header on the first page, it must be established before any text appears in the file. A footer takes effect on the page on which the command occurs.

nroff treats the header and footer as having three sections: left, center, and right. A header or footer can contain any or all of the parts. The left section is left aligned, the center section is centered on the page, and the right section is right aligned. The two macro sets give you different ways to specify the headers and footers.

Headers and Footers with the ms Macro Set

With the **ms** macro set, you can turn off the default value or specify different contents of each section in a "title variable" in the **.ds** command in which you define the string. Figure 9.7 lists the variable names.

Variable	Description
LH	left header
CH	center header
RH	right header
LF	left footer
CF	center footer
RF	right footer

Figure 9.7 **ms** *header and footer variables*

If you want to have your name in the upper left corner and the word *confidential* in the lower right, with no values in the right or center sections, you could use these commands:

```
.ds LH Ruth Ashley
.ds CH
.ds RH
.ds LF confidential
.ds CF
.ds RF
```

If you want to include the current page number, use the symbol *%*. The default **ms** page number was defined as **.ds CH -** *%* **-** to cause the page number to appear between two hyphens. If you want it to appear in the lower right preceded by the word *page*, you could use this command:

```
.ds RF page %
```

When you use a page number symbol, the current page number prints in that location in the header or footer.

Headers and Footers with the mm Macro Set

In the **mm** macro set, you specify all three sections (i.e., left, center, and right), or at least the ones you want to use, in the same command. Each part of the header or footer is enclosed in single quotes, and the entire string is enclosed in double quotes. Here is how the header and footer strings might look:

```
"'left'center'right'"
"'''confidential'"
"'Ruth Ashley'x'July 8, 1990'"
```

The first example shows the format of the string, which is the same for a header or a footer. The second example shows no values (null) for the left and center sections, with the word *confidential* appearing on the right.

You can use any of the following six commands to specify header and footer strings:

Command	Description
.PH *string*	Header on every page
.PF *string*	Footer on every page
.EH *string*	Header on even pages
.EF *string*	Footer on even pages
.OH *string*	Header on odd pages
.OF *string*	Footer on odd pages

You can specify both odd and even headers or footers for the same file. You can specify additional header and footer commands to change the string in the course of the document. A header command takes effect on the next formatted page. A footer command takes effect on the current page.

You can include a page number specification in any section of the header or footer string. **mm** looks for the page number in a register named **nP**. For various internal reasons, you must include four backslashes to quote the page number register name four times when you use it. For example, the default header command could be replicated as follows:

```
.PH "''- \\\\nP -''"
```

This uses null left and right sections with the page number surrounded by hyphens in the center of the page. You could put the page number preceded by *Page* at the lower right corner of the page with this command:

```
.PF "'''Page \\\\nP'"
```

Keeping Text Together

When text is divided into pages, **nroff** generally just pages at the appropriate line with no regard for the content. You may want a certain block of text kept together; if it won't all fit on the current page you want it all put on the next. This block of text is often referred to as a **keep**. You can specify keeps with macros; they are defined and handled exactly the same in both **ms** and **mm** macro sets.

To mark a block to stay together on a page, use the **.KS** command to start the keep and **.KE** to end it; if you don't end the block, the output won't be at all what you expect.

Suppose you mark off a quoted paragraph with **.KS** and **.KE**. If there isn't room on the current page, **nroff** starts the next page and places it at the top and then continues with the file. There may be a lot of white space left on the page that was ended early. If the keep must be printed in sequence, you can't prevent that. But suppose you have a table or list in the text that you want kept together, but it doesn't have to be in the same exact location in relation to the rest of the text. You can define it as a block to be kept together, but let it float to the top of the next page; in this case (called a floating keep), other text will be moved up and printed so no inordinate amount of white space results. You mark the start of the floating keep with **.KF**; like a standard keep, it ends with **.KE**. The only difference is in the use **nroff** makes of the bottom of the page.

One problem occurs with **ms** in some versions of Unix. If the file is being double spaced, a keep may appear in single space. If this happens to you, just include a **.ls 2** command immediately following the first **.KS** command; then all keeps will be double spaced just as the text is.

Preventing Formatting

Sometimes you have a block of text you want to appear exactly as you have it set up in **vi**. Such text should be copied to the formatted output file on a line-by-line basis. This block is often referred to as a **display**; as with a keep, you must mark the beginning and the end of a display. The commands that mark displays and the effects are also the same with the **ms** and **mm** macro sets.

A standard display is copied to the output with each line indented a standard amount, usually five spaces. If you want it kept all on one page, use the **.DS** command to start it; if the display is not a keep as well, use **.ID** to start it. All types of display blocks are ended with **.DE**.

You can also specify a flush left display, one that is not indented. Use **.DS L** to specify a flush left display that is also a keep, or **.LD** to start one that can be split. If you want the display lines centered, you can use **.DS C** if it is to be kept together, or **.CD** if it can be split.

Keep and Display Summary

Figure 9.8 shows the basic commands that establish and end keeps and displays in both macro sets. You can use them any time you need them in a file.

Remember that you must specify the macro set when you execute **nroff** if the commands are to have any effect.

Your system undoubtedly has additional options for defining and handling keeps and displays. After you have learned to handle these basic functions, you may want to check your documentation to see what else is available.

Keep Commands

Command	Description
.KS	Start standard keep.
.KF	Start floating keep.
.KE	End current keep.

Display Commands

Command	Description
.DS	Start standard display and keep.
.DS L	Start flush left display and keep.
.DS C	Start centered display and keep.
.ID	Start indented display, not keep.
.LD	Start flush left display, not keep.
.CD	Start centered display, not keep.
.DE	End current display.

Figure 9.8 Keep and display commands

Footnotes

Many people need to include footnotes in reports or documentation. Footnotes are a real pain to handle on a typewriter, but **nroff** makes them almost a snap. You'll use the same basic commands in both macro sets, but the effects differ somewhat between the two sets. A **footnote** is some reference to a block of text at the bottom (or foot) of the page. You can mark the reference with a symbol such as an asterisk (*) or let **nroff** use sequential numbering. You mark the start of a footnote with **.FS** and the end with **.FE**. Figure 9.9 (see following page) shows how the commands look in the unformatted file and the result when the file is formatted with **ms**.

Original File:

```
In the process, it was noted that
every time the eccentric enchanter attempted to levitate,*
.FS
*As noted in the annals of yore
.FE
he became enraged at the minimal effect on gravity.
```

Formatted Output:

```
In the process, it was noted that every time the
eccentric enchanter attempted to levitate,* he
became enraged at the minimal effect on gravity.
 .
 .
 .
 -------------------------
*As noted in the annals of yore
```

Figure 9.9 Symbol footnote with **ms**

Notice that the footnote commands do not cause a line break. When the document is formatted the line is continuous with the symbol (*) in position. The symbol is typed in the text at the point where the footnote is referenced, as well as at the beginning of the footnote itself. **nroff** puts in the dashed line and figures out how much space to leave for any footnotes required on a page.

The same effect is handled just a bit differently with the **mm** macro set. Figure 9.10 shows the original file appearance and the formatted result.

Original File:

```
In the process, it was noted that
every time the eccentric enchanter attempted to levitate,*
.FS *
As noted in the annals of yore
.FE
he became enraged at the minimal effect on gravity.
```

Formatted Output:

```
In the process, it was noted that every time the
eccentric enchanter attempted to levitate,* he
became enraged at the minimal effect on gravity.
  .
  .
  .
  -------------------------
*As noted in the annals of yore
```

Figure 9.10 Symbol footnote with **mm**

Just as in the **ms** macro set, the footnote commands don't cause a line break. But with the **mm** macro set you can specify the symbol only once, in the **.FS** command itself. The symbol is automatically placed at the reference point and before the footnote.

If you want sequenced footnotes with the **ms** macro set, you'll need to insert the numbers yourself just as you do with the symbols; **ms** doesn't check or maintain them for you. The **mm** macro set, on the other hand, can number the footnotes for you automatically. Immediately following the text where the footnote is to be referenced, type ***F**, then press **Return** and type the **.FS** command without any arguments. Follow it with the footnote text and the **.FE** command as usual. When the document is formatted and printed, the footnotes will be numbered in sequence. If you examine the formatted document on screen, the footnote references will look strange, as will the formatting, but the document will print just fine. If your printer isn't capable of superscripting, the numbers will be printed in line with the rest of the text. If you expect to use many footnotes, automatic numbering is a good reason to use **mm** as your primary macro set.

Specifying Types of Paragraphs

To **nroff**, a paragraph is a set of lines or block of text with one or more blank lines above it and below it. Each macro set has a group of commands to specify types of paragraphs. While they differ a bit, the paragraph commands have the same intent, to let you use a single command to specify multiple effects. **nroff** has standard values stored in registers for a paragraph indentation and block quote paragraphs. You may be able to change these values, but you should be sure to check the defaults first. The standard unit of measure is the character; use **i** following the number to specify inches.

You can easily specify two types of paragraphs with **mm** macros and four types with **ms** macros. These make good initializing macros. When used, these macros cause a line break but don't insert a blank line. You use different commands to specify the different types of paragraphs.

mm	ms	Type of paragraph
.P 1	.PP	Standard paragraph
.P	.Lh	Left block paragraph
	.IP	Indented paragraph
	.QP	Block quote paragraph

Both macro sets support the **standard paragraph**, which starts with an indented line and has all the other lines filled. Both also support a **left block** or **justified** paragraph with all lines filled; the first line is not indented. An **indented** paragraph has all its lines indented; if you want this feature with **mm**, you must use the basic **nroff .in** commands. The **block quote** paragraph has all lines indented on both sides; if you want this with **mm**, you can generate the effect with several basic **nroff** commands. You'll probably want to create a macro of your own to handle it if you use block quote paragraphs often with **mm**.

The **ms** macro set lets an indented paragraph take one of three forms. If you use **.IP** without any arguments, it generates a standard indented paragraph; all lines are indented the standard amount from the left margin. You can create a hanging indent if you specify an argument in the command; the argument appears at the left margin and the indent takes effect as usual. For example, suppose your text has these lines:

```
.IP 2.
The hanging indent is especially useful in
preparing documentation for users, since it
produces a useful display for reading and
locating information.
.sp 1
.IP (a)
The levels can be specified in any way you want.
.sp 1
.LP
No technical writer can completely avoid hanging indents,
since they are so ...
```

When it is formatted with **nroff** and the **-ms** macro set, you get this result:

```
2.   The hanging indent is especially useful in preparing
     documentation for users, since it produces a useful
     display for reading and locating information.

(a)  The levels can be specified in any way you want.

No technical writer can completely avoid hanging indents,
since they are so ....
```

You can specify a hanging indent with a nonstandard amount of indentation by including the amount (in character spaces) in the command. For example, if you use **.IP Explanation: 14**, the specified word starts at the left margin and the other lines are indented to column 14. If the text you include with **.IP** includes any spaces, enclose it in double quotes. For example, you would use **.IP "Line 6:" 10** to cause the specified string to start at the left margin and have a nonstandard indentation of 10 columns.

Many versions of Unix let you specify inches instead of spaces for the indent; try **1.5i** in the command to see if it works in your system.

Additional Macros

Both **ms** and **mm** offer many additional macros. You can change the built-in defaults, for example. After you are comfortable with the basic formatting commands covered in this section, you might want to examine the documentation available at your installation to learn what else you can do to help format your documents.

Unix System Exercise 9.4

Purpose: Practice using commands for a particular macro set.

1. Bring up **format.ms** or **format.mm**. Insert an appropriate initializing macro at the beginning. Remove all **.in** and **.ti** commands from the file. You might want to **nroff** the file at this point and see how it looks.

2. Set a header that has your name on the left and the page number on the right. Set a footer consisting of the centered phrase "rough draft." Format it and see how it looks; if the defaults still appear, set them to null. Be sure to get the header and footer working before you continue.
3. Set the left margin about one inch further in from the left edge of the page. **nroff** it to see the result.
4. Set the first three paragraphs to be standard paragraphs, with a first-line indent. Set the next paragraph to have all lines indented from the left but not from the right. Set the next to be indented from both sides. The rest of the paragraphs can be whatever type you want. **nroff** the file and examine the result.
5. Check your formatted file and locate a paragraph that is split across two pages. Define that paragraph as a keep, and **nroff** the file again. Examine the output.
6. If you expect to ever use footnotes, put two of them on the first page of your file. Be sure to mark the end of the text. Use **nroff** to see the result.

If it doesn't work:

A. Be sure you are using the commands for the correct macro set and specifying **-ms** or **-mm** in the **nroff** command line.

B. Remember to remove default values for the header and footer.

C. Each paragraph needs a blank line or paragraph command preceding it.

SUMMARY

This chapter has covered the basic commands you can use to format files you produce in **vi** with **nroff**. You have learned to do the following:

- Control line filling and justification with **.nf**, **fi**, **.na**, and **.ad** commands.
- Cause line breaks with spaces or **.br** commands.
- Control line spacing and line length with **.ls**, **.sp**, and **.ll** commands.
- Force a new page with a **.bp** command.
- Center lines with the **.ce** command.
- Set the left margin with the **.po** command, the **.RS** and **.RE** macros or the **-rO** option on the **nroff** command line.
- Control indentation with the **.ti** and **.in** commands.
- Define and use new macros with the **.de** macro.
- Define headers and footers for the **ms** and **mm** macro sets.
- Define keeps and displays for the **ms** and **mm** macro sets.
- Define footnotes for the **ms** and **mm** macro sets.
- Use appropriate paragraph commands for the **ms** and **mm** macro sets.

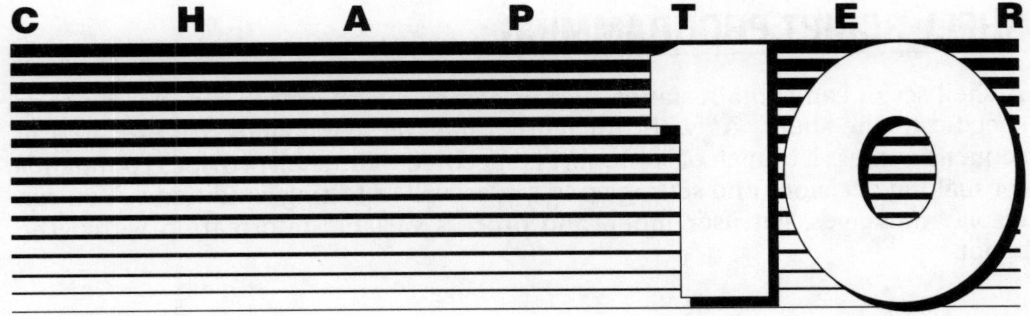

PROGRAMMING THE BOURNE SHELL

Many features of Unix shell programming are common to all shells. You should read this chapter even if you generally use a different shell for your Unix sessions. You'll be able to create and execute files containing Bourne shell commands from any Unix shell.

The Bourne shell doesn't just interpret your commands to Unix and provide an interface between you and the operating system. It also includes a complete programming language that you can use to create new commands and perform new operations from the monitor. This chapter won't cover all there is to know about programming the Bourne shell, but you will learn enough to create and use practical shell command files called **scripts**, using some of the shell features. You'll be able to find more information in your system's documentation.

In the first part of this chapter you'll learn to create simple Bourne shell scripts, make them executable, and run them from your terminal. You'll see how to use some variables and create a simple decision structure, or loop, within the script. In the rest of the chapter, you'll learn some of the underlying principles and concepts you'll need for more advanced shell programming and learn some more control structures you can use in creating your own shell scripts.

SHELL SCRIPT PROGRAMMING

A shell script can contain standard Unix commands as well as other commands specific to the shell. As with other programs, the commands are executed in sequence unless a branch of some sort is specified. The shell provides commands for making decisions and setting up loops, as well as testing conditions. You can display messages, get user input, and process variable information within the script.

Creating a Shell Script

Suppose you frequently use the command line **grep -vn C.*t suppliers.*** to produce a list of the lines in any of the specified files that don't contain the given pattern. Because this command is fairly complex to type, it would be convenient to have a shortcut. You can create a shell script, using **vi**, that contains this single line. Then you can execute it by typing just the file name.

You can use **vi** or any other ASCII editor to create shell script files. You can include comments in any script file. A comment begins with the symbol #, and the shell ignores anything following this symbol on the line. A Bourne shell script cannot begin with a comment, however, because if the shell sees the # symbol as the first nonblank character in a script file, it assumes you have a C shell script and processes it accordingly. If you use comments in your script files, remember not to use one on the first line of a Bourne shell script.

Storing Script Files

While shell scripts can be stored in any of your directories, it is most convenient to have them all together in one location. The Unix system uses the **bin** or **/usr/bin** directory for its program files. If you expect to have more than one or two shell scripts and programs, you should create a directory named **bin** in your own directory structure. Your default search path most likely already includes this directory, even if you haven't created it yet.

The search path tells Unix where to look when you enter a command. It always includes the standard **bin** and **/usr/bin** directories if you have access to all the standard commands. You can check your search path by examining your startup **.profile** file on your home directory. You will see a command that starts with **PATH=**; the rest of the command specifies directories to be searched in sequence.

A colon (:) separates the directory names. If your own **bin** directory isn't included, you can add it to this command through **vi**.

Executing a Shell Script

So far, the script file containing the Unix **grep** command is just an ordinary file. Before you can use it as a program, you must make it executable. Once a file or program is executable, you can enter its file name as a command and Unix executes the file. Normally, you don't have execute access to files. When you start creating script files, however, you will want to be able to run them. You can give yourself execute access with the **chmod** command. Assume the file is named **getlines**; here is how you can make it executable (the commands you type appear in bold to help you distinguish them from the screen responses):

```
$ ls -l getlines
-rw-rw-r--  1  carson                    159  Jun 23  09:43  getlines
$ chmod u+x getlines
$ ls -l getlines
-rwxrw-r--  1  carson                    159  Jun 23  09:43  getlines
$ _
```

Once the file is executable, you can enter its name as a command, just as with standard Unix commands such as **ls**, **sort** or **grep**. Here's how the output from this command looks when you execute it:

```
$ getlines
suppliers.89:1:AT&T
suppliers.89:2:Blue Cross Insurance
suppliers.89:3:Bullinger's
suppliers.90:1:American Express
suppliers.90:2:AT&T
suppliers.90:3:Bell Implements
suppliers.90:4:Blue Cross Insurance
suppliers.90:5:California Dreamin'
$ _
```

Another Example

Suppose that whenever you want a directory listing, you want a full listing, including the hidden files, paged to the screen with **more**, and you want a message at the end telling you to go ahead with the next command. You can use **vi** to create a file named **lsl** containing the following lines:

```
ls -la | more
echo 'Enter your next command'
```

You make this file executable with the command **chmod u+x lsl**. Now whenever you want to get a listing in your preferred format, just enter **lsl**; it works just like the standard commands. If you have placed the file in a directory in your search path, you can use the command from anywhere in the system.

DISPLAYING MESSAGES

Shell scripts can display messages on the screen through the **echo** command, as you saw above. You can use **echo** to display text or values read in from the keyboard or the command line. The **echo** command in a shell script has the same effect as at the keyboard; it displays the text and any variables included in the command and then moves to the next line. If the **echo** command is at the end of the script, the standard prompt is displayed next. You can include the **-n** option to cancel the line feed and cause the next command output or prompt to appear on the same line. Figure 10.1 shows a shell script that displays an extensive message, along with the output from the script.

Notice that output from **echo** commands that include the **-n** option are followed by the next command output or prompt on the same line. You can use this option as needed to format the screen output of any Bourne shell scripts you write.

CHANGING SHELLS

If you generally work in the C shell, you might want to temporarily change to the Bourne shell to see how these features work at the command prompt. Just type the command **sh** to change to the Bourne shell. To return to the C shell, use **csh**. You won't have to change to execute Bourne shell scripts, but to use the Bourne shell commands at the keyboard when you see the command prompt, you must be in the Bourne shell.

Shell script:

```
echo 'Which file do you want to choose?'
echo ' '
echo -n '1 - members.1985          '
echo    '4 - members.1988 '
echo -n '2 - members.1986          '
echo    '5 - members.1989 '
echo -n '3 - members.1987          '
echo    '6 - members.1990 '
echo ' '
echo -n '  Type the number and press Enter '
```

Resulting Display:

```
Which file do you want to choose?

1 - members.1985      4 - members.1988
2 - members.1986      5 - members.1989
3 - members.1987      6 - members.1990

Type the number and press Enter $ _
```

Figure 10.1 Specifying line feeds

If you can't change from the C shell to the Bourne shell at your terminal, you must create small Bourne shell scripts to try out the commands. If you want to change your default login shell to the Bourne shell, see your system administrator.

USER VARIABLES

You will frequently need to use variables in your scripts. For example, to get user input from the keyboard, you must assign a variable to hold that input; you can then use the variable in a later command. You can also include variable information in the command line. In this chapter, you will examine variables you can define within the Bourne shell. Variables are declared differently when you work in the C shell, as you'll see in Chapter 11.

You can establish user variables and assign values to them and then use the variables at the keyboard or in script files. If you set a variable at the keyboard, it maintains that value until you change it or end the session. If you set a value in a script file, it is local to that script; it isn't automatically passed on to other scripts or back to the shell.

Suppose you want to use the value **bb** instead of **blackboard** to refer to that word. You could use this series of commands:

Keyboard	**Script file tryscript**
`$ bb=blackboard`	`bb=blackboard`
`$ echo bb`	`echo bb`
`bb`	`echo $bb`
`$ echo $bb`	`$ tryscript`
`blackboard`	`bb`
`$ _`	`blackboard`
	`$_`

If you have a file named **blackboard**, you could display it with the command **cat $bb**. Similarly, you could assign a complex path or file name you use frequently to a keyboard variable and use it (preceded with $) during a session.

You declare the variable by specifying it on the left side of the equal sign, placing the value on the right side. You can't use spaces around the equal sign with the Bourne shell. Notice that when you use the dollar sign before the variable name in other commands, it acts as a variable and displays the value, rather than the string itself. Here's how you might do it in a shell script:

```
fname='Ruth Ashley'
echo 'Hello, ' $fname
echo 'Thanks for coming.'
```

When you use a value that includes spaces or a special character, you must enclose that value in single quotes, or apostrophes ('). If the value is to be the output of a command, include the command name in accent marks (`). For example, in the script command **input_list=`who`**, the output of the **who** command is assigned to the variable **input_list**. Another way to declare a variable is to name it in a **read** command, which you will learn to do shortly.

The Bourne shell also lets you assign *readonly* status to a variable, which means it can be read but not changed. By default, user variables can be read and changed at will. Four variables are given values at the keyboard in the following commands:

```
$ bb=blackbeauty
$ catalog='1989 Sears & Roebuck'
$ me=carson
$ you='monty python'
$ readonly catalog
$ echo $catalog
1989 Sears & Roebuck
$ readonly bb me
$ bb=beastofbaluchistan
bb: is read only
$ readonly
readonly bb
readonly catalog
readonly me
$ _
```

The value that includes spaces is enclosed in single quotes. Three variables are given the *readonly* attribute; note that you can specify one or more variables in the **readonly** command. If you try to assign a new value to a variable that has *readonly* status, it doesn't work; the message informs you that the variable can only be read—not modified. The **readonly** command by itself results in a list of all user variables that have *readonly* status. You get the same effects when you include the commands in a script file.

There is no easy way to remove the *readonly* attribute from a variable. When you end the session, any keyboard-created variables are dropped. When a script file ends, any variables established in it are forgotten.

Handling Numeric Values

All variables used in a Bourne shell script are string variables. If you must use one as a numeric variable, you can use the **expr** command to process it. The **expr** command won't be covered in detail in this book, because it is much easier to handle numeric values through the C shell, which has similar functions built in. If you find you need numeric variables in a Bourne shell script, check out the use of the **expr** command in your documentation.

Getting Keyboard Input

While you may occasionally want to set a user variable in a shell script, most variable information will come from the keyboard, either as part of the command line or in response to a message from the script. You can use the **read** command to get keyboard input and assign it to a user variable in one step, as in the following example:

```
echo -n 'Please type your full name:'
read fname
echo 'Hello, ' $fname
echo 'Thanks for coming.'
```

When this script is executed, you'll see this interaction on the screen (the keyboard entry appears in bold):

```
Please type your full name: Ruth Ashley
Hello, Ruth Ashley
Thanks for coming.
$ _
```

Notice that you don't need quotation marks here; whatever the user types at the keyboard before pressing **Return** is automatically assigned to the user variable supplied in the **read** command. The script can then display or process the variable as you see above. Following is another example:

```
echo 'Which file do you want to choose?'
echo ' '
echo -n '1 - members.1985          '
echo    '4 - members.1988 '
echo -n '2 - members.1986          '
echo    '5 - members.1989 '
echo -n '3 - members.1987          '
echo    '6 - members.1990 '
echo ' '
echo -n '  Type the number and press Enter '
read file_number
```

Notice that the **read** command has been added to the script shown earlier in Figure 10.1; after the messages are displayed on the screen, the user types a number and presses **Return**. The script can then use the value and continue processing; you'll see other versions of this script later in the chapter.

UNIX SYSTEM EXERCISE 10.1

Purpose: Write and execute simple shell scripts.

1. Use **vi** to create a file named **lsl**. It should display the long form of the current directory and pipe it to the screen with **more**. If you like, add a short message to the file.
2. Create a script file named **both** that asks the user to enter the first name; it should be entered on the next line. Assign that value to **fname**. Then ask for the last name entered on the same line as the message and assign it to **lname**. Display both values in the same line, then display "Good bye, now" and end the script.
3. Check the contents of **.profile** in your home directory to see if the **PATH** command includes **$HOME/bin**. If not, add this to the end of the **PATH** command; it won't take effect until you start your next Unix session.
4. Create a new directory named **bin** and move both scripts to it. Then make both scripts executable.

continued on following page. . .

Exercise 10.1 continued. . .

5. Run the scripts from the **bin** directory. If they don't work correctly, edit them until they do. Then try running them from other directories.

If it doesn't work:

A. The **lsl** file should contain this command: **ls -l | more**. A message with **echo** can precede or follow it.

B. The **both** file should contain commands like these:

```
echo 'Please type your first name.'
read fname
echo -n 'Now type your last name.  '
read lname
echo 'Thank you, ' $fname $lname
echo 'Good bye, now.'
```

C. Be sure to use **chmod u+x lsl** and **chmod u+x both** to make the scripts executable.

D. If your scripts won't run unless you are in the directory that contains them, your **PATH** command isn't working properly. Make sure you preceded your directory name with a colon (**:**) in the **PATH** command. Try logging off and back on again.

USING COMMAND-LINE VARIABLES

The Bourne shell provides variables for command-line arguments you can use to execute a shell script. Just as you can use various arguments with standard Unix commands, so can you set up a shell script so it requires or uses command line arguments. You can specify as many arguments as needed. The Bourne shell assigns the first nine arguments included in the command line to variables named *$1* through *$9*. If you use fewer than nine arguments (the usual case), the higher variable names are set to null and have no value. If you use more than nine arguments, you need a special command (**shift**) to access them.

You can use these variable names to refer to the arguments within the script. For example, you have already seen a script file named **lsl** that produces a long listing of the current directory, including hidden files, and pipes it to the screen with

more. Suppose now you want to be able to specify any directory name in the command. You could modify the **ls** command in **lsl** to look like the following:

```
ls -la $1 | more
```

When you use **lsl /usr/bin** as a command, the value */usr/bin* is substituted for the variable *$1* in the file and the long listing of the named directory is produced and piped to the **more** filter which displays it to the screen one page at a time. If you don't provide a value for *$1*, it is given a null value; in that case, you'll get the paged output from a listing of the current directory, just as if you didn't include the variable in the script file.

You can use as many variables as you need in a shell script file. The first one in the command line is assigned to *$1*, the second to *$2*, and so forth. Suppose you want to be able to copy a file into up to three different directories or file names in a single command. You want the first argument to specify the file to be copied and the rest to specify targets. In that case, the shell script **mcopy** might appear as follows:

```
cp $1 $2
cp $1 $3
cp $1 $4
```

If a **cp** command contains only one argument, the named file is copied into the current directory. The command is invalid if the only named file is in the current directory. Any error messages that appear on the screen won't invalidate the commands that are already completed. For example, using the previous **mcopy** shell script, the command **mcopy savedir copy1 copy2 copy3** copies the contents of **savedir** (*$1*) to all three target files (*$2*, *$3*, and *$4*, respectively). The command **mcopy savedir copy1 copy2** copies the contents of **savedir** (*$1*) to the two named target files (*$2* and *$3*, respectively) and produces an error message for the last target (*$4*). The command **mcopy savedir copy1** copies the contents of **savedir** (*$1*) to the named file (*$2*) and produces an error message for each of the others.

Processing Arguments

As you've seen, the shell assigns arguments to its numbered variables in sequence. It provides two additional variables you can use to process or display the arguments. The variable *$** represents all the command-line arguments. If you use a command such as **echo $***, all the command-line arguments are displayed on the screen. The variable *$#* contains the integer count of the command-line arguments. You could modify the **mcopy** file to look like this:

```
echo 'There are ' $# ' named files.'
echo $*
echo 'All except ' $1 ' are target files.'
cp $1 $2
cp $1 $3
cp $1 $4
```

This version of **mcopy** displays the number of arguments supplied and lists them and then specifies the source file name as the only one that isn't a target file.

Using More Arguments

Although you are limited to nine shell variable names in a script file, you can use the **shift** script command to make more variable names available if they are entered with the command line. When you use **shift**, the current value of *$1* becomes unavailable, the value of *$2* is assigned to *$1*, and so on until a value beyond *$9* is assigned to *$9*. Basically, the **shift** command shifts the values of all the variables to the next lower variable name. You won't need to use **shift** unless you write scripts that require more than nine variables. However, you can use it with fewer variables and it has the same effect. After **shift**, the former value of $1 is no longer available. Remember that any of these variables that isn't given a value from the command line is set to null. You'll see an example later in this chapter.

USING DECISION STRUCTURES

Making decisions in a script file is essential. You may want to check the number of variables and display different messages for different values. You might want to perform a completely different action depending on what the user enters at the keyboard. You might want to access a particular file the user has selected from a menu. The Bourne shell provides several variations on IF commands that you can use to make decisions in your scripts. All of them depend to a great extent on a **test** command that establishes a condition.

The test Command

In the Bourne shell, you have to use a **test** command to specify a condition to be tested; you won't need to use it in C shell scripts, where you can specify the expressions directly. Figure 10.2 (see following page) shows the **test** command format, including the types of expressions you can test. The expression criteria may determine if a variable exists, if two strings are identical, if one number or expression is larger than another, or if a file is available. In this section, you'll see how to use several different types of expressions.

The expression is the heart of the **test** command. You can test a string, an integer, or a file name. You can use parentheses around the **test** command if you want, but they aren't required. If you write complex or combination expressions, you may need parentheses within them. If you are a programmer, don't try to get any more complex here than you do in programs; if you don't program, you should limit yourself to very simple **test** commands.

If you test a string for any condition other than "not null," the string must exist or you'll get an error message and the script file processing will be aborted. The command **test $fname** is true if the user variable *$fname* has been specified on the right side of an equal sign or in a **read** command. If you use **test $fname = 'Ruth'** when the variable *$fname* doesn't exist, you'll get an error message and the script file processing is aborted. If a string exists, it is not null; you can also tell if the length is greater than zero (has some contents) or if it has a length of zero, which means it exists but has no value. You can use = or != to test whether two strings are equal or not. When you compare two strings, one can be a variable and one a constant if you wish; use a $ before a variable name and double quotes around a constant string.

You can compare two integer values with any of the six relational operators shown in Figure 10.2 (see following page). As with strings, one can be a variable and one a constant if you like, or you can specify two variables; you don't need quotes around an integer constant. If you use an exclamation point (!) before the operator, it is negated. Thus, the command **test $1 !-lt 0** is true if the current value of variable *$1* is not less than zero.

Command: **test**

Purpose: Test input or verify file access; specifies a condition that is true or false.

Format: **test** *expression*

Expression criteria:

String expressions

criteria	true if:
string	not null
-n *string*	length > 0
-z *string*	length = 0
string1 = *string2*	equal
string1 != *string2*	not equal

Integer expressions (*int1* relational operator *int2*)

criteria	true if:
-gt	*int1* is greater than *int2*
-ge	*int1* is greater than or equal to *int2*
-eq	*int1* is equal to *int2*
-ne	*int1* is not equal to *int2*
-le	*int1* is less than or equal to *int2*
-lt	*int1* is less than *int2*

file name expressions

criteria	true if:
-r *file-name*	exists and read access
-w *file-name*	exists and write access
-f *file-name*	exists and not directory
-d *file-name*	exists and is directory
-s *file-name*	exists and size > 0

Examples:

1. `( test $fname='Ruth' )`
2. `( test $1 -gt 500 )`
3. `test $# -ge 4`
4. `test -f-w $2`

Results: True or false, depending on variable values.

Figure 10.2 The **test** *command*

You can check a file name, either as a constant or a variable, to make sure it exists, to be sure you have the appropriate access, and to determine whether it is a directory or an ordinary file. If you have a script in which you edit a file named in the command line, for example, you might want to use a command such as **test -w -f $1** before entering the editor to make sure it is a file to which you have write access.

You can specify more than one condition in forming the expression; however, if you are new to programming, you will be wise to keep your conditions very simple. If you know what you are doing, you can use **-a** to AND separate conditions or **-o** to OR them.

Basic if Commands

IF commands are very similar in most programming languages. Figure 10.3 (see following page) shows the basic formats of the **if** command for the Bourne shell; The words that appear in bold are required whenever you use the IF structure. Parentheses around the **test** command are optional. Notice that the **if** command scope is terminated by the **fi** entry on a line by itself. The indentation from the left margin is optional; most programmers find that regular indentation helps them keep the structure of **if** commands in mind. Notice that the strings in the **test** command require double quotes while the message in the **echo** command is enclosed with single quotes; some versions of Unix will accept either quote style, but if you have trouble with these commands, change the quote style and see if it works better.

When the shell encounters any **if** command, it first evaluates the **test** command to determine if it is true or false. The **test** command must be valid; that is, a string must exist if you are testing for any condition other than null. If the condition is true, the commands that follow **then** are executed in sequence until either **else** or **fi** is encountered. Either terminates the **then** commands. If the condition is false, the commands that follow **then** are skipped, and Unix goes to the commands that follow the next **else** or **fi** that it encounters. If both **then** and **else** are included in the same **if** structure, they are not both executed—either the **then** or the **else** section is processed.

When you use the IF-THEN structure, you don't specify any special commands to be processed when the **test** command evaluates as false. No matter what the value of the condition, any commands following **fi** are processed. If the script requires false condition processing, you'll need to use the IF-THEN-ELSE structure. The first IF-THEN-ELSE example in Figure 10.3 compares the first command line variable to a constant. If they match, one message is sent to the terminal; if not, a different message is sent.

IF-THEN

Format: **if** *test-command*
then *commands*
fi

Example:

```
if (test $1 = "Ruth")
    then echo 'Ruth has signed on'
fi
```

IF-THEN-ELSE

Format: **if** *test-command*
then *commands*
else *commands*
fi

Example 1:

```
if (test $1 = "Ruth")
    then echo 'Ruth has signed on'
    else echo 'So where is Ruth?'
fi
```

Example 2:

```
echo -n 'Please type your full name: '
read fname
if (test -n $fname)
    then echo 'Welcome, ' fname
         echo 'Thanks for following instructions.'
    else echo 'You didn't enter any name.'
         echo 'Try again.'
fi
echo 'Script continues'
```

Figure 10.3 Formats for **if** *commands*

The second IF-THEN-ELSE example in Figure 10.3 is a more complete script than the first. Here the **echo** command displays a request for input, which the **read** command accepts and assigns to a variable. The **test** command makes sure the user entered at least one character before pressing **Return**. If so, the entry is used in the messages displayed next; if not, the user is asked to try again and follow instructions this time. Then the script continues.

If you want to use a structure in which there are commands to be executed when the condition is false but none when it is true, you can use the negation symbol (!) in the **test** command to reverse the condition and allow you to use a standard structure.

Using if Commands

You can use **if** commands wherever necessary in a script. For example, you could polish up the **mcopy** shell script shown earlier with **if** commands to modify processing based on the number of command-line variables. Here is how it might look:

```
if (test $4)
  then cp $1 $4
fi
if (test $3)
  then cp $1 $3
fi
if (test $2)
  then cp $1 $2
  else echo 'You omitted all target files.'
fi
```

In the previous **if** commands, a variable is null if it wasn't given a value in the command line. The test doesn't verify that the source file exists or that it can be copied. To do that, you could include a test of *$1* for existence and/or read access before testing for the presence of the target files.

Unix System Exercise 10.2

Purpose: Use command-line variables and decisions in script files.

1. Create an **mcopy** script that copies the first named file to one, two, or three named target files. Modify it to check for more than three targets and display a message showing which copies are not attempted.
2. Modify the **both** script to ask the age, and then show one message if it is over 65, a different one if it is under 21, and no special message if the age is between these points.
3. Create a new script that will let you display the contents of a file on the screen. If no file name is provided in the command line, ask the user to enter one at the keyboard and use that in the **cat** command instead.
4. Store all your script files in your **bin** directory and make them executable, then test them. Modify them until they work the way you want them to.

If it doesn't work:

A. Your **mcopy** script should be similar to the ones you've already seen in this chapter, with a command similar to this added:

```
if (test $# -gt 4)
   echo 'File ' $1 ' not copied to $5 $6 $7 etc.'
fi
```

B. In **both**, you need commands similar to these between the two current **echo** commands:

```
echo -n 'Type your age in years: '
read age
if (test $age -gt 65)
   then echo 'You are a senior citizen.'
fi
if (test $age -lt 21)
   then echo 'You are a minor.'
fi
```

continued on following page...

Exercise 10.2 continued. . .

C. Your new script should look something like this:

```
if (test $1)
   then cat $1
   else echo -n 'What file do you want displayed? '
        read keyfile
        cat $keyfile
fi
```

MORE COMPLEX DECISIONS

You have seen how to use basic decision structures in your script files. In this section, you'll see how you can use more complex decision constructions if necessary. In most cases, however, it is safer to keep the decisions in a script file as simple and clear as possible. Provide plenty of onscreen feedback for users so they know why it doesn't work if problems arise.

IF-THEN-ELSEIF

Nesting IFs can become very awkward. In fact, some Unix systems only allow you to nest IFs in one particular way. Figure 10.4 (see following page) shows the format and examples of this construction.

Format: **if** *test command*
  then *commands*
  elif *test command*
    then *commands*
  ...
    else *commands*
fi

Example 1:

```
if (test $age -lt 21)
    then echo 'You are a minor.'
    elif (test $age -gt 65)
        then echo 'You are a senior citizen.'
        else echo 'You are a relatively standard age.'
fi
```

Example 2:

```
echo 'Enter your age in years ==> '
read response
if (test $response -lt 21)
    then echo 'You are a minor'
    elif (test $response -lt 37)
        then echo 'You are still young'
        elif (test $response -lt 55)
            then echo 'You are middle aged'
            elif (test $response -lt 66)
                then echo 'You are getting on in years'
                else echo 'You are a senior citizen'
fi
```

Figure 10.4 The IF-THEN-ELSEIF structure

You can use as many **elif** sets as you want, as demonstrated in Example 2 of Figure 10.4. In Example 2, the user is asked to input an age in years. The IF-THEN-ELSEIF structure uses the age to determine which message to send to the screen. Note that an **else** line follows only the last **elif**.

You can use the IF-THEN-ELSEIF structure to select from several possibilities. Following is an example of how you might use it to perform the appropriate action after the user has selected an option from a displayed menu:

```
echo 'Which file do you want to choose?'
echo ' '
echo -n '1 - members.1985                  '
echo    '4 - members.1988 '
echo -n '2 - members.1986                  '
echo    '5 - members.1989 '
echo -n '3 - members.1987                  '
echo    '6 - members.1990 '
echo ' '
echo -n '  Type the number and press Enter '
read file_number
if ( test $file_number -gt 6 )
  then echo $file_number ' is an invalid selection'
  elif ( test $file_number -eq 1 )
    then cat members.1985
    elif (test $file_number -eq 2 )
      then cat members.1986
      elif (test $file_number -eq 3 )
        then cat members.1987
        elif (test $file_number -eq 4 )
          then cat members.1988
          elif (test $file_number -eq 5 )
            then cat members.1989
            elif (test $file_number -eq 6 )
              then cat members.1990
              else echo $file_number ' invalid'
fi
```

Case Structures

A case structure allows you to specify any number of different actions (or sets of commands) for different values of a variable. For example, you could display different messages, perform completely different commands, or even execute completely different scripts from within a script. Figure 10.5 (see following page) shows the format and an example of a case structure. In the example, the user has been asked to type a number from 1 to 5, indicating the age range from the displayed message. The case structure produces a different response for each choice.

Format: **case** *test string* **in**
pattern-1) commands;;
pattern-2) commands;;
pattern-3) commands;;
...
esac

Example:

```
read response
case $response in
   1) echo 'You are a minor';;
   2) echo 'You are still young';;
   3) echo 'You are middle aged';;
   4) echo 'You may be getting on in years';;
   5) echo 'You are a senior citizen';;
   *) echo 'You entered an invalid value. Run the program again';;
esac
```

Figure 10.5 Case structure

Note that this case structure is similar in effect to the second example in Figure 10.4. The case structure can often be accomplished through a series of **if** commands, but **case** produces a much cleaner script. Some versions of Unix let you omit the semicolons.

Here is how you could use the case structure to accomplish the same effect you saw in the previous IF-THEN-ELSEIF structure:

```
read file_number
case $file_number in
   1) cat members.1985;;
   2) cat members.1986;;
   3) cat members.1987;;
   4) cat members.1988;;
   5) cat members.1989;;
   6) cat members.1990;;
   *) echo $file_number ' invalid';;
esac
```

With a case structure, you specify the exact value for each pattern and the action to be taken for each. The last pattern in the figure is an asterisk, which means any value not included in earlier patterns in the case structure. You can use a vertical bar or square brackets to specify alternate values. For example, if the choices offered are letters rather than numbers, you could use patterns such as **A|a** and **B|b** or **[Aa]** and **[Bb]**. If you want several choices to have the same effect, you can accomplish that too. Suppose you want the same message for a choice of 3 or 4 in the example in Figure 10.5. The case structure could replace those two lines with **3|4) echo 'You are middle aged';;**.

LOOPS AND TESTING

You have seen how to make decisions in a Bourne shell script. You may want to create a loop as well. You can do this in several ways, just as you can in any programming language. The methods will be examined here briefly, with a few examples to help you use similar structures in your own script files.

Using for Loops

A **for** command lets you set up a series of commands that will be processed for every value in a list. Figure 10.6 shows the format of the command and two examples. Notice that the words **do** and **done** enclose the commands that are repeated. The *loop index* is generally a variable name that takes on a different value each time through the loop.

Format: **for** *loop-index* **[in** *argument-list***]**
do
commands
done

Example:

```
for filen in $file1 $file2 $file3 $file4 $file5 $file6
   do
   grep -n [Dd]uo[Tt]ech $filen >> saveall
   done

for args
   do
   grep -n [Dd]uo[Tt]ech $args >> saveall
   done
```

Figure 10.6 Using **for** *loops*

When you include **in** and a list of arguments, the commands enclosed by **do** and **done** are executed for each argument you supply. In the first example in Figure 10.6, the **grep** command is executed for each of exactly six command-line variables. You would use the **in** argument list primarily when these values are supplied through the keyboard. If you want to cycle through the variables supplied in the command line, you can omit the **in** and the list as in the second example. All the command-line arguments are processed in turn by the loop, for up to nine command-line arguments. The second example in Figure 10.6 executes the **grep** command once for each of up to nine command-line arguments.

Suppose you want to use a **for** loop to perform a multiple copy as you did in **mcopy** earlier in this chapter. You can't just omit the **in** option because then the first variable (the source, *$1*) will be copied onto itself. The easiest method is to use two user variables in addition to the command-line variables, one to hold the source of the copy and one to hold each target file in turn. You can use the **shift** command to dispose of the source file after assigning it to another variable name. Here is one way to do it:

```
source=$1
shift
for target
   do
      cp $source $target
   done
```

The variable *target* is defined by its appearance following **for**. Because the **for** command as written here refers to command-line variables, *target* refers to the first command-line variable (formerly *$2* in the previous **mcopy** script) the first time the **cp** command is executed. When run with the command **mcopy newstuff new1 new2 new3 new4**, the new version first assigns the file name **newstuff** to the user variable *source*, and then uses the **shift** command to move all values down one variable. The **for** loop then copies the file to the remaining target files.

Conditional Looping

Like many programming languages, the Bourne shell lets you specify conditional looping either until a condition becomes true or while it remains true. Figure 10.7 shows the formats of both structures along with examples. Note that the structures are identical except for the words **until** or **while**. As with **for** loops, the words **do** and **done** enclose the commands included in the loop. The **test** command options are the same as those in the **if** command.

Format: **until** *test-command*
do
commands
done

Example:

```
echo 'Enter your name: '
read name
until (test $name)
   do
     read name echo 'Please type something before pressing Enter'
   done
echo 'Thanks, ' $name
```

Format: **while** *test command*
do
commands
done

Example:

```
if (test $# -gt 1)
     newvar=$1
     while (test $2)
          do
               shift
               cp $newvar $1
          done
fi
```

Figure 10.7 Conditional looping structures

The first example shows the use of the **until** command to ensure that the user has entered something valid before going on to the next step. In this case, the user is asked to enter anything at all; in a real-life situation, you would probably use several commands here to give some help. The second example shows another way of using **mcopy** to handle any number of target files. The **if** first makes sure at least one target file is named and then sets the source file variable. The **while** loop sets each target file in turn and performs the copy until there are no more files available.

Unix System Exercise 10.3

Purpose: Use complex control structures in Bourne shell script files.

1. Modify your current version of **mcopy** so that it uses the IF- THEN-ELSEIF structure.
2. Modify **mcopy** again so that it can handle up to five targets with a CASE structure.
3. Create a new script that will use a loop structure; this one should accept any number of command-line values and display a listing of whether or not each is included in the current directory.

If it doesn't work:

A. For problem #1, your new version of **mcopy** could contain lines such as the following:

```
if (test $# -gt 4)
   echo 'File ' $1 ' not copied to $5 $6 $7 etc.'
else if (test $# -gt 3)
   cp $1 $4
else if (test $# -gt 2)
   cp $1 $3
else if (test $# -gt 1)
   cp $1 $2
else
   echo 'No target files specified'
fi
```

continued on following page...

Exercise 10.3 continued...

B. For problem #2, the case structure with **mcopy** could contain these lines:

```
numbargs=$#
case $numbargs in
    1) echo 'No target files specified';;
    2) cp $1 $2;;
    3) cp $1 $2
       cp $1 $3;;
    4) cp $1 $2
       cp $1 $3
       cp $1 $4;;
    3) echo 'File ' $1 ' not copied to $5 $6 $7 etc.';;
esac
```

C. For problem #3, your new script might look like this:

```
for filename
  do
  if (test -e $filename)
      echo $filename 'exists'
  fi
  done
```

ADDITIONAL SHELL INFORMATION

You have seen how to construct scripts using the control structures, user variables, and command-line variables. In the rest of this chapter, you will learn about more Bourne shell variables you can use in scripts. You will also see how you can nest scripts and pass variable values on to a nested script. Finally, you will learn a technique for running a command or script in the background, which allows you to do other work at the terminal while it executes.

Bourne Shell Variables

Shell variables are automatically defined by the shell and are ready for you to use in shell scripts or at the terminal. They are different in each shell, although some of the effects are the same. The command-line variables (*$1*, *$2*, and so forth) are shell variables. You have already seen two other Bourne shell variables.

HOME contains your default working directory; it is set in your **.profile** startup file whenever you log on. If you want to change your default working directory, you can change *HOME* there or enter another command to reset it. The command **HOME=/usr/carson/practice** changes the value of *HOME* from the keyboard. When you use **cd $HOME/exercise**, the new value is used (**exercise** must be a child directory of practice).

Earlier in this chapter, you saw how to use the *PATH* shell variable, which is also established in the **.profile** file. You can modify your default path as well.

Using the $0 Variable

You have seen that the variable *$1* represents the first argument supplied in the command line. The variable *$0* (dollar sign zero) holds the value of the script file name itself, the command you use to call the current program. If you type **echo $0** at the keyboard, you'll see that the current program is **-sh**, which is the shell itself. If you include the command **echo 'Program ' $0 ' was used to produce this.'** in a shell script named **sendmessage**, you could have this interaction:

```
$ sendmessage
Program sendmessage was used to produce this.
$ _
```

The current value of the variable is included in the output to replace the variable name. The *$0* variable is a *readonly* variable; you can't change the status or value of *readonly* variables. The shell takes care of assigning values to *readonly* shell variables.

Additional Shell Variables

The Bourne shell has several more variables, most of which you can change if necessary. Figure 10.8 summarizes several variables you can use directly at the keyboard or include in your **.profile** startup file. *PS1* and *PS2* establish nondefault prompts for your Unix sessions. *IFS* establishes a nondefault field separator for the command line.

If you use any of the shell variables at the keyboard, they affect your entire Unix session until you log off or change it again. If you use any in a script file, they affect only that script.

HOME — **Your logon working directory; using cd without an argument makes this directory current.**

PATH — **Your search path; Unix uses this to locate executable files that aren't in the working directory.**

PS1 — **Your shell prompt; the default Bourne shell prompt is the dollar sign followed by a space. To use a combination such as = = >, you could enter PS1='= = > '.**

PS2 — Your shell secondary prompt, defaults to >; you see this when a command hasn't been completed. Typing a single quote often restores your primary prompt. You could use **PS2='Finish command or type single quote '** as a secondary shell prompt.

IFS — **Your standard interfield separator; by default you can use Spacebar or Tab to separate fields on a command line. If you want to use a colon, you could use IFS=: and then use a colon to separate fields.**

Figure 10.8 Shell variables

Unix Processes

When you log on to Unix, a copy of the shell is provided for you as a new separate process; it has a separate process ID number that you can see if you enter **echo $$**. Many Unix commands, and most separately compiled programs or executable shell scripts, create a new process with a new process ID number. Each process is separate, with its own set of variables, and variables aren't automatically passed from one process to another. In order for values of shell or user variables to be passed to a new process, they must be exported. The **.profile** file includes an **export** command that allows the default *PATH* and *HOME* values to be available to other processes.

When you enter a command name, the shell first checks to see if the command is executable. If it is, the shell checks to see if it is a compiled program; if so, the shell "spawns" a new process to handle the program. If the executable command is not a compiled program, the shell assumes it is a shell script and creates a new process (called a **child process**) to execute it. Each new process generally involves a **subshell**, a newly generated copy of the original shell, and has a different process ID number. The subshell reads the commands in the shell script and executes them as specified.

You can tell what process is currently running with **echo $$**; you can include this command in shell scripts to see what process is running at any particular time.

Each process takes up memory in the system. Since it also begins with a new set of variables, you might want to run a script or program without starting a new process. You can prevent this when you run the script. Suppose you want to run **lsl** without starting a new process. First add a line containing **echo $$** to the script file so you can track the process ID. Following is an example of how the interaction might look:

```
$ echo $$
01268
$ lsl
01285
$ echo $$
01268
$ . lsl
01268
$ _
```

The first **echo** command shows that the shell is process **01268**. When **lsl** is executed the first time, it shows a new process number of **01285**. Note that the basic shell process ID has not changed. When **lsl** is executed following the period, it is in the basic process ID. When you use a period and space to start a script file, no new process is begun. You can also use the **exec** command to run a script or program without starting a new process by typing **exec lsl**.

Nesting Scripts and Passing Variables

You can call a script from within another script, just as you can use any other Unix command within a script. When a new process starts, user and command-line variable values from the previous process are not passed on automatically; a new set of shell variables is generated and the new process receives only the command-line variables from the command line that invoked the new process. If you run a nested script without generating a new process, the variable values can be changed and used by the nested script and the changes affect the original script as well.

You can cause values to be passed to a new process by the Bourne shell by exporting those values specifically. If you use the **export** command and name the variables, they can then be read and changed in the nested script, but no changes are passed back to the outer script. The **.profile** script includes an **export** command that allows the *PATH* and *HOME* variables to be used and changed by generated processes. You can change these variable within a generated process, but when control returns to the logon shell, its variables will be just as they were before.

You can name as many variables as you want in an **export** command. The named variables are all passed by value; that means a variable's value is passed to the new process and can be used, changed, or whatever by specifying the name of the variable. But, as mentioned previously, the changes are not passed back to the higher level process.

If you want a called script to change a variable that is accessible to the script that called it, don't let the calling script generate a new process. Use **exec** *scriptname* or the "period space" technique to execute a nested script within the same process as the calling one.

Processing in the Background

When a process runs in the background in any shell, you can continue working at the terminal on other processes. This is useful when a process takes a while and doesn't require any keyboard input from you. For example, sorting a long data file or using **awk** to process a database may take quite a while. Many application programs you may use can take a great deal of time, as do compilers and linkers.

You can specify any command or script to run in the background by typing an ampersand (&) before pressing **Return** to end the command line. When you do, Unix displays the process ID number of the background process; it is important to note this number in case you need to cancel the process later on. Following the process ID number, you'll see the standard shell prompt.

If the background process sends output to the screen, it will do so no matter what you are doing at the screen, so it's a good idea to redirect any output before going on to other work. If the background process expects standard input, it uses a null string.

Cancelling a Process

If you know its process ID number, you can cancel a process with the **kill** command while working in any shell. While the command has additional options, the simple form allows you to terminate one or more processes by listing the process numbers following **kill**. If you don't know the process numbers of current background processes, use the **ps** command. Following is an example:

```
$ sortall &
01299
$ ps
  PID TTY     TIME CMD
01268 5m      0:10 -sh
01299 5m      0:07 sortall
01326 5m      0:02 ps
$ kill 01299
01299 terminated
$ _
```

The first command starts a process in the background; note the process ID number is shown. The **ps** command then shows the ID numbers and names of all active processes; you can use the **-l** option to get additional information just as you can with the **ls** command. The **kill** command then requests that the background program be ended, and the message confirms this.

Unix System Exercise 10.4

Purpose: Use Bourne shell variables and experiment with processes and background processing.

1. At your keyboard or in a script file, display the current process ID. Then run **ps** and see what its process ID is.
2. Put the **ps** command at the end of your **lsl** script, by preceding it with a period and a space. Execute the script and note the resulting process ID numbers.
3. Within the current **lsl** script, add a line to display the value of *$0*. Execute it to see the result. Then remove this line and the **ps** command from the script.

continued on following page. . .

Exercise 10.4 continued. . .

4. At the keyboard, change the value of *PS1* to **= = >**, try a command, and then change back to the standard prompt.
5. If you have any long-running programs (more than two minutes), run one of them in the background. Note the process number of that program, and then terminate it with the **kill** command.
6. Create a new script named **showthem** to list the values of the target files in **mcopy**. Nest a reference to this script within **mcopy**. Try it without exporting the variables or running it as part of the same process. Then try export or "period space" to see the difference.

If it doesn't work:

A. If you have trouble restoring the standard prompt, use a backslash to quote each character.

B. If you don't have a long running program, try using **sort** or **awk** to do some work.

C. The **showthem** script mentioned in problem #6 might contain this line:

```
echo $2 $3 $4 ' are all target files.'
```

The **mcopy** script should contain one of these lines:

```
. showthem
exec showthem
```

SUMMARY

This chapter has covered a great deal about shell script programming in general and Bourne shell programming in particular. You have learned to do the following:

- Create, store, and execute script files.
- Display messages from a script with the **echo** command.
- Establish and reference user variables for the Bourne shell.

- Receive keyboard input to a Bourne shell script with the read command.
- Use command-line variables in a Bourne shell script.
- Adjust command-line variables with a **script** command.
- Set up Bourne shell conditions with the **test** command.
- Set up Bourne shell decision structures with the **if** command.
- Set up Bourne shell decision structures with the **case** command.
- Set up loops in a script with the **for** command.
- Set up conditional loops in a Bourne shell script with **while** and **until** commands.
- Use Bourne shell variables *PS1*, *PS2*, *IFS*, *HOME* and *PATH*.
- Identify active processes with **ps**, and stop them with the **kill** command.
- Pass variables to a new process with the **export** command.
- Prevent the starting of a new process with "period space" or the **exec** command.
- Run a process in the background with **&**.

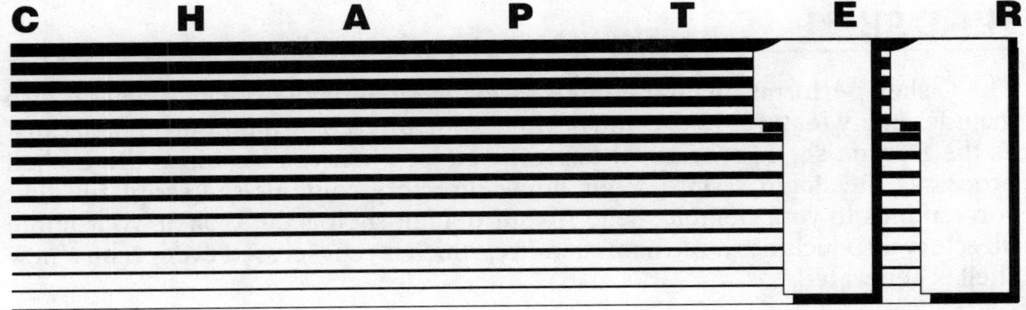

PROGRAMMING THE C SHELL

The C shell includes sophisticated keyboard features and a complete programming language that you can use to create new commands and perform new operations from the keyboard. You can execute a C shell script from within any shell, but you must be using a C shell to take advantage of its keyboard features. This chapter won't cover all there is to know about programming the C shell. You'll learn to use the history feature and you'll learn enough to create practical shell scripts with many of the shell features. You can find more information in your system's documentation.

THE C SHELL

The C shell performs much the same basic functions as the Bourne shell. It also includes many features above and beyond those offered by the Bourne shell. Just as the Bourne shell processes the **.profile** script when you log in, so the C shell processes the **.login** script. Your home directory contains the script file that corresponds to your default shell. If your default shell is the C shell, your home directory also includes a file named **.cshrc**, which is reprocessed every time a new shell is generated.

At any given time, you'll be using either one shell or the other, although you may be able to switch back and forth during the course of a session. If you prefer a different default shell than the one assigned to you, see your system administrator. You can create and use scripts for either shell, regardless of the shell interface you are using.

This chapter will focus on features of the C shell that are different from those in the Bourne shell. Features that are much the same will be passed over briefly. You cannot mix features; a script must be written for one shell or the other.

You will find some of the C shell features very useful during a Unix session; however, keep in mind that many of its features are oriented more toward programmers than toward end users or text editing users. The more experience you have with Unix, the more useful you will find these C shell script facilities.

CHANGING SHELLS

When you log on to Unix, you are placed in your default shell. If you see the $ prompt, you probably are in the Bourne shell. If you see the % prompt, you are probably in the C shell. In most Unix installations, you can change shells during a session; use **chs** to generate a new C shell or **sh** to generate a new Bourne shell.

The C shell often includes an event number by default, starting with 1 for the first prompt in the session, 2 for the second, and so forth. Every time you start a new shell, the event numbers start over again. Some installations don't use the event number; you'll see how to get it or dispose of it shortly.

While you are in the C shell, all your Bourne script files will still run the same. Unix recognizes a C shell script as having a # symbol as the first nonblank character. The # introduces a comment line, which can be used in either type of shell script; just make sure you never begin a Bourne shell script with a comment and that you always begin a C shell script with a comment. If the script file processor finds a # first, it treats the script as a C shell script; otherwise, it treats the script as a Bourne shell script. Any script that includes decision making or looping control structures will not work for both shells because of syntax differences.

If you generally use the Bourne shell, you may have trouble logging off from the C shell. Try your usual command. If it doesn't work, press **Ctrl-D**; you'll either exit or see instructions on what to do next. If you've generated additional shells with **chs** and **sh** commands, you may need to exit several levels of shell to reach the login prompt.

EVENT NUMBERS

The C shell assigns a number to each command you give it, starting with 1 for each session; most C shell prompts include the event number. If your system doesn't show an event number, you can set the prompt with a command such as the following: **set prompt = '!% '**. If you have trouble making this command work, try using the backslash to quote each symbol within the single quotes. The C shell then substitutes an event number for the ! symbol and follows it with the percent prompt and a space. If you prefer, you can put a space between the two symbols. The C shell requires you to include a space on each side of the equal sign in any command.

EVENT HISTORY

The reason you want to see your event numbers is that the C shell keeps a record of the commands you give it so you can reissue a command by specifying its event number. You can even edit or change the command before reissuing it. Actually, the C shell keeps a history even if you don't see the event numbers; the event numbers are generated and used internally in any case.

The C shell generally has an internal default of the number of events it stores for each user. You can find out what this default is by typing **history** at a C shell prompt. You will see a display similar to the following:

```
13% history
    4 ls
    5 ls -l
    6 cat temp.x
    7 rm temp.x
    8 cat fixall.x
    9 lpr fixall.x
    10 mail monty < fixall
    11 mail monty < fixall.x
    12 vi fixall.x
    13 history
14% _
```

In this case, the default history size is 10 events; the C shell saves commands you used for the last ten events and shows them to you when you ask. If you use the **history** command and don't see a listing, you don't have a default value. If you see a longer listing, the C shell saves more events as a result of a larger default value. You can change to saving 15 events with a command such as **set history = 15**. The event numbers will appear in a history listing even if they don't appear as part of your prompt.

Reexecuting an Event

Using the history list, you can execute any event again by referring to the history list, by using its event number, by specifying where the event was in relation to the most recent event, or by specifying a particular string included in the command. In this section, you will learn how to use all these methods. Then in the next section, you'll see how to modify an event when you reexecute it.

Reexecuting the Previous Event

When you reexecute any event, you start with an exclamation point (!) to tell the shell what you are doing. To reexecute the event just completed, type two exclamation points (!!). Your screen might appear as follows:

```
14% ls f*
fandango.tex
fandango.wva
frost_bite
15% !!
ls f*
fandango.tex
fandango.wva
frost_bite
16% _
```

Whatever the previous command was, typing **!!** at the prompt repeats it.

Reexecuting an Earlier Numbered Event

You can execute any earlier numbered event that is saved in the history list, whether or not you use the **history** command. You can reexecute any event within the number saved by the history feature. Just type the event number you want following the exclamation point. The screen might look like this:

```
16% !11
mail monty < fixall.x
17% _
```

In this case, command number 11 (see the earlier history listing) is reexecuted. Note that **vi fixall.x** has been executed in the interim, so the same data is not necessarily being sent, just the same file name.

You can also specify an event relative to the current one. If you use **!–3**, the third command before the current one is used. If the prompt shows event 17, typing **!–3** reexecutes event 14.

Reexecuting an Event Based on Command Text

Sometimes you may not recall the event number but you remember the command. To save time and avoid typing **history**, you can just type the first part of the command you want to reexecute. When a string of text follows the exclamation point, the C shell finds the most recent event that begins with that string. The following history listing has been included to show you the effect:

```
17% history
    8 cat fixall.x
     9 lpr fixall.x
     10 mail monty < fixall
     11 mail monty < fixall.x
     12 vi fixall.x
     13 history
     14 ls f*
     15 ls f*_
     16 mail monty < fixall.x
     17 history
18% !m
mail monty < fixall.x
19% !lp
lpr fixall.x
20% _
```

Event 18 requests that the most recent event starting with the string *m* be executed; that happens to be event 16. Event 19 requests the most recent event starting with *lp*; that is the **lpr** command in event 9.

If you want to reexecute an event based on a string within the command, rather than one at its beginning, use a question mark (?) before and after the string. The final question mark can be omitted if it immediately precedes **Return**. Following is an example of how it might look:

```
20% !?monty?
mail monty < fixall.x
21% _
```

Selecting Words from Historical Commands

You can select specific portions of a previous event for reexecution if necessary. The shell numbers the words in each event starting with 0 for the command itself; the command can't be changed in this type of reexecution. The first argument is number 1, the second 2, and so forth. Much as in search commands, you can represent the first argument as a caret (^) and the last argument as a dollar sign

($). When you request the command be reexecuted by number, you can indicate the specific arguments you want to use following the event number and a colon. The command **!24:3** means to reexecute event 24 using only argument 3. The command **!24:2-4** means to reexecute event 24, using arguments 2 through 4. The command **!24:3-$** means to reexecute event 24, using arguments 3 through the last one. Suppose your history contains the following commands:

```
38 mcopy lsl x1 x2 x3 x4 x5
39 ls x?
40 vi lsl
41 rm x1 x2 x3
```

You could reexecute the **mcopy** command to use your shell script to copy the source file to the first three targets with this command: **!38:1-4**.

Modifying Reexecuted Events

Suppose you make a simple typing error in a command and receive an error message. You certainly don't want to retype the entire command or reexecute it as it stands. The C shell lets you include a substitution instruction in the reexecute command. Just use a colon followed by **s** and a forward slash (/), and then type the existing pattern followed by a slash, followed by the substitution pattern. Here is an example:

```
64% lr /usr/carson/exercise/comm.doc /usr/carson/practice/comm.x
lr: Command not found
65% !!:s/lr/lpr
lpr /usr/carson/exercise/comm.doc /usr/carson/practice/comm.x
66% _
```

The reexecution request **!!:s/lr/lpr** supplies the substitution modifier, and the command is modified and executed. Whenever you reexecute a command, the C shell displays it so you know the result of your request. Actually, you can make an even shorter correction to the most recent event.

If you are making a change to the most recently executed event, as in the previous example, you can use a shorter form of command. You can even drop the exclamation points. Type a caret (^), followed by the incorrect pattern, followed by another caret and the pattern you want. You could enter event 65 in the previous example as **^lr^lpr**. This gives you a very quick way of correcting a command entered incorrectly. You'll need the form shown earlier for any modifications to events before the immediately previous one, however.

Figure 11.1 shows a number of additional modifiers you can use following the colon in an event reexecution request. The **g** modifier appears before the **s** to change all the occurrences of the string. The command **!65:gs/carson/davis** reexecutes event 65, changing all occurrences of *carson* to *davis.*

Modifier	Meaning	Effect
s	substitute	Substitute, as in **s/lr/lpr/**.
gs	global	Substitute all in line.
p	print	Show result, but don't execute it.
q	quote	Quote modifications to prevent recursion.
&	repeat	Repeat the previous substitution.
t	tail	Keep only the last element of a path name.
h	head	Remove the last element of a path name.
r	root	Remove the file name extension.

Figure 11.1 Reexecution modifiers

Most of the modifiers affect path names or file names. Because a path name, with or without a file name at the end, contains no spaces, it is a single word. If you try these modifiers, append the **p** modifier to see the effect; then, if you are satisfied, use **!!** to execute the modified event. Here is an example:

```
48% lpr /usr/davis/exercize/grease /usr/davis/exercize/britain
(error message)
49% ^cize^cise
can't access (error messages)
50% !48:gs/cize/cise/:p
lpr /usr/davis/exercise/grease usr/davis/exercise/britain
51% !50:s/ase/ece/:p
lpr /usr/davis/exercise/greece usr/davis/exercise/britain
52% !!
request id is (printer id) (2 files)
```

If you want to select a word or series of words and then modify it, reference the word or series of words first, and then use the modifier. If you don't use the **p** modifier, the shell tries to execute the command. You may get an error message if your modifier causes the command to try to access a nonexistent file. Following are a few examples:

```
65% !!:s/lr/lpr
lpr /usr/carson/exercise/comm.doc /usr/carson/practice/comm.x
66% rm fillall.x
67% !65:r
lpr /usr/carson/exercise/comm /usr/carson/practice/comm.x
68% !65:2:r
lpr /usr/carson/practice/comm
69% !65:t
lpr comm.doc /usr/carson/practice/comm.x
70% !65:2:h
lpr /usr/carson/practice
71% !67:p
lpr /usr/carson/exercise/comm /usr/carson/practice/comm.x
```

In event 67, the **r** modifier causes the root only of the first argument to be used, so the file name extension is dropped. Event 68 uses only the second word, modified to use only the root. In event 69, the tail of the first word is used; only the last element of the path is included in the specification. Event 70 requests the head of the second word, so it drops the first word and the last element in the pathname. Event 71 shows event 67 again, and assigns it to event number 71. You can combine some of these modifiers. Be sure to append **p** to a request if you want to see the resulting command before you execute it.

Unix System Exercise 11.1

Purpose: Practice manipulating events in the C shell.

1. If you aren't in the C shell, switch to it with **csh**. If you don't see an event number with the prompt, get one with **set prompt = '!% '**. You may need a backslash before the exclamation point.
2. If your event number is less than 10; issue a series of commands which include variations of **ls** and some of your script files. Try sending some mail to yourself. Type an incorrect command such as **kp** for **cp**. Then check the history listing. If it shows fewer than ten events, adjust it to record ten or fifteen events.

continued on following page. . .

Exercise 11.1 continued. . .

3. **Practice using and modifying earlier events. Correct typographical errors, make replacements, and so forth.**

4. **Copy a file from one directory to another, using a full path name for each. Then try modifying the file names and path names with the modifiers in Figure 11.1.**

If it doesn't work:

A. **If you can't change to the C shell, you can't use the history feature. You can still create C shell scripts, however.**

B. **Practice manipulating the reexecution functions; they become more useful as you get more comfortable with them.**

USING THE alias FEATURE

The C shell provides a feature you can use to create new commands and provide new names for old commands. The **alias** command lets you provide a new name for a command with options and/or arguments. You can even redefine an existing command name to have a different effect if you want. For example, suppose you always want a long directory listing. The command **alias ls ls -la** sets up the first word listed (**ls**) as an alias for the rest of the command. So whenever you type **ls**, the C shell substitutes **ls -la** for it and you get a long listing. Figure 11.2 shows the format and variations of the **alias** command. To change an incorrect alias, you can just define another with the same name. To remove an alias altogether, use **unalias** with the defined alias name.

Command: **alias**

Purpose: Establish new name for existing command.

Format: **[un]alias [*new-command-name* [*substituted-command*]]**

Examples:

1. `alias ls ls -la`
2. `alias md mkdir`
3. `alias ls`
4. `alias`
5. `unalias ls`

Results:

1. Typing **ls** will now result in the command **ls -la** being executed.
2. Typing **md** will now result in the command **mkdir** being executed.
3. Displays current alias for **ls**.
4. Displays current list of all aliases.
5. Removes alias for **ls**.

Figure 11.2 The **alias** *command*

Notice that the command **alias** without any options results in a list of the current aliases. Naming a single argument in the command results in a display of the alias for the command represented by that single argument. If you include more than one argument, all arguments following the first argument become the substitution value for the first argument. For example, if you frequently send mail to a group of five people, you might use the command **alias mailq mail monty carson judi steve ruth**. From then on, whenever you use the command **mailq**, the entire alias (i.e., **mail monty carson judi steve ruth**) is substituted for it. The **unalias** command requires a previously established alias as its single argument and removes the substitution value. For example, if you entered **unalias mailq,** entering **mailq** would no longer cause the command **mail monty carson judi steve ruth** to be executed.

Every time you enter a command line, the C shell locates the commands and substitutes aliases for every command that has an alias. Then it repeats the process, so if you have an alias that includes another defined alias, the nested alias will be identified and substituted. The C shell recognizes when an alias includes its own reference, as in **alias ls ls -la** and won't substitute it again on a second pass.

For example, if you use a command such as **ls exercise**, the command **ls** is replaced with its alias (**ls -la**), and then the command **ls -la exercise** is executed, resulting in a long listing of the **exercise** directory with any hidden files included. If you use a command such as **ls lsl**, the C shell performs the substitution on the command **ls**, but it doesn't affect the characters *ls* in the argument; it simply executes the command **ls -la lsl.**

You can use modifiers in **alias** command-line arguments much the same way as you use them in reexecuting events. The modifiers shown earlier in Figure 11.1 can be used in **alias** commands as well as in reexecution commands.

USING VARIABLES IN THE C SHELL

The C shell includes more shell variables than does the Bourne shell. Like the Bourne variables, these variables are all strings. But the C shell provides a way to handle variables that contain numeric values as numeric variables. As in the Bourne shell, variables are recognized by the initial $; if a variable has been established, that variable's current value is substituted when the shell encounters that variable name.

You can quote the $ character (with a backslash, as in **\$**) to prevent substitution if you want $ treated as an actual dollar sign character; however, if the variable name appears within double quotes, the backslash does not prevent substitution. If the variable appears within single quotes, substitution doesn't occur regardless of quoting. This is not the same as the effect in commands such as **set prompt = ' \$ '** in which the $ symbol is not used as a variable but as a constant.

Declaring String Variables

You can establish user variables and assign values to them and then use those variables at the keyboard or in script files. If you set a variable at the keyboard, it maintains that set value until you change it or end the session. If you set a value in a script file, you can specify that that value be local to that script or that it be made global and passed to any nested scripts. Variables in the C shell are always strings, but you can define numeric strings so that you can process them in arithmetic; however, keep in mind that even numeric values are really still strings.

You use the **set** command to define a standard string, the @ symbol to define a numeric string, and the **setenv** command to store a variable in the environment so that it will be automatically passed to other scripts and programs.

Suppose you want to use the value *bb* instead of *blackboard* to refer to that word. You could use this series of commands at the keyboard:

```
23% set bb = blackboard
24% echo bb
bb
25% echo $bb
blackboard
26% _
```

If you have a file named **blackboard**, you could display it with the command **cat $bb**. Similarly, you could assign a complex path name or file name you use frequently to a keyboard variable and use that keyboard variable (preceded with $) during a session instead.

You declare the variable in the **set** command by specifying that variable on the left side of the equal sign and placing the value for the variable on the right side; with most implementations of the C shell, you must use a space on each side of the equal sign. When you use the dollar sign before the variable name in other commands, it acts as a variable and displays the value of the variable rather than the variable name. Figure 11.3 (see following page) shows the format and variations of the **set** command. It shows how to declare a string array as well.

Using **set** by itself results in a list of all currently set user and shell variables. Using **set** with just a variable name, without the equal sign and value, gives it a null value. You can use the **unset** command to remove the definition of a user variable. When you enclose a list of values in parentheses, you declare an **array**. You can just list the values, separated by spaces. To give them null values, use sets of single quotes as in the example in Figure 11.3. If you don't assign values in the array declaration, you must supply the values later. The first element in the array declared in Example 4 of the figure is referenced as *$student[1]*. Arrays will be discussed in more detail later in this chapter.

Command: **set**

Purpose: Declare a C shell variable.

Format: **[un]set** [*variable name* [= *value*]]
[un]set *array name* = (*list of values*)

Examples:

```
1.    set fname = Ruth
2.    set fname
3.    set
4.    set student= ('' '' '' '' '' '' '' '')
5.    unset fname
```

Results:

1. Declares the variable *fname* and gives it the value **Ruth**.
2. Declares the variable *fname* and gives it a null value.
3. Displays list of all current variables and their values.
4. Declares an array of eight variables and gives a null value to each.
5. Removes the variable *fname*.

Figure 11.3 The **set** *command*

Declaring Numeric Variables

To declare a variable to be used in numeric operations, you use the @ symbol instead of the **set** command, in the format @ *variable name operator expression*, as in the examples that follow. The *operator* here is one of the standard C assignment operators, including =, + =, -=, *=, /=, and %=. A space is required to separate components of the assignment.

```
23% @ quantity = 0
24% @ quantity += 4
25% echo $quantity
4
26% @ quantity ++
27% echo $quantity
5
28% @ student_count = 17
29% echo $student_count
17
30% _
```

To declare a numeric array, you must first use **set** to establish the array size. Then you can assign values with the @ symbol, as in the following:

```
32% set scores = (0 0 0 0 0 0 0 0 0 0)
33% @ scores[1] = 100
34% @ scores[2] = 90
35% @ scores[3] = 95
36% @ subtot = $scores[1] + $scores[2] + $scores[3]
37% echo $subtot
285
38% _
```

In this example, event 32 establishes a ten-element array, assigning a value of zero to each element. You can include nonzero values in the declaration if you prefer. Events 33 through 35 assign numeric values to three elements of the array. Event 36 declares a new numeric variable, *subtot*, and assigns it a value. Elements of a numeric array work just like numeric variables when you include the element number in square brackets. If you refer to the array name without an element number (as in *$scores*), you refer to the entire set of values. The special variable reference *$#scores* contains the number of elements in the array.

Expressions for Numeric Variable Declaration

The expressions you can use in numeric variable processing can consist of constants, variables, and various **operators**, which are very similar to those you can use in C programs. Figure 11.4 summarizes these operators in decreasing order of precedence (i.e., the top operator in the left column has highest precedence, and the bottom operator in the right column has the least precedence.). If you aren't comfortable with these operators, check your C documentation before using any of the unfamiliar ones in a script.

Parentheses

( )	Change order of evaluation

Unary operators

~	One's complement
!	Logical negation

Arithmetic operators

%	Remainder
/	Divide
*	Multiply
–	Subtract
+	Add

Shift operators

> >	Right shift
< <	Left shift

Relational operators

>	Greater than
<	Less than
> =	Greater than or equal to
< =	Less than or equal to
! =	Not equal to
= =	Equal to

Bit operators

&	AND
^	Exclusive OR
|	Inclusive OR

Logical operators

Figure 11.4 Operators in expressions

In expressions, use at least one space to separate most operators, constants, and variable names. The only exceptions are when the operator follows an open parenthesis or precedes a close parenthesis, and when the operator itself requires two symbols. The C shell treats any number beginning with 0 (zero) as an octal (base eight) value. Any missing or null argument is treated as zero, and any result is always a decimal value. If you need further information on construction of expressions for numeric variables, check your C programming documentation.

Setting Global Variables

You can set global variables, which affect any child processes or scripts as well as the current one, by using the **setenv** command and specifying the variable name after declaring the variable. You'll see several examples of **setenv** in your **.login** and **.cshrc** files.

Counting Array Variables

When you declare an array for string or numeric variables, the variable *#array-name* holds the number of elements in the declared array. You can't change this value directly, but you can assign it to another numeric variable and change it there if you want to track the number. If you have declared a ten-element array called *scores*, the value of *#scores* is 10, no matter what values are assigned to elements of the array.

Variable Existence

Whenever a variable has been declared, you can test if it exists by checking the variable *?variable-name*. If you have used the command **set fname = Ruth**, variable *?fname* has a value of 1. If you later use **set fname**, *?fname* still has a value of 1; even though *fname* has no value, the variable still exists. If you then use **unset fname**, *?fname* has a value of 0 because the variable no longer exists. Any test of a variable when it doesn't exist results in an error message, so you'll want to use this special variable in scripts when you aren't sure whether a variable exists or not.

C Shell Variables

The C shell has many more shell variables than does the Bourne shell; some are similar, but most are unique. They will be summarized in this section, with greater attention to the more useful ones. You'll be able to find additional information on all of them in your system's documentation.

Variables with Values

- The *argv* variable is an array that contains all the current command-line arguments. A reference to *$#argv* gives you the number of elements in the *argv* array. It will be covered in more detail shortly.
- The *cdpath* variable affects how the **cd** command works. It lets the shell look for a directory of the single name you specify even if it isn't a child of the current directory. This variable is usually set in the **.login** file.
- The *child* variable is given the value of the process ID number of a process running in the background. It is automatically unset after the background process terminates.
- The *history* variable controls the number of events that you can execute by specifying the event number. You saw how to set and use it earlier in this chapter.
- The *home* variable has the value of the path name of the home directory of the user, much like the *HOME* variable of the Bourne shell. The **cd** command with no options returns you to this directory.
- The *path* variable has the value of a search path, much like the *PATH* variable of the Bourne shell.
- The *prompt* variable has the value of the current shell prompt; it works much like the *PS1* variable of the Bourne shell. The prompt is generally set in the **.cshrc** file. You've already seen how to change it with the **set** command.
- The *shell* variable contains the path name of the current shell.
- The *status* variable contains the exit status of the last command. It has the value 0 if the command was successful or 1 if the command was unsuccessful. You can also set the status in a special **exit** command in a script; you'll see how to do that later in this chapter.
- The *$* variable contains the current process ID number, just as in the Bourne shell. Use **echo $$** to display the process ID number.

C Shell Variable Switches

Several of the C shell variables act as **switches**; they are either set or not. If the variable is declared, the action is taken, otherwise it isn't. Many of these variables may be set for you automatically in either the **.login** or **.cshrc** when you log on or start a new shell, but they may not all be available in every C shell implementation.

- The *echo* variable causes the C shell to display each command before executing it.
- The *ignoreeof* variable causes the C shell to ignore **Ctrl-D** when it causes an exit from the shell. If the command **set ignoreeof** has been issued, you must use **exit** or **logout** to terminate the shell.
- The *noclobber* variable protects files from accidental destruction. When **set noclobber** has been issued, redirection (>) won't overwrite an existing file and appending (>>) won't create a new one. You can override the effect by adding an exclamation point to the redirection symbol, as in **>!** or **>>!**. By default, *noclobber* is generally not set.
- The *noglob* variable prevents the expansion of ambiguous file names; the term "globbing" is sometimes used to refer to the expansion of such file names. If you use **set noglob**, then characters such as *, ?, and [ ] in the command line are not expanded. If *noglob* is not set, you would have to quote these symbols to prevent expansion.
- The *nonomatch* variable lets the C shell pass an ambiguous file name that doesn't have any valid matches on to a program being called without expanding it. Otherwise the shell generates a *no match* message and ignores the command.
- The *verbose* variable causes the C shell to display the words of each command following a reexecution of that event, as you saw in the examples earlier in this chapter.

These switches can all be turned on with **set** commands or turned off with **unset**. Many are set in your startup files; you can edit those files to remove or change **set** commands if necessary.

Unix System Exercise 11.2

Purpose: Use the **alias** feature and try variables at the keyboard.

1. If your default shell is the C shell, check the contents of **.login** in your home directory to see if the **set path** command includes **$home/bin**. If not, add this to the end of the command; it won't take effect until you start your next Unix session. Check the values of any shell variables set there. Examine a file named **.cshrc** for variables as well. If your default shell is the Bourne shell, you have already adjusted the PATH variable to include your **bin** directory.
2. Use **set** to check any variable settings. Change the setting of **echo**, then run and reexecute a few commands and see the different effect. Restore **echo** to its original value.
3. Set a variable at the keyboard. Try to display it by name.
4. Declare an array of four variables containing four different names or user IDs. Display one or two elements at the keyboard. Display the count of the number of elements in the array.
5. Check any set variables again. Remove any you don't want.
6. Declare a numeric variable and give it the value 6. Add six to it and display the result.
7. Set a variable at the keyboard to your own name. Display its value. Set it to null and display the value. Unset it and try the value once more.
8. Set an alias for the **cat** command called **show** so that you can type **show** *file-name* to see the contents of a file. Try it out, then check any other aliases that might be available.

If it doesn't work:

A. If the **alias** feature doesn't work, check your documentation.

B. You shouldn't have trouble setting user variables and arrays. If you have trouble with numeric variables, be sure you are using the correct operators, such as + =.

C SHELL SCRIPTS

Like a Bourne shell script, a C shell script can contain any standard Unix commands; in addition, it can include commands specific to the C shell. Shell script commands are executed in sequence unless a branch is specified. The C shell provides commands for decision making and setting up loops, similar to those used in the Bourne shell. The C shell also includes a **goto** command and labels, as well as commands to break out of a loop or continue in it.

The first nonblank character in a C shell script must be the pound sign, also know as the sharp symbol (#). This character also causes the rest of the line to be treated as a comment. If you don't enter the # symbol first, Unix processes the script as a Bourne shell script no matter which shell you called it from; because the syntax generally differs somewhat between the two shells, the process won't run the way you expect. Be sure to include a comment as the first line in a C shell script, as shown below:

```
# sample C shell script
grep -vn C.*t suppliers.*
```

Storing Script Files

In general, it is most convenient to keep all your script files together in one location. The Unix system uses the **/bin** or **/usr/bin** directory for its program files. Most users create a directory named **bin** below their home directory to hold their own script and program files. You have probably already added this directory to your default search path. You probably created the directory during the Chapter 10 exercises. You can store all types of executable script files and programs in this directory. Of course, you can store other files here too, if you want.

In your **.login** file, you'll see a command that starts with **set path =** ; the rest of the command specifies directories to be searched in sequence. A space separates the directory names. If your own **bin** directory isn't included, you can add it to this command through **vi**.

Executing a Shell Script

C shell scripts are executed just as are Bourne shell scripts or standard Unix programs. You have to make script files executable first, of course, with the **chmod** command. Once a file is executable, you can just use its name as a command.

Suppose that whenever you want a directory listing, you want a full listing, including the hidden files, paged to the screen with **more**, and you want a message at the end telling you to go ahead with the next command. You can use **vi** to create a C shell script file named **lsl** containing the following lines:

```
# C shell for long listing
ls -la | more
echo 'Enter your next command'
```

Notice that this is very similar to the Bourne shell script in Chapter 10; the only difference is the comment on the first line. You can make this file executable in the same way, with **chmod u+x lsl**. If you modify a working Bourne shell script to turn it into a C shell script, it is already executable. Then, whenever you want to get a listing in your preferred format, just type **lsl**. As long as the shell sees the # symbol first, the script is treated as a C shell script.

Displaying Messages

C shell scripts can display messages on the screen through the **echo** command, much as Bourne shell scripts do. You can use **echo** to display text or values supplied in the command line, calculated in the script itself, or taken from any variable. The **echo** command displays the text and any variables included in the command, then moves to the next line. The C shell doesn't support the **-n** option to cancel the line feed, so your output or prompt appears on the next line on the terminal.

Getting Keyboard Input

Many implementations of the C shell don't have a built-in way to get user input directly from the keyboard. Others let you use redirection to assign keyboard values. If you find that the redirection technique shown in this book doesn't work on your system, check with your system administrator. Someone may have prepared a C program you can call to accomplish the task. Chapter 12 includes a sample C program you could use to accomplish keyboard input during C shell script execution.

Variable information for a C shell script is generally supplied in the command line or is generated internal to the script itself. If you really need keyboard input, you may be better off using a Bourne shell script. Following is an example of how you can use redirection to intercept standard input and assign it to a user variable in some C shell implementations:

```
echo 'Please type your full name: '
set fname = $<
echo 'Hello, ' $fname
echo 'Thanks for coming.'
```

When this script is executed, you will see the following interaction on the screen (the keyboard entry appears in bold):

```
Please type your full name:
Ruth Ashley
Hello, Ruth Ashley
Thanks for coming.
$ _
```

Whatever is typed at the keyboard up until the user presses **Return** is automatically assigned to the user variable supplied in the **set** command. If the system doesn't support the technique shown, you'll see a message such as *variable syntax* or a similar indication that the command didn't work.

USING COMMAND-LINE VARIABLES

Just as you can use various arguments with standard Unix commands, so can you set up a shell script that requires or uses command-line arguments. You can specify as many arguments as needed. You've already seen the C shell array variable *argv* that automatically contains any command-line arguments used to execute a shell script.

Variable *argv[0]* represents the name of the C shell script—the command used to execute it; this is the only element of the array that you won't be able to change. The shell assigns the first argument included in the command line to *argv[1]*, the second to *argv[2]*, and so forth. The reference *$argv[*]* or its abbreviation, *$**, references the entire array. The variable *#argv* automatically contains the number of variables included as command-line arguments.

You can choose to abbreviate references to command-line argument variables as *$1*, *$2*, and so forth; these abbreviations look just like the command-line variables you use in Bourne shell scripts. Values are assigned only to the number of elements that are supplied in the command line; you can use *$?argv[n]* as a command to see if an element exists, where *n* represents the element in question. You can use these variable names to refer to the arguments within the script.

Suppose you already have a script named **lsl** that produces a long listing of the current directory, including hidden files, and pipes that listing to the screen with **more**. You want to be able to specify any directory name or ambiguous file name when you invoke the command. You could modify the **ls** command in **lsl** to look like this:

```
# C shell script
ls -la $1 | more
```

When you use **lsl /usr/bin** as a command, the value */usr/bin* is assigned to the array element *argv[1]* and is substituted for the variable *$1* in the file. As a result, the long listing of the named directory is produced and piped to the **more** filter, which displays it to the screen one page at a time. If you provide an ambiguous file name, use a backslash to quote special characters such as ***** and **?**; otherwise they won't be processed properly. If you don't provide a value for *$1*, it is set to null; in that case, you'll get the paged output from a listing of the current directory, just as if you didn't include the variable in the script file.

Suppose you want to be able to copy a file into up to three different directories or file names in a single command. You want the first argument to specify the file to be copied and the rest to specify targets to be copied to. Here is how the C shell script **mcopy** might look:

```
# copy to several targets
cp $1 $2
cp $1 $3
cp $1 $4
```

The script works exactly like its Bourne shell counterpart. The command **mcopy savedir copy1 copy2 copy3** copies the contents of **savedir** ($1) to all three target files (*$2*, *$3*, and *$4*). The command **mcopy savedir copy1 copy2** copies the contents of **savedir** (*$1*) to the two named files (*$2* and *$3*) and produces an error message for the last (*$4*). The command **mcopy savedir copy1** copies the contents of **savedir** (*$1*) to the named file (*$2*) and produces an error message for each of the others (*$3* and *$4*).

Processing Arguments

As you've seen, the C shell assigns arguments to the *argv* array in sequence. The variable *argv[*]* or *$** represents all the command-line arguments. If you use a command such as **echo $***, all the command-line arguments are displayed on the screen. The variable #argv or $# contains the integer count of the command-line arguments. You might modify the **mcopy** file to look like this:

```
# copy to several targets
echo 'There are ' $# ' named files.'
echo $*
echo 'All except ' $1 ' are target files.'
cp $1 $2
cp $1 $3
cp $1 $4
```

This version displays the number of arguments supplied and lists them, then specifies the source file name as the only one that isn't a target file.

Unix System Exercise 11.3

Purpose: Write and execute simple C shell scripts.

1. Use **vi** to create a C shell script file named **lsl**, or modify your Bourne shell script of this name. It should display the long form of the current directory and pipe it to the screen with **more**. If you want, add a short message to the file.
2. Create a C shell script file named **keyboard** that asks the user to enter a string. Assign that value to **keyin**. Display the value on the next line, then display the message *Good bye, now* and end the script.
3. If you don't already have one, create a new directory named **bin** and move both scripts to it. Then make both scripts executable.
4. Run the scripts from the **bin** directory. If they don't work correctly, edit them until they do. Then try running them from other directories.
5. Create a new C shell script file that will accept a list of user IDs as arguments. In the script file, display the number of arguments, the full list of arguments, and the second one. Make it executable and test it.

If it doesn't work:

A. The new **lsl** file should have a # symbol as the first nonblank character. The next line should contain this command: **ls -l | more**. A message with **echo** can follow it.

B. First try the **keyboard** file with commands such as these:

```
# trying keyboard input
echo 'Please type your name.'
set keyin = $<
echo 'You typed ' $keyin
echo 'Good bye, now.'
```

If it doesn't work properly, try using a **set** command to establish a value for **keyin** before echoing it to the screen. Take time to check out whether your system allows any of the keyboard input techniques discussed in this chapter. If not, you'll need to use Bourne shell scripts when you need keyboard input.

continued on following page...

Exercise 11.3 continued. . .

C. Be sure to use **chmod u+x lsl** and **chmod u+x keyboard** to make the scripts executable.

D. In your command-line input script, use *$#argv* to represent the number of arguments, *$** to represent the entire list, and *$2* or *$argv[2]* to represent the second argument.

E. If your scripts won't run unless you are in the directory that contains them, your **path** (or **PATH** if you default to the Bourne shell) command isn't working properly. Make sure you preceded your C shell directory name with a space. Try logging off and back on again.

USING DECISION STRUCTURES

Making decisions in any script file is essential. You may want to check the number of variables and display different messages for different numbers. You might want to perform a completely different action depending on what the user enters at the keyboard. You might want to access a particular file selected by the user from a menu. The C shell provides several variations on IF structures that you can use to make decisions in your scripts. While the structures are similar to those used in the Bourne shell, the syntax and conditions differ somewhat. The same effects can be achieved, however.

The Condition or Expression

The expression you include in an **if** command specifies a condition to be tested; the shell determines whether the condition is true or false. A condition may determine if a variable exists, if two strings are identical, if one number or variable is larger than another, or if a file is available. String and numeric expressions can use any of the operators shown in Figure 11.4 earlier in this chapter. In addition, you can use several more operators to test file names. You can enclose the expression in parentheses if you want; many people do this just to be clear in their own minds about what constitutes the expression. You'll see several examples in the next section of this chapter. Most of these expressions are identical to those you use in C programs.

You can test a string or a numeric variable. To see if a string exists, use an expression in the form *$?variable*; the result is 1 if the variable exists and 0 if it does not. If you reference a variable name when it doesn't exist, you'll get an error message and the script file processing will be aborted. You can use = = or != to test if two values are equal or not. When you compare two strings, one can be a variable and one a constant if you want; use a $ before a variable name (which must exist) and double quotes around a constant string. To see if the current value of *fname* matches a constant, you might use an expression such as (**$fname = = "Judi"**).

You can compare two numeric values with any of the six relational operators shown earlier in Figure 11.4. As with strings, one value can be a variable and one a constant if you like, or you can specify two variables. You don't need quotes around a numeric constant. If you use an exclamation point (!) before the operator, that operator is negated. Thus the expression (**$1 !< 0**) is true if the current value of variable *$1* is not less than zero.

Figure 11.5 shows several expressions you can use to evaluate the status of file names used as arguments. You can check a file name, either as a constant or a variable, to make sure it exists, to check that you have the appropriate access, and to determine whether it is a directory or an ordinary file. If you have a script in which you use the input and edit a file included in the command line, for example, you might want to use an expression such as (**-w -f $1**) before entering the editor to make sure it is a file to which you have write access.

You can specify more than one condition in forming the expression. If you are new to programming, it is wise to keep your conditions very simple, however. If you know what you are doing, you can use **&&** to AND separate conditions and || to OR them.

Expression	True if:
-e *file-name*	exists
-r *file-name*	exists and allows read access
-w *file-name*	exists and allows write access
-f *file-name*	exists and not a directory
-d *file-name*	exists and is a directory
-s *file-name*	exists and size is 0

Figure 11.5 Additional expression conditions

Basic if Commands

Decision-making commands have similar effects in most programming languages. Figure 11.6 shows the three basic formats of the **if** command for the C shell, with an example of how each command format might be used. Notice that the **test** command is not used and that parentheses are required around the expression that is evaluated.

IF

Format: **if (*expression*) command**

Example:
```
if ( $?fname ) goto goodname
```

IF-THEN

Format: **if (*expression*) then**
command(s)
endif

Example:
```
if ( -r $1 ) then
    echo 'Processing ' $1
    grep if $1
endif
```

IF-THEN-ELSE

Format: **if (*expression*) then**
command(s)
else
command(s)
endif

Example:
```
if ( $1 == "Ruth" ) then
    echo 'On track'
else
    echo $1 ' not on track'
endif
```

Figure 11.6 Basic **if** *command formats*

The basic form of the **if** command lets you specify the expression (enclosed in parentheses) and a single command to be processed if the expression evaluates to true; when you use this format, the command appears on a single line. In the example in Figure 11.6, the expression tests that the file name specified as the first command-line argument exists. The command **if ($?fname) goto goodname** tests for the presence of the variable, transferring control if it exists. You will see how to use the **goto** command to transfer control a bit later.

For all of the more complex formats, the **if** command scope is terminated by the **endif** entry on a line by itself, as you can see in the IF-THEN and IF-THEN-ELSE structures. The indentation from the left margin is optional; most programmers find that regular indentation helps them keep the structure of **if** commands in mind.

Notice that the strings in expressions require double quotes while the message in the **echo** command is enclosed with single quotes; some C shell implementations accept either type of quote in certain commands, but if you have trouble with these commands, change the quote style to see if it works better.

When the shell encounters any **if** command, it first evaluates the expression to determine if it is true or false. The expression must be valid; that is, a string must exist if you are testing it, except for the special variable reference *$?variable*. If the expression is true, the single command is executed. In an extended command, any commands that follow **then** are executed in sequence until either **else** or **endif** is encountered. Either **else** or **endif** terminates the **then** commands, and commands following **endif** are processed next. If the expression evaluates to false, the commands that follow **then** are skipped, and Unix goes to the commands that follow the next **else** or **endif** that it encounters. If both **then** and **else** are included in the same **if** structure, they are not both executed.

When you use the basic IF or the IF-THEN structure, you don't specify any special commands to be processed when the condition evaluates as false. If it is false, control goes to the command following the **endif**. If the script requires false condition processing, you'll need to use the IF-THEN-ELSE structure. The IF-THEN-ELSE example in Figure 11.6 compares the first command-line variable to a constant. If they match, one message is sent to the terminal; if not, a different message is sent.

If you want to use a structure in which there are commands to be executed when the condition is false but none when it is true, you can use the special **continue** command in the **then** portion of the structure. The **continue** command acts as a placeholder to bypass the **then** or **else** portion of an **if** command.

Using if Commands

You can use **if** commands to make decisions and expand the usefulness of a script. For example, you could polish up the **mcopy** shell script shown earlier with **if** commands to modify processing based on the number of command-line variables. Here is how it might look:

```
# Sample C Shell Control Structures
if ($#argv == 4 ) then
   cp $1 $4
   cp $1 $3
   cp $1 $2
endif
if ($#argv == 3 ) then
   cp $1 $3
   cp $1 $2
endif
if ($#argv == 2 ) then
   cp $1 $2
endif
if ($#argv < 2 ) then
   echo 'No target files specified'
else
   set all = $#argv
   @ all -= 1
   echo 'You asked for ' $all ' copies.'
   echo 'Up to three requested copies made.'
endif
```

Transferring Control

Unlike the Bourne shell, the C shell offers a **goto** command and labels you can use to unconditionally transfer control in your scripts. It also provides an **exit** command to immediately leave the script and return to the calling process.

In accordance with good programming practices, you'll want to minimize the use of **gotos**, but occasionally they are very useful. Here is how you could use the **goto** command in another variation of the previous IF structure used to enhance the **mcopy** script:

```
# Sample C Shell Control Structures
if ($#argv == 4 ) then
   cp $1 $4
   cp $1 $3
   cp $1 $2
   goto alldone
endif
if ($#argv == 3 ) then
   cp $1 $3
   cp $1 $2
   goto alldone
endif
if ($#argv == 2 ) then
   cp $1 $2
   goto alldone
endif
if ($#argv < 2 ) then
   echo 'No target files specified'
   goto message
endif
if ($#argv > 4 ) then
   echo 'Too many target files specified'
   goto message
endif
message:
   echo 'Please run with from one to three targets.'
alldone:
   echo 'End of script.'
   exit
```

The previous scripts don't verify that the source file exists or that it can be copied. To do that, you could include a test of *$1* for existence and/or read access before testing for the presence of the target files.

The **exit** command can be used at the final point in a script or to cause an exit at an earlier point. You can include an integer in parentheses in the **exit** command to set the status switch if you like. The command **exit (3)** sets the value. A command beginning **if ($status = = 3)** could be used to test the status value.

Unix System Exercise 11.4

Purpose: Use decision structures in script files.

1. Create a C shell version of the **mcopy** script to check for more than three targets and display a message showing which copies are not attempted. You could just modify your Bourne shell script if you want.
2. Modify your Bourne shell **both** script to take the name and age from command-line variables, and then show one message if the age is over 65, a different one if it is under 21, and no special message if the age is between these points.
3. Create a new script that will let you check if a file name provided as a command-line argument is a standard file and, if so, display the contents on the screen. If not, provide an error message for the user instead.
4. Store all your script files in your **bin** directory and make them executable, then test them. Modify them until they work the way you want them to.

If it doesn't work:

A. In **mcopy**, you need a command similar to this:

```
# check for more than three targets
if ($# > 4) then
   echo 'File ' $1 ' not copied to $5 $6 $7 etc.'
endif
```

B. In **both**, you need commands similar to these, if *$2* represents the age provided:

```
# Check age supplied as second argument
if ($2 > 65) then
   echo 'You are a senior citizen.'
endif
if ($2 < 21) then
   echo 'You are a minor.'
endif
```

continued on following page...

Exercise 11.4 continued...

C. Your new script should look something like this:

```
# C shell script
if ( -f $1 ) then
    cat $1
    else
        echo 'You did not provide a valid file name.'
endif
```

MORE COMPLEX DECISIONS

You have seen how to use basic decision structures in your script files. In this section, you'll see how you can use more complex decision constructions if necessary. In most cases, however, it is safer to keep the decisions in a script file as simple and clear as possible. Always be sure to provide plenty of onscreen feedback for users so they know why it doesn't work if problems arise.

IF-THEN-ELSEIF

Nesting IFs can become very awkward; some Unix systems will only allow you do it in one particular way. Figure 11.7 shows the format and and some examples of this construction.

You can use as many **else if** sets as you want. Notice that an **else** line follows only the last **else if**. In the examples in Figure 11.7, the user includes an age in the command line. The IF-THEN-ELSEIF structure uses the age as the second argument to determine which message to send to the screen.

Format: if (*expression*) then
command(s)
else if (*expression*) then
command(s)
...
else
command(s)
endif

Example 1:

```
if ( $2 < 21 ) then
   echo 'You are a minor.'
else if ( $2 > 65 ) then
   echo 'You are a senior citizen.'
else
   echo 'You are a relatively standard age.'
endif
```

Example 2:

```
if ( $2 < 21 ) then
   echo 'You are a minor'
else if ( $2 < 37 ) then
   echo 'You are still young'
else if ( $2 < 55 ) then
   echo 'You are middle aged'
else if ( $2 < 66 ) then
   echo 'You are getting on in years'
else
   echo 'You are a senior citizen'
endif
```

Figure 11.7 The IF-THEN-ELSEIF structure

The following example shows how the IF-THEN-ELSE structure can be used to simplify the **mcopy** (multiple copy) script you have been working with in this chapter.

```
if ( $#argv > 4 ) then
   echo 'Too many target files specified'
else if ($#argv == 4 ) then
   cp $1 $4
   cp $1 $3
   cp $1 $2
else if ($#argv == 3 ) then
   cp $1 $3
   cp $1 $2
else if ($#argv == 2 ) then
   cp $1 $2
else
   echo 'No target files specified'
endif
```

Case Structures

A case structure allows you to specify any number of different actions (or sets of commands) for different values (or patterns) of a variable. For example, you could display different messages, perform completely different commands, or even execute completely different scripts from within a script. Figure 11.8 shows the format and an example of a case structure. The example uses a number corresponding to an age range. The number is entered as the second argument in the invoking command. For each case, a particular program is executed after the message is sent to the screen. If the number were assigned earlier in the script based on an actual age entered in the command line, the **case** statement would use a user variable instead of a command-line variable. The rest of the case structure would be the same.

The case structure can often be accomplished through a series of **if** commands, but the case structure shown in Figure 11.8, starting with the **switch** command produces a much cleaner script.

Format: **switch** (*variable*)
case *str1:*
  commands
  breaksw
case *str2:*
  commands
  breaksw
...
case *strn:*
  commands
  breaksw
default:
  commands
  breaksw
endsw

Example:

```
switch ( $2 )
case 1:
   echo 'You are a minor'
   minorsub
   breaksw
case 2:
   echo 'You are still young'
   youngsub
   breaksw
case 3:
   echo 'You are middle aged'
   middlesub
   breaksw
case 4:
   echo 'You may be getting on in years'
   middlesub
   breaksw
case 5:
   echo 'You are a senior citizen'
   seniorsub
   breaksw
default:
   echo 'You entered an invalid value. Run the program again'
   breaksw
endsw
```

Figure 11.8 Case structure

With a case structure, you specify the exact value for each option and the action to be taken for each option; the last command in each action is **breaksw**, which breaks out of the case structure and branches ahead to the **endsw** point. You can use square brackets to specify alternate values. For example, if the choices offered are letters rather than numbers, you could use patterns such as **[Aa]** and **[Bb]**. Suppose you want the same message for a choice of 3 or 4. The case structure could replace those two sections with these lines:

```
case [34]:
   echo 'You are middle aged'
   middlesub
breaksw
```

The last branch in the format is named **default**:, and it includes any value not included in earlier parts of the case structure. The **mcopy** script becomes even more streamlined when coded with a case structure:

```
switch ( $#argv )
case 1:
   echo 'No target files specified'
   breaksw
case 2:
   cp $1 $2
   breaksw
case 3:
   cp $1 $2
   cp $1 $3
   breaksw
case 4:
   cp $1 $2
   cp $1 $3
   cp $1 $4
   breaksw
default:
   echo 'Too many target files specified'
   breaksw
endsw
```

LOOPS AND TESTING

You have seen how to make decisions in a C shell script. You may want to create a loop as well. You can do this in several ways, just as you can in any programming language. They will be examined here briefly, with a few examples to help you use similar structures in your own script files.

Standard goto Loops

You can construct a standard **goto** loop with a label, a set of commands, including **if** as needed, and a **goto** command to loop back to the label. You can use the **break** command to leave the loop when appropriate. Here is an example:

```
if ( $#argv > 1 && $#argv < 5 ) then
     set targetct = $#argv
 looplabel:
   cp $1 $#argv[$targetct]
   @ targetct -= 1
   if ($targetct == 1 ) exit
   goto looplabel
else
 echo 'Specify from one to three targets'
endif
```

Using foreach Loops

A **foreach** command works like a standard **for** loop, processing the arguments in turn. It lets you set up a series of commands that will be processed for every value in a list. Figure 11.9 shows the format of the command and two examples. Notice that the word **end** marks the end of the commands that are repeated. The *loop-index* is declared by its appearance in the **foreach** statement; it is generally a variable name that takes on a different value each time through the loop. Notice that an array name can be specified, as in the second example in Figure 11.9.

Format: **foreach** *loop-index* (*argument-list*)
command(s)
end

Example 1:
```
foreach filen ( $1 $2 $3 $4 $5 $6 )
    grep -n [Dd]uo[Tt]ech $filen >> saveall
    end
```

Example 2:
```
set count = 0
foreach argument ( $argv[*] )
    @ count += 1
    echo $count ' contains ' $argument
    end
```

Figure 11.9 Using **foreach** *loops*

The commands enclosed between **foreach** and **end** are executed for each argument you supply. All the arguments are processed in turn by the loop, no matter how many there are.

Suppose you want to perform a multiple copy as in **mcopy** with a **foreach** loop. You have to adjust the loop index, which can be done with **shift**, much as with the Bourne shell. Here is an example:

```
set source=$1
shift
foreach argument ($argv[*])
    cp $source $argument
    shift
    end
```

When run with the command **mcopy newstuff new1 new2 new3 new4**, the new version first assigns the file name **newstuff** to the user variable source. The **foreach** loop then shifts out the first argument and copies the saved source file to each of the remaining arguments.

Conditional Looping

As in many programming languages, the C shell script can specify conditional looping while an expression evaluates to true. Figure 11.10 shows the format and an example. As with **foreach** loops, the word **end** marks the end of the loop. The expression options are the same as those in the **if** command.

Format:

```
while ( expression )
  command(s)
  end
```

Example:

```
# Using a while loop for multiple copies
echo 'demonstration of while '
set count = 1
set total = $#argv
while ( $count < $total )
   @ count += 1
   cp $1 $argv[$count]
   end
```

Figure 11.10 Conditional looping

The example in Figure 11.10 shows the use of the **while** command in a loop that copies the first argument to files named in all the rest of the arguments. Notice that two user variables are used to control the loop. It is generally safer not to change the value of *#argv* directly through the loop.

An expansion of the example is shown below. Here an **if** command makes sure at least one target is specified, then the **while** loop copies to each target file in turn until no more are available.

```
# Multiple copy with while
if ( $#argv > 1 ) then
   set count = 1
   set total = $#argv
   while ( $count < $total )
      @ count += 1
      cp $1 $argv[$count]
      end
else
   echo 'You must specify at least one target.'
endif
```

Unix System Exercise 11.5

Purpose: Use complex decision structures and branching in a C shell script.

1. Create a new C shell script that takes one of four values as input and displays a different message for each. Use the IF-THEN-ELSEIF structure.
2. Create another version of your script that uses the CASE structure.
3. Make both versions of the script executable, and test them until they work correctly.
4. Create a script that uses a loop to display every argument included in the command line. Use a standard **goto**, **foreach**, or **while** loop. Test it.
5. Modify your loop script so that it uses a different looping technique. Test this one as well.

If it doesn't work:

A. Compare your coding to the examples in this chapter. Be careful of the syntax because the C shell is very picky. If you use any special characters in the command line, be sure to quote them.

B. Try reproducing the multiple copy (**mcopy**) examples from the text if you have trouble with this exercise. Once you have one script working, you should be able to create similar scripts.

SUMMARY

This chapter has covered special features of the C shell, as well as commands and techniques for creating scripts for this shell. You have learned to do the following:

- Access a list of previous events with the **history** command.
- Change shells with **sh** and **csh** commands.
- Reexecute and modify previous commands by event number, by relative position, or by content.

- Set up names for command-line words with the **alias** command.
- Establish user variables and arrays with the **set** command.
- Establish numeric variables with the @ symbol.
- Use variables to reference an entire array, a particular element, and the number of elements.
- Use C shell variables as needed.
- Display messages with the **echo** command.
- Use redirection to get keyboard input, if allowed on your system.
- Use command-line variables in C shell scripts.
- Create expressions for condition testing.
- Set up decision structures using the **if** command.
- Transfer control with **goto** and **exit** commands.
- Set up case decision structures with the **case** command.
- Set up loops with the **foreach** command.
- Set up conditional loops with the **while** command.

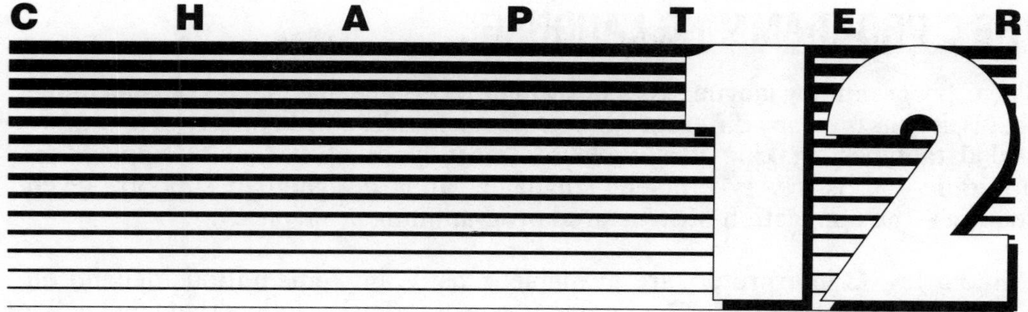

BASIC C PROGRAMMING TOOLS UNDER UNIX

While Unix is an operating system that supports many applications, it also supports various programming languages. Each language has its own set of tools you can use to progress from ASCII source code modules to a fully executable program. Such tools include preprocessors, compilers, assemblers, interpreters, linkers, and debuggers. Because Unix is primarily written in the C programming language, however, tools for handling C programs are more readily available and are more likely to be incorporated into Unix at your installation than tools for handling programs in other languages. This chapter discusses the basic C programming tools of Unix.

THE C PROGRAMMING LANGUAGE

The C programming language is a fairly high-level language that is **transportable**; that is, it runs on many different systems. It can handle a wide variety of operators and data types, making it suitable for most types of system or application programs. C is a very efficient language. It is designed to support—even require—the application of structured programming principles.

While a few C interpreters are available, most C implementations depend on **compilers**. Unix includes a C compiler as one of its basic services that you invoke with a simple command, along with various other tools you can use in a C programming environment.

Figure 12.1 shows a simple C program that enables a C shell script to receive keyboard input. Once this program is compiled, you can reference it in a script with a command such as **set variable = `read`** following the request for user input; notice that the program name is enclosed in accent marks rather than single quotes to result in the **read** program output. This program could be interpreted or compiled on virtually any C interpreter or compiler you might encounter. It includes the essential components of any C program.

```
/* read routine for C Shell */
#include  <stdio.h>
main()
{
char character;
while ((character = getchar ()) != '\n')
    {
    putchar (character);
    }
}
/* end of read program */
```

Figure 12.1 C **read** *program*

Notice that the program includes a **preprocessor directive (#include)**, a request for a **header file (stdio.h)**, and the need for the standard library of C functions, which includes the **while** function. You can prepare C source programs with any ASCII editor; **vi** works just fine. You will find the autoindent feature especially useful for typing source code.

Using the cc Command

Once a source code program is prepared, you are ready to compile it. Unix includes several steps in the C compiler (**cc**) command. It automatically calls the preprocessor (**cpp**) as the first step; it automatically calls the linkage editor (**ld**) as the last step.

Figure 12.2 (see following page) shows the format and options of the **cc** command. Only the very basic options are included. Your installation most likely has many additional options that customize the command. Once you've learned to use the basic **cc** command, you can check your installation's documentation and try out its additional features.

The file names you specify in the **cc** command line can consist of any combination of C source programs (indicated by extension **.c**), assembler language source programs (indicated by extension **.s**), and object code files (indicated by extension **.o**). If any source programs are specified, the appropriate compiler or assembler is invoked first; the preprocessor is executed as the first pass if necessary. After the compilation and/or assembly is complete, the resulting object programs are linked with any named object files into a single executable output file; by default, this file is named **a.out**. The **-o** option lets you name a nondefault file to hold the output; don't use an extension that **cc** assumes to be something else, such as **.c**, **.s**, or **.o**. By default, any temporary object files are removed at the end of the link process. If you want to keep the object code files for later use, specify the **-c** option to prevent linkage; this saves the object code resulting from C and assembler source programs in files with the same basic names but with extension **.o**. These object files can be included in later **cc** commands.

If you want to compile C programs and leave the output in corresponding assembly language source programs with extension **.s**, use the **-S** option. These files can be processed in a later **cc** command, alone or in combination with other source and object files. The **-S** option differs from the **-c** option in that it results in source files rather than object files. Both types of files can be used in later commands, however. If the file names include only object files, the **cc** command calls the linkage editor (**ld**) only.

The **-l** option names a library; the entry here is appended to the default search library path for your installation. If you use **-lm**, it actually searches in the standard math library, **/lib/libm.a**. Put the **-l** option at the end of the command line; then it will apply to unresolved references in any of the previously named files.

Command: cc

Purpose: Compile a C source program; includes invoking the preprocessor and linkage editor; stores executable output in **a.out.**

Format: **cc** [*options*] *file-name(s)*

Options:

-c Compile only; don't link.
-o *file-name* Stores executable output in named file instead of **a.out.**
-O Optimizes output; may have additional specifiers.
-S Compile only; store assembly source code in *file-name*.s.
-l *lib-name* Search for unresolved external references in *lib-name*; put at end of command.

Examples:

1. `cc demoprog.c`
2. `cc demoprog.c -o compdemo.test`
3. `cc demo1.c demo2.s demo3.o -o compdemo.test`
4. `cc -c payroll.c`

Results:

1. C source program **demoprog.c** is processed through the preprocessor, the C compiler, and the linkage editor. Executable output is stored in file **a.out.**
2. Same as Example 1, except that the executable output is stored in file **compdemo.test**.
3. Compiles C source program, assembles assembly language program, and links both results with the object code file; executable output is placed in file **compdemo.test**.
4. Compiles C source program and places object code in file **payroll.o**.

Figure 12.2 The **cc** *command*

The make Facility

C programs are often composed of several source programs and modules, put together in several levels. A program may include several header files, functions, and even library references. The Unix C programming environment includes a facility to help programmers manage the program development process. The **make** command takes its input from a previously prepared file called a *makefile*. The *makefile* includes dependency information about relationships between files. Any module that a target file depends on is a prerequisite for that target file. The target file can't be created if all the prerequisites aren't present. Because the target file depends on all the prerequisites, the prerequisites are often called **dependencies**.

Each dependency line in the *makefile* specifies a target file that is dependent on one or more prerequisites. The first line specifies the ultimate target, the executable module that will result. Each prerequisite may be a target file on later lines in the **makefile**, until the entire system of dependencies is defined. If any prerequisite file has been modified since its target file was last modified, the **make** command updates the target file based on information in the *makefile*.

Figure 12.3 (see following page) shows the format and basic options of the **make** command. The **-f** option lets you specify a *makefile* with a nondefault name; if you omit this option, **make** gets input from a file named **makefile** or **Makefile** in the working directory.

You can use the **-n** option to cause the command to display the commands it would use to update the target file but not execute them. This lets you see what would happen without actually updating the target file. The **-t** option updates modification times of target files, but it doesn't change anything else. Its effect is similar to the Unix **touch** command, which updates the time of the named file without otherwise changing it. You would use **-t** if you knew that the changes to the dependent files won't affect compilation; this would be true if you only added comments, for example.

If the **make** command doesn't include any target files, it affects the first target file in the processed *makefile*; the result is to process the entire file. If you name a particular target file in the makefile to be processed, only that file and its dependencies will be examined. You don't need to specify a target file if you want the entire dependent structure defined in the *makefile* to be processed.

Command: make

Purpose: Keep a set of programs and their dependencies current.

Format: **make** [*options*] [*target files*]

Options:

-f *file-name*	Use named file as input instead of **makefile**.
-n	No execution; display commands only.
-t	Update modification times of target files; no other changes.

Examples:

1. `make`
2. `make -f payroll.make`
3. `make -n -f payroll.make`
4. `make -t payroll.c`

Results:

1. Process commands for the first target file in **makefile** in the current working directory.
2. Process commands for the first target file in **payroll.make**.
3. Display commands that would be processed in **payroll.make**, but don't execute them.
4. Update modification time of target file **payroll.c** in **makefile**.

Figure 12.3 The **make** *command*

makefile Contents

As you might expect, a *makefile* has a specific format, with a dependency line, followed by construction commands to be processed if necessary, followed by other similar sets as needed. The first set refers to the ultimate output, usually an executable program. Each dependency line contains the target file name followed by a colon and the file's prerequisites. The target file depends on the prerequisites being present and up to date. Each construction command must be preceded by a tab. Construction commands are ordinary commands that Unix uses to construct the target file; they usually include at least one **cc** command. Suppose you have created a file called **makefile** that contains these lines:

```
payroll: gross.c expenses.c
        cc gross.c expenses.c -o payroll
```

You can execute this file with the simple command **make**, which locates a file named **makefile** in the working directory. When you use **make** rather than **cc** to compile and link the **payroll** program, the compilation will be performed only if either **gross.c** or **expenses.c** has been modified since the last compilation. Each prerequisite can also be treated as a target file farther down in the *makefile*. The execution of the *makefile* continues until all dependencies are taken care of. Following is an example:

```
payroll: gross.o expenses.o
        cc gross.o expenses.o -o payroll
gross.o: gross.c special.h
        cc -c gross.c
expenses.o: expenses.c special.h
        cc -c expenses.c
special.h: math.h table.h
        cat math.h table.h > special.h
```

The first target file, **payroll**, depends on the presence of the two named object files; the construction command uses the **cc** command to link the two object files into an output file with the target file name. The next two target files are those two object files, each created by compiling it with a specially named header file. For both these target files, the **cc** command includes the **-c** option so that the output is the desired object file. The last dependency creates the header file **special.h** from a combination of two other header files. Any commands can be used for processing the dependencies, as you can see in the last entry here which uses a **cat** command.

Normally, you'll have more than one *makefile* to work with, so you'll give them more descriptive names. If the previous example *makefile* were named **make.payroll**, you would execute it with the command **make -f make.payroll**. If you omit the **-f** option, Unix treats the file name you provide as a target file rather than as a *makefile*.

Implied Dependencies

The **make** command relies on implied dependencies and implied construction commands as well as specific ones, which simplifies the creation of *makefiles*. If you don't include a dependency line for a file, the system assumes that any object code programs are dependent on source code files. If you include **sales.o** as a dependency to a target file and don't specify **sales.o** as a separate target file, **make** looks for a source code file that corresponds to it. Using its own defaults, it looks in the working directory for the same file with extension **.c** for C source, **.s** for assembler source, or another character for one of the other compilers it supports. The **make** command supplies a default construction command to call the proper assembler or compiler and create the object file.

OTHER C PROGRAMMING TOOLS

Different C compilers include different tools you can use to prepare, polish, and debug programs. You should check the facilities available with your installation of Unix.

You will most likely have a program to "beautify" your programs. One variety is called **cb**; this program uses a C source program as input and outputs a source program in which the spacing and indentation demonstrate the structure of the program.

Another tool may help you make your programs more efficient by identifying possible bugs, unreachable code, unused variables and functions, and even loops not entered at the top. One version of this tool is called **lint**.

Most C programming environments include a preprocessor command (**cpp**) and a linkage editor command (**ld**) that you can use separately if necessary, although these programs are called when needed as part of the standard **cc** command execution.

Some sort of debugger, often an online debugger, is part of most Unix programming environments. You should check your installation's documentation to see what is available for you to use.

EXECUTING PROGRAMS

Once a program is executable, you can execute it just like any other Unix program. Using the **cc** command automatically provides execute permission for any executable output. In fact, it gives others execute permission as well, so you might want to remove this permission. The executable form should be placed in a program directory, your own or the system's, depending on who will be using it. While programs are still being tested, you'll probably want to keep them in your own **bin** directory.

Unix System Exercise 12.1

Purpose: Find out what is available for C programming, and try a simple compilation.

1. In Chapter 8, you prepared a file called **demoprog.c** containing a short C program. Locate it and compile it with the **cc** command. If you get any error messages on the screen, check the source code again; it may contain a typographical error. Fix it up and compile it again.
2. Check your directory for a file named **a.out**. Note that it is executable. Try running it. If you get a runtime error, check the source code and correct any typing errors. This program should run correctly in any Unix installation.
3. Try to create a *makefile* named **compdemo** that will compile the program and store the executable output in a file named **rundemo**. When the file is created, run the **make** command to execute it. Use **touch demoprog.c** to force an update.
4. Find out if your installation has a "beautification" program (try the command **cb** *file-name*), an "efficientizer" (try **lint** *file-name*), and a debugger of some sort.
5. If you have a C program of your own, prepare it for execution and try it out. If you use the C shell, you might want to enter and compile the program shown in Figure 12.1, and then try it out in a C shell script. Use as many C programming tools as you have available.

continued on following page. . .

Exercise 12.1 continued. . .

If it doesn't work:

A. Check back in the instructions in Exercise 8.4 (page 187) to see how **demoprog.c** should look. This program should not give you any serious problems, but feel free to write your own if you prefer.

B. If the **make** command doesn't seem to work, be sure you used the **-f** option preceding the name of your *makefile*.

SUMMARY

This chapter has covered the basic C programming tools of Unix. You have learned to do the following:

- Create an executable C program with the **cc** command.
- Compile C source modules with the **cc** command.
- Link object modules with the **cc** command.
- Create a specification of target files and dependencies that represents all the prerequisites for an executable program in a **makefile**.
- Execute a **makefile** with the **make** command.
- Execute a program.

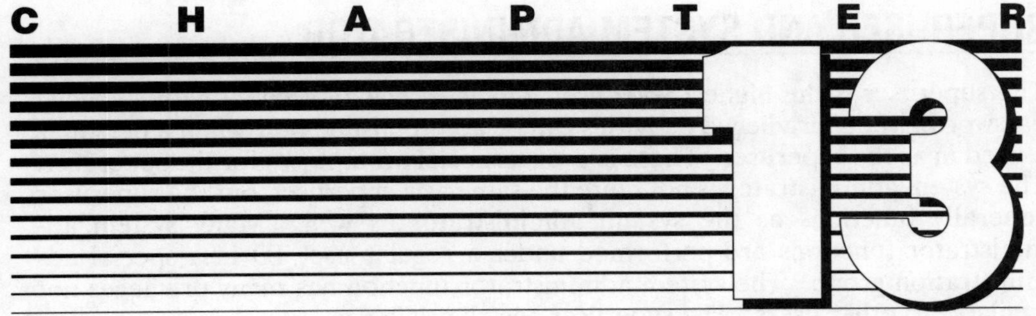

UNIX SYSTEM ADMINISTRATION

The Unix system administrator, who may actually be a group of people, has the ultimate responsibility to keep the Unix system operating. As a user of the Unix system, you do not have access to the entire system. But the system administrator, in the superuser guise, does. This person has full access to all files of all users. Only this person can create new users and groups, shut down the Unix system normally, and back up and recreate the entire file system.

In this chapter, you will get an overview of the responsibilities of the system administrator and see how you can help to keep your Unix system running smoothly. Finally, you will see how you can create backups of your own in situations where you have a diskette drive available for your use.

SUPERUSER AND SYSTEM ADMINISTRATOR

The superuser is the highest level user; this level has an account with a special password. Many privileged activities can be accomplished only when a person is logged in as the superuser. There is even a special prompt (#) for the superuser. The system administrator is not quite the same as a superuser, but the superuser generally functions as the system administrator as well. Many system administrator functions are performed under a regular user ID in a special administration group. The system administrator function has many privileges not available to other users. The superuser has all privileges.

Because the superuser has every possible privilege, it is possible to do damage to the Unix system when logged in as superuser. For example, a superuser might shut the system down while others are online, in which case their current work might be lost. He or she could inadvertently erase or overlay a critical system file. Most superusers have an ordinary user ID and password in addition to the superuser ID and password. They limit the use of the superuser ID for system maintenance functions. They also carefully limit access to the superuser password for security reasons.

When the term **system administrator** is used, it refers to the person who makes the decisions and has access to the superuser account. This person will function as superuser when necessary. If your installation is large enough to have separate people fulfilling the two functions, check with your group leader if you need advice concerning where to go for help.

When you see the words "see the system administrator" in this chapter, you need not take them literally. You can accomplish many of the tasks covered in this chapter by talking to your group leader or sending a mail message to whoever is in charge.

UNIX SYSTEM BACKUP

Every operating system ever developed has the potential for crashing, and any file you create or use has the potential for going bad. There is no way of preventing this. But a good backup system can help ameliorate any problems that may result. Your Unix installation has a backup system, whether it is based on a regular schedule or an occasional one. The system administrator backs up files on tape or disk, depending on the hardware available. If necessary, the files on the backup medium can be restored to the file system in use. Even the complete set of files can be restored if necessary.

How It Affects You

If you accidentally erase or otherwise destroy a file, that file can probably be restored from the system backup files. You will need to make the request, of course, and it may take some time for the restoration to be performed. If a hardware problem wipes out any of your files, let the system administrator know; the problem undoubtedly affected other files as well, and they can all be restored at the same time.

In some Unix installations, files may be automatically removed from the system if they are not used within a predetermined period of time. If you have files that disappear, check with the system administrator. They probably still exist on a backup tape or disk somewhere in the system or on the shelf. Don't wait too long before you check, however; backup files aren't kept forever.

If you want your files to appear active to Unix, you can update the modification date occasionally. The easiest way to do this is with the **touch** command. Just use the command **touch ***, and all files in the working directory are given the current date. Don't overdo this, however. The **touch** command overrides the actual last-modification date, which can make it difficult for you to identify files.

If you have files you don't need any more, get rid of them. You might be able to copy them to diskette if you have a diskette drive available to you. This saves files out of reach of the system administrator. You can restore the files later when you need them again.

MANAGING USERS

The system administrator can set up user accounts, assign new user IDs and passwords, and even give you a second user ID if you need one. In addition, the system administrator can assign or change groups and other default conditions associated with your login ID.

The system administrator cannot find out a user's password, but he or she does have access to all other information about a user, as well as read, write, and execute access to all files. If you forget your password, however, there is help available. The system administrator can assign you a new one without knowing your old one. When you get a new password issued, change it to one you can remember the next time you log on. As always, don't create a password that others can easily figure out.

If you aren't satisfied with the terminal setup when you log on, you may be able to make some changes yourself. For example, you can change the shell variables that set up your home directory and search path in your **.profile** or **.login** file, using **vi**. If you want to change the shell you start in automatically or the type of terminal you use, see the system administrator.

The system administrator can also let you know who else is in the same group and what other groups use the system. You can use the **who** command to find out what users are currently on-line.

MAINTAINING FREE SPACE

One problem with most operating systems is maintaining enough free space on disk. The system administrator oversees this process, but cooperation from the users is essential.

Disk space gets filled with files, some of which are vital, such as the files and programs that make up the Unix operating system. If your system includes online documentation you can access through the **man** command, that takes up space. A spelling checker or thesaurus takes up a great deal of space for storing alternative words and meanings. Every application, whether it is a word processor, an accounting package, a graphics handler, or even a telecommunications network, consists of files that take up space. And this is only the official, administrator-managed space.

Directories take up space as well; when a directory contains more than 30 files, it takes up much more space than for just a few files. And one that contains more than 256 files takes up immensely more space. Once a directory reaches a size that makes a disk space jump (30 or 256 files), removing a file doesn't lessen the space required for the directory.

Files you create take up space. Even the smallest file takes some space. Spreadsheets and databases can get very large. Some files are temporary; they may be created by an application program or utility and then not be removed when the program ends. You may have copied a file to another directory for easier use and then neglected to remove the original copy. Make it a point to remove files when you don't need them any more. Don't keep extra copies on the disk. And don't keep too many versions of the same file. You may need one or two generations at hand, but earlier versions should be removed or backed up.

You may get a message from the system administrator asking that old, large, or seldom used files be examined. In this case, check them out. Get rid of what you can. You won't get such a message unless there is a disk space problem.

What You Can Do

Occasionally check your directories in time sequence (**ls -lt | more**) to see how long it has been since the files have been modified. Check them in size sequence (**ls -ls | more**) to see what the largest files are. Be sure to check all your directories; if the same large file occurs in more than one directory, you may be able to remove some copies. You may even find a directory you haven't used in months. It might be time to get rid of it.

As a matter of routine, try not to keep temporary files. If you use **nroff** to create a printable formatted file, for example, use **lpr -r** to print it so the file is removed after it is printed. Use piping whenever you can to avoid temporary files.

If you want to check your disk usage, try the **du** command; this isn't always available to general users, but sometimes you can use it. Without any options, **du** gives you the **d**isk **u**sage of the working directory and any subdirectories; you can specify any directory name instead. The output gives you the number of blocks used by files in the directory and its subdirectories. The block size varies among Unix installations, but it gives you the relative size of the directories.

EMERGENCY PROBLEMS

The system administrator or superuser handles various emergency problems that may occur. Software problems may be handled by someone else.

Terminal Problems

When a terminal stops responding, the problem may be minor, major, or anything in between. If it is minor, you may be able to solve the problem yourself.

Your terminal may be responding just fine, but not echoing (displaying) characters. This qualifies as minor, so try to fix it. Press **Ctrl-J**; you may see some messages. The messages are a good sign; they mean that Unix knows you are out there doing something, but you can ignore them at this time. Type **stty echo** or **stty sane** and press **Ctrl-J** again. You won't see the command on the screen, but

Unix should recognize it. Then type **ls** and see if the system echoes the command. If so, great. If not, try the other **stty** option. If it still doesn't respond, there is some other problem.

The next step is to check other terminals to see if they have problems. If all are locked up, there may have been a system crash. You can try calling the computer room, but don't be surprised if no one answers; the people there are working frantically to get Unix back up.

If other terminals work fine, send a message to the system administrator, giving the terminal ID of the nonfunctional terminal. Most terminals in large installations have an external terminal ID label for just this purpose. Through the superuser account, the terminal can be disabled and enabled again. Even if you decide to continue your work at a different terminal, be sure to report the problem. And if you can't log off, report that too.

System Crash

A real system crash is an emergency for all users. A panic message of some sort appears on the system console (the main terminal, usually where Unix is started up) and no other terminals respond at all. This usually results from some interruption in the power source or from inadvertent damage to one or more of the system files. The system administrator and the computer room crew do all they can to get the system going again. They may need to reinstall the system from its original form or restore the system and its files from backup disks, so be patient.

Printer Problems

If a printer isn't working correctly, the problem may be local or general. Make sure the power is on, of course. A local problem may be a paper jam or an out-of-paper condition. You can probably handle either of these. If everything looks fine but it doesn't print, either with or without a message on your terminal, contact the system administrator.

Another type of printer problem occurs if a process is in a loop and continues printing garbage. If it resulted from a Unix print command, you should be able to stop it with a **cancel** command specifying either the printer device number or the print queue number. If it resulted from a process you started, perhaps while debugging, find out the process ID number (with **ps**), and then terminate the process with the **kill** command. If this doesn't do it, try **kill -9** *processID*. If the process still isn't dead, contact the system administrator. Just turning off the printer won't help in the long run, although it may save paper in the short run.

HANDLING DISKETTES

If you work at a terminal with a diskette drive available, you may be able to transfer your files to diskette for extra security or to transport them to another Unix system. This section explains how to format diskettes. Your installation will be able to provide the commands it uses for transferring files to and from diskettes.

Formatting Diskettes

A diskette must be formatted under Unix before it can be used to store data. If the system supports diskettes of various sizes, you must tell the system which capacity the diskette is for. The basic command is **format**; to format a diskette in the default way, insert the diskette into the only drive or the first drive (on top or on the left) if you have more than one, and issue the **format** command. If you aren't asked any questions, the diskette is formatted.

Most systems require that you specify the drive involved (usually a: or b:) and type of diskette if there is a choice. The exact data you enter depends on your system, of course, but most systems allow you to enter just the **format** command and respond to prompts for any additional information.

Transferring Data Files

You may be able to copy data files to a diskette yourself; you may even be able to set up a complete file system of your own on the diskette. Check with the documentation for your system. The command **tar** works on Xenix systems. You may also be able to make copies of diskettes directly. The command **diskcp** works on Xenix systems.

Unix System Exercise 13.1

Purpose: Try out a few system commands and clean up your exercise directories.

1. Try the **who** command to see what terminal you are working at. Check if the terminal has an external label that gives that ID.
2. Check the current logged in users; notice the terminal ID for each.
3. Try the **du** command in your home directory. Then try **du ../** to see the disk usage of other users. If you want to examine the output in detail, pipe it to **more** or redirect it to a file.
4. Erase any files you have created through the exercises in this book, unless you want to keep them for some reason. Take time to clean out your directories and remove any except **bin** that you created for these exercises.

If it doesn't work:

A. You shouldn't have any problems with these exercises. If you have trouble, see a colleague or check with the system administrator.

SUMMARY

This chapter has presented an overview of the system administrator's responsibilities in terms of how they affect the Unix user. You have learned to do the following:

- Depend on system backups to restore files.
- Update your files' modification date with the **touch** command.
- Get a new password if you have forgotten yours.
- Conserve disk space.
- Check disk usage with the **du** command.
- Check out and report a terminal problem.

- Check out and report a printer problem.
- Identify and respond to a system crash.
- Format diskettes for personal backup use.

D

O

P

W

Symbols